HELPING AMERICA'S FAMILIES

HELPING AMERICA'S FAMILIES

Alfred J. Kahn *and*
Sheila B. Kamerman

TEMPLE UNIVERSITY PRESS
Philadelphia

Temple University Press, Philadelphia 19122
© 1982 by Temple University. All rights reserved
Published 1982
Printed in the United States of America

Library of Congress Cataloging in Publication Data

Kahn, Alfred J., 1919–
    Helping America's families.
    Includes bibliographical references and index.
    1. Family—Services for—United States.   I. Kamerman,
Sheila B.   II. Title.
HQ536.K33   362.8'2'0973   81-14549
ISBN 0-87722-212-6   AACR2
ISBN 0-87722-213-4 (pbk.)

Contents

Preface

In recent years scholars and expert groups have joined in urging more attention to the creation of family support systems. Kenneth Keniston and his colleagues proposed "comprehensive and universally accessible public services to support and strengthen . . . families in the rearing of their children."[1] The Advisory Committee on Child Development, National Research Council/National Academy of Sciences, called for "the creation of a broad system of supports for the family."[2] Urie Bronfenbrenner placed these recommendations in the context of a behavioral science rationale.[3]

We were impressed several years ago with the need to take the next step: to clarify the concept of family support systems, to develop a picture of what is in place, and to see what the possibilities might be. The domain proved to be extensive and the characterization difficult. This report claims to do no more than to initiate efforts at specification.

This book asks: Who offers help to American families? What kinds of services are available? Who uses the services? Are they at all adequate to the needs—or to the demand, to use the economists' term? The search for answers has required attention to the social and demographic circumstances of American families and to emerging trends. It took us to the public sector, to voluntary nonprofit social agencies, to church programs, to the self-help movement, and to the marketplace. It also required exploration of the state of the art in helping families and in delivering services.

We have been studying family policy and social services in the United States and other societies over the past decade, attempting to assess what is in place and to clarify what, if anything, can and should be done to assist modern society as it adapts to change and seeks to ensure the quality of primary group life in the industrial, urban world. In the course of this effort we have moved back and forth between social benefits, on the one hand, and personal social services and their delivery, on the other.

As we have stressed elsewhere, personal social services can never be viewed as a substitute for adequate income, jobs, health and medical care, or housing. But neither can social benefits substitute for adequate services. Good social or family policy requires consideration of both benefits and services. Here, we focus on services only—the range and variety of services, provided under diverse auspices, that many families and family members view, or say they view, as helpful. Our goal is not to direct attention away from the urgent need for improved social benefits, about which we continue to write, but rather to highlight the growing importance of the service sector in contributing to a better quality of life for all people, rich and poor alike.

The reader will note that our explorations, carried out over a three-year period, have required substantial cooperation by executive personnel and line staffs in many kinds of organizations and agencies, by leadership in standard-setting organizations, and by public officials. We are grateful for this help and hope that our report of what became a wide-ranging exploration will be seen both as offering useful, if sometimes critical, perspectives and as making a case for needed future development.

This work could be initiated and carried through because of the support by the Robert Sterling Clark Foundation and its executive director, Margaret Ayers. Only others who carry out similar work know the importance of moral and financial backing accompanied by patience. We are indeed grateful.

In the course of producing this volume, we have relied on the intelligent and conscientious work of Felicity Howlett, who typed its several versions, and on the editorial wisdom of our Temple University Press colleagues, Doris Braendel and David Bartlett.

HELPING AMERICA'S FAMILIES

1   Families Have Problems

Definitions of "the family" vary from the traditional to the change-oriented. Thus:

A family is "an association between a man and a woman and the children she bears" (Margaret Mead).[1]

A family is "a group of two or more persons related by blood, marriage, or adoption, and residing together" (the Census Bureau).[2]

A family is "the sphere of intimate others, usually co-residents in the household" (Rosabeth Kanter).[3]

A "familial constellation" is "a person-to-person mutual aid system which intends to provide on a sustained basis for a variety of necessary functions: the provision of emotional support to all its members and the assurance of economic and physical survival of the total constellation. Functional, familial behavior is characterized by intimacy, commitment to the constellation, and continuity and intensity of the relationship over time" (Family Service Association of America).[4]

The family as a support system is "collector and disseminator of information about the world; feedback guidance system; source of ideology; guide and mediator in problem-solving; source of practical service and concrete aid; haven for rest and recuperation; reference and control group; source and validator of identity; and contributor to emotional mastery" (Gerald Caplan).[5]

Experts thus differ in their relative emphasis on family structures or family functions in describing what it is or what is desirable. People everywhere vary in their satisfaction with or concern about families generally. Thus, conservatives ascribe many of our contemporary social problems to the "deterioration" of the family, by which they usually mean the changes occurring in family structure and family roles; some, for example, identify family permissiveness as the cause of many of our problems today and gear their efforts toward restoring "old" values and patterns. Others, in their dissatisfaction with traditional family practices, reject the traditional family as being dysfunctional in today's world. Some spokesmen for the counterculture trace many contemporary societal defects to rigid, alienat-

3

ing households and urge upon us a new type of extended family. Still others take the family as a given and advocate a larger role for public policy in intervening between the family and the perpetuation of educational and income inequality. Still others who work with the family as is want to help it change itself or strengthen itself to adapt, cope—and assure its members a richer life. Many advocates select elements of several of these orientations as they formulate their own.

Despite the debate about the nature of the family, how it functions, how it initiates social change and is in turn affected by such change, there are very few experts who argue anything other than the centrality of the family in contemporary, as in past, history. Whatever the social problems, the solutions must be family-related unless there is a good reason to the contrary. For most Americans ask with Robert Nisbet: Where is there evidence of a creative society where people have no place in a kinship group?[6] And, similarly, Americans would concur with Margaret Mead's reminder that "the evidence indicates that the couple, together with their children, biological or adopted, are everywhere at the core of human societies, even though this 'little family' (as the Chinese call the nuclear family) may be embedded in joint families, extended families of great size, class, manorial systems, courts, harems or other institutions that elaborate on kin and material relations."[7]

Our concern in this book is not with accounting for or further analyzing the detailed ways in which social change is affecting or is affected by families. Others have addressed this subject, as we have elsewhere. Instead, we would take the family as it is, and as it changes, assuming that it is "here to stay."[8] Our focus is on how families are adapting to, coping with, and modifying today's realities, and how the society is responding or helping in a diversity of ways. Ultimately, our interest is in how families seek to strengthen themselves, and the resources they use in so doing.

In the chapters that follow, we offer an overview: What kinds of problems, needs, or wants do today's families have? What do families say they need or want in the way of help? What kinds of services do families seek? What are they offered, what do they receive, and what do they use? What, if anything, is known about the consequences of using these kinds of help or services? And, quite specifically, what are the considerations that operate in offering families information, advice, support, counselling, mutual aid, practical assistance?

What definition of the family will guide us? For formal purposes, the Census is helpful: "Two or more persons related by blood, marriage, or adoption and living together." Most families meet this definition. But those who plan or offer family supports, and those who make social policy, are concerned, ultimately, with the quality of the environments in which children are born and socialized, in which adults find intimacy, satisfaction, and support, in which communities find richness and mutual support. Thus, in discussing services and help, our focus will be on the primary living unit, or the primary relationship unit, whether connected in the formal terms of the Census or by mutual ties and commitments, whether two-parent or one-, whether children are in the household, already gone, or not yet there. We stress a "family" focus, not to exclude individuals who live alone, but to emphasize the importance of primary groups as they seek, obtain, and use help.

Our mode in this volume is exploratory. We ask our readers to join us in finding what prove to be only partial answers and additional complex questions. At most we shall be able to propose experimentation and possible starting points for relevant policy development. We shall question some of our own previous positions as well as some values long held in the helping professions about the future of service delivery. We shall suggest that something new is occurring, and that something new is needed in response.

We begin by listening to some families as they ask for help. The range of requests is wide, yet almost all reflect problems, some practical, some in relationships, some internalized. Some are true dilemmas; others may be new and unfamiliar situations to the people involved. Still others are simply circumstances for which people are prepared to use a service.

"The principal called me at work. He said my Jimmy is fighting with all the kids and the teacher can't manage him. He asked me if something is wrong at home. What could I say except the truth: My husband gets drunk and hits me and Jimmy gets angry. He can't do anything because he's too little, but he's old enough now to understand what is happening. What can I do?"

"We've been married for thirty years and my husband suddenly announced he's leaving me. He says he wants a divorce. I don't know what to do. I need some help."

"My wife wants to leave. She says I don't talk and maybe she's right. I would like to try to change; so we thought maybe we would both come for counselling."

"We want to make our marriage better. Some friends told us about how they went away with a few couples together—you know, not couples in trouble but with good marriages, like ours—who've been married fifteen or so years and want to work at a kind of marriage renewal."

"My husband has just been transferred again—for the fourth time in fifteen years. The kids really like it here. They don't want to move. We thought maybe we could sit down together and get some perspective on all this. Maybe Bill should look for another job if they don't let him stay here.

Or maybe I should stay a year or so here until the kids would be changing schools anyway; Bill could commute weekends until then. Or maybe there's something we could do to get the kids excited about the new place—except now they're afraid to get excited about another place."

"He just walked out one day and never came back. Never called or wrote or anything. After I had the baby, the social worker helped me get on welfare. But I have no one here—I don't know anyone. My parents don't want any part of me now. I have barely enough to eat, no one to talk to and the baby cries a lot. I think it would be better if I had a job, but I don't know what to do with the baby. Sometimes I'm so depressed I think I could kill myself, and other times I feel so trapped I could kill her—or just walk out. I don't know what to do."

"We fight all the time: over money; over how the kids should behave; over my brother and his mother. It's no good for us and it's no good for the kids. We've got to do something."

"My mother broke her hip last month. The doctor told me she's eighty-three and she shouldn't be living alone anymore. But she told me she'd kill herself if I put her in a home. I'd take her in with us, but my husband has a problem with his mother too, and we can't bring them both into our house. We haven't enough room, and besides, they don't get along."

"We've agreed to disagree. We're getting a divorce. I've got a good job, and I'm not asking for alimony, just some support for Sarah, our six-year-old. What we're fighting over is custody. John refuses to give me custody and I won't let him have her, especially since he travels so much for work. We just have to get someone to help us work this out."

"I thought I had everything—a good job with a real future, a wonderful husband who's at least as successful as I am, a beautiful home, a healthy, enchanting baby. I read all the books. I've talked to my two friends who have babies. But nothing prepared me for having a baby, and a job and a household too. I wake up in the middle of the night, listening. If there's no noise, I'm afraid the baby's dead. If he's crying, I'm sure something is wrong. During the day, I find myself constantly calling home to make sure everything is all right. When I'm taking care of him on the weekends, I'm afraid I'll make some terrible mistake. I'm tired all the time and worried most of the time. How do you know what's 'normal' behavior for a baby? What kinds of things should I be worried about? Does it matter if someone else takes care of him?"

"Beth's been at three different family day care homes in the past three months, and I've used five different sitters. She used to be the friendliest of kids, but now she whimpers if someone new comes into the house, and grabs my hand tight if I try to leave her at someone's house. I've got to work if we're going to eat. Isn't there a decent child care service someplace in this town, at a price a working mother like me can afford?"

"The managing partner just called. He thinks it would be a good idea if I brought my new client home for an informal dinner. I'd like to, but given our schedules, plus two pre-schoolers, dinner at home is more like a three-ring circus. My husband said he's seen an ad for a special 'dinner like mother used to cook,' brought to the house all ready to serve. He couldn't remember the name of the store, so I thought I'd try you."

Some of these requests are related to normal life events that require new services, resources, or arrangements: a child to be cared for, a proposed job transfer, an aged parent needing personal care. Others reflect a breakdown in a relationship or role. Such divisions, of course, are not precise: Some people regard it as wrong for a mother to work, even though the majority of mothers, married and unmarried, do so. Some regard a shift in marital preferences appropriate and "normal," while others define this as break-down. Some regard obtaining assistance from others rather than "doing it oneself" as an indication of inadequacy and dependence, even though much of our economy is based on just this, the provision and consumption of services. The range becomes a bit more clear if we examine requests for personal or family help in one explicitly labelled "helping" agency, a family service agency.

The most characteristic requests for help at many such agencies are telephone calls from women, requesting some sort of counselling for a marital problem. The details may vary but the essential request is, I'm having some problems with my marriage and I'd like to come in for some counselling:

"My husband and I are having trouble communicating. We were very much in love when we first got married seven years ago, but for the past year or so everything seems to be going downhill. It's just no good any-more, and I'd like to come in and get some help."

"We were married thirty years last week and now Bob wants a divorce. I want to come in for counselling."

"I just discovered my husband has been having an affair. I don't know what to do."

The second most typical request for help, also largely from women but occasionally from men, is the plea for help regarding a child, or a parent-child problem:

"My sixteen-year-old daughter stole some money from her father's girlfriend while she was visiting him on one of his weekends. I don't know how to handle it."

"My son and I have been fighting more and more. He's having problems at school and his grades have fallen down. But when I talked to his teacher she didn't seem to know what to do about it. I'm divorced and my ex-husband doesn't see Larry. He says Larry isn't really his anyway, since we adopted him. I just don't know what to do."

"The principal says my children are cutting school and that they have learning problems. She says I have to get some help for them."

"My fifteen-year-old son ran away from home. I'm separated from my husband and I have nobody to turn to. Kenny's back now, but he's very angry and upset." (The boy had been hospitalized previously and had been given medication that he no longer was taking. The mother was referred to a mental health clinic in the community.)

"My wife and our ten-year-old son are constantly fighting. I'm sure it isn't good for the boy. My wife and I seem to be fighting more too. I'm worried about money. I have some big debts coming due soon, and Marylin isn't helping. She's a terrible spender. Do you provide family therapy?"

Other types of requests for help are also brought to these family service agencies:

"Something's happened to our sex life since the baby was born last year. We used to have sex almost every night but now my wife is always tired, or she's tense listening for the baby. When I try to talk to her about it, she says it's all my fault. I think maybe we need some help."

"My father came to live with us three months ago, after my mother died. He's eighty-three. Now, my thirteen-year-old daughter tells me that the old man tried to molest one of her friends yesterday. I don't know what to do."

"My wife has been terribly depressed ever since our baby died last year. Our physician suggested we should get some counselling."

"I'm pregnant and my boyfriend wants to marry me, but I'm not sure I'm ready. I don't think I want an abortion either. We're still in school and I don't want to drop out, but I can't support a baby by myself. I need to talk to somebody."

"We've just found out my husband has terminal cancer. He's very depressed, and he's being very hard on the children. Our older boy is coming home late and staying out in the evening, and the younger one is suddenly having trouble at school. I'm worried about the children, about being left alone, about money, about Gene's turning into an invalid—or worse. I'd like to make an appointment for counselling."

"Until two years ago, my eighty-nine-year-old mother lived alone and took care of herself. Then she fell on an icy sidewalk and broke her hip. When it didn't heal right she came to live with us so we could help her. But she's become forgetful in the last couple of months. Twice she turned the burner on to heat up water and then forgot to turn it off. My husband says she's not safe left alone during the day. I work with my husband in the store, so I can't be home. My husband says she should be in a nursing home. My mother cries when I mention it to her. I need some help in deciding what to do, and how to do it."

Still others who come to family agencies ask for help with landlords, with bureaucracies, with employers. Or they ask for help for themselves or someone else in their family, for alcohol or drug problems.

Sometimes a staff member of another agency calls to refer a family for help. Sometimes a woman calls the agency seeking help for a friend. Or someone may come to the agency in person. Occasionally, a couple may drop in. The specifics vary, but for many of those requesting help, the pain is individual, personal, and unique.

There are those who say all of this just demonstrates how severely troubled is the state of the American family. We would disagree. We would say, rather, some families certainly do have troubles; other families have needs; and still others have wants. Some family troubles could even be described as illness, breakdown, pathology, or severe deviance. Others have troubles that are characteristic of life's stages, circumstances—the need to adapt or adjust to death, separation, divorce, remarriage that unites two families with children and parents, difficult moves, the entry of a second parent into the labor force—and so forth. Still other families are, by any reasonable criterion, functioning very well—but need or want additional assistance. They may turn to "outside" sources for information, advice, child care, house maintenance, vacation arrangements. Our questions are: When families are in situations like some of those we have described, where do they go for service or help? Who helps or serves them and how? Does the help or service they get really help? Does it alleviate the pain, solve the problem, meet the need, satisfy the want? This is the subject of this book.

There are many studies and books about services for the psychiatrically disordered and severely handicapped. The problems of adoption and substitute care for dependent, neglected, and abused children have had attention. We and others have written about protective services for the aged and for children, and about adolescent delinquents and persons in need of supervision. These are high-priority groups, but they are not our focus here. We shall attempt in this present work to emphasize the more "typical," "average," "normal" family situations. In short, the notion of family support presented here is not treatment or maintaining functioning for the severely ill, handicapped, disturbed, disordered.

It will soon become clear, however, that our objective is illusive and our answers incomplete. The boundary between service to the normal-average and the very disturbed varies by problem, client, place, and viewpoint. And it is not easy to escape from the usual categorical orientation in social services and to achieve a more holistic approach, whether on family principles or on some other basis. The reader should be alerted to these problems; we shall return to them time and again. By now it should be clear that we have found it necessary to suggest our range by constantly repeating the words *help* and *service* even though the words mean different things at various points in our society and our distinction could be maintained only artificially. From now on, the repetition will not be sustained. Whenever the words are used, they imply a response to a want or a need subjectively defined or felt in the family, or to a socially defined problem or situation, whether average-typical-normal, or related to breakdown, crisis, or pathology. Similarly, since our search for family supports is oriented to the normal and typical, we will rely on words like *preventive, developmental, enhancement, secondary prevention*, even though we recognize that boundaries are uncertain.

The domain we are surveying is large, active, and growing. In this exploration, we cast a wide net in order to consider the phenomenon as a whole. Americans throughout the country are asking for and taking help and service for themselves and for their families. They have created and supported a diversity of helping services: dating services, marriage counselling, and divorce counselling; debt counselling, consumer and credit services; family therapy; family social services and personal services for families; pastoral counselling; and community mental health assistance. They flock to family life education sessions conducted under many names and auspices. They assemble together with or without professional leadership in programs for "marriage enrichment," "parent effectiveness," mutual aid, and "consciousness-raising for couples." They "retreat" for weeks or weekends to improve the way they communicate, or their capacity to "relate." And they read millions of paperback and hardcover books and millions of popular magazines that regularly describe family problems, propose substantive or process solutions, and encourage self-help through personal insight or through general understanding of interpersonal or societal processes.

A self-organized coalition of agencies attempting to influence the shape of the 1980 White House Conference on Families included groups such as the American Home Economics Association, the Family Service Association of America, the National Urban League, the American Association of Marriage and Family Counselors, Future Homemakers of America, Parents Without Partners, the National Council on Family Relations, and the U.S. Catholic Welfare Conference. A directory listing "helping services" in a major city is even longer and more varied. And even then it is unclear whether the diversity of these resources for families is fully identified by such a listing. Indeed, after an extensive survey of the types of help sought and used by American families today, an important part of what we discovered is the complexity and range of service or help sought and obtained.

Although providing help to America's families sustains both a large industry and a substantial self-help movement, its domain is decentralized, diverse, changing, in flux, and somewhat ephemeral. It has no well-defined parameters, nor any precise dimensions. Therefore, there are no complete data on the number of families seeking help, the number of helping services available, the amount of money expended on obtaining help, or the results achieved.

Nonetheless a picture is needed. We shall describe what we have discovered: the kinds of help provided, by whom, and to whom. We also shall report what is known about effects. But we must begin with a review of the overall context: what American families look like now, what their problems are, and how families go about seeking help.

The American Family

What is "the American family"? For the most part, we use the Census Bureau's formal definition of a family that we cited earlier: "a group of two or more persons related by blood, marriage, or adoption, and residing together." This does not mean, however, that the desires and needs for service and help of people living in other household arrangements should be ignored. Nor do we believe one should question what individuals may mean by "family" when they come to ask for help.

According to the Census Bureau definition, there were over 57 million families in the United States in 1979, almost all of whom were primary families maintaining their own households. A small additional number, about 260,000, were secondary subfamilies living in households maintained by other persons or family groups.[9]

Fifty-three percent of these families included at least one child under eighteen, about 23 percent had a child under six, and 13 percent had a child under three. Thus, although the number of families increased during the 1970s, the proportion of families with children, and those with children at each age, has decreased. In addition, among those families with children, there has been about a 20 percent decline in the number of children, from about 2.4 in 1968 to fewer than 2.0 in 1979.

The number of families headed by women has increased dramatically over the last twenty years from 4.5 million in 1960 to 8.5 million in 1979. The most rapid growth in one-parent families occurred in the 1970s from 11 percent of all families with children to 19 percent, an increase of 78 percent as contrasted with 55 percent in the 1960s.

The women maintaining these families are more likely to be young, to have children, to be divorced or never married, and to be black than were their 1960 counterparts. The number of families maintained by women under thirty-five has more than tripled since 1960, and these families now constitute more than a third of all female-headed families. Divorced women now head four times as many such families as in 1960, and today account for a third of the total number of women who head families. Although 71 percent of the total number of female-headed families are headed by white women, only 12 percent of white families are headed by a woman while 39 percent of all black families are female-headed.

Female-headed families constitute 19 percent of all families with children (over 20 percent if we include subfamilies).[10] Among white families with children, 14 percent are female-headed; among black families with children, 46 percent are female-headed. Almost 20 percent of all children today, about 11 million, live in a one-parent family, overwhelmingly female-headed. This is a 50 percent increase since 1970. And 46 percent of all children born in the mid-1970s are likely to live in such a family by the time they are eighteen.

More women, especially women with children, entered or re-entered the labor force in the 1970s than ever before in U.S. history. Specifically, there has been a marked growth in the number of two-earner families with children and in the number of single-parent, sole-earner families maintained by women.[11] Thus, at the same time that the total number of children dropped from 65.8 million in 1970 to 58.1 million in 1980, the number whose mothers worked or looked for work increased by 36 percent, from 25.5 million to almost 31 million. For the first time in our history, more than half the children under eighteen have working mothers, regardless of whether they live with a sole parent or two parents.

Although more school-aged children than pre-school-aged children are likely to have working mothers, the rate of growth in labor force participation of mothers with young children (under six) has been more rapid than for any group, and particularly so for mothers of very young children (under three). In 1980, 54 percent of the mothers of children aged three to five were in the labor force, and 42 percent of the mothers of children under three. A recent survey of married women between the ages of eighteen and thirty-four with at least a youngest child under five reveals labor force participation rates that are astonishingly high:[12]

Age of Youngest Child	Percent of Mothers in Labor Force
less than 1 year	29.0
1 year	33.7
2 years	41.0
3 years	44.4

Indeed, most (72 percent) of the 1970s growth of labor force participation by married mothers occurred among those aged twenty-five to thirty-four, 66 percent of these women were in the labor force in 1980 and over half of them had children under six. Moreover, by 1980 close to one-third of the mothers of pre-school-aged children who worked at all during the year worked full time all year round, combining a full work life with full-time household and child care responsibilities.

In a survey of married women who had given birth within the previous year, almost 42 percent had worked during their pregnancy.[13] Clearly, women are increasingly likely to be combining employment and family life, and the popularity of this life style is likely to increase during the 1980s.

Regardless of race, ethnic origin, or family type, children whose mothers are in the labor force live in families with considerably higher income than do children with at-home mothers. More black children than white in two-parent families have working mothers; the pattern is reversed for one-parent families. Hispanic children are least likely of all groups to have a working mother. Of all family types, female-headed families are the most likely to be poor (32 percent) and about half of all families in poverty are female-headed.

In March of 1980, more than half of all two-parent families with children contained two working parents. Clearly, the two-parent, two-wage-earner family has emerged as the dominant family type: more than half of all white mothers in two-parent families and 62 percent of all black mothers in these families were in the labor force.

As the increase in female-headed families might suggest, the divorce rate in the United States climbed from 2.2 per 1,000 population in 1960 to a historic high of 5.1 per 1,000 in 1978, a rate that surpassed even the previous high of 4.3 immediately following World War II. Given a marriage rate of 10.3 per 10,000 population, the ratio is one divorce for every two marriages. If the current level of divorce continues on a lifetime basis, the likelihood is that 40 percent of those now marrying will subsequently divorce. By far the greatest rate of increase has occurred among couples in the age range of twenty-five to thirty-nine years, the range within which 60 percent of all divorces occur.

The number of children involved in divorce has tripled over the last two decades. By 1976 the average number of children per divorce fell to about one per divorce, while the number of divorces involving no children increased to 43 percent (from 37 percent in 1964). Despite this trend, the rising divorce rate caused the total number of children involved in divorce to climb to an all-time high of 1.1 million in 1976.

Most divorced women remarry, especially if they are young. Seventy-five percent of those women who had divorced before the age of thirty had remarried at the time of a 1975 survey. The average time between divorce and remarriage was a little more than three years.

Nearly all children under eighteen (96 percent) lived with one or both parents in 1980. The proportion living with both parents, however, declined sharply from 91 percent in 1960 and 89 percent in 1970 to 81 percent in 1980. In the same period, the proportion living with only one parent more than doubled from 9.4 percent (8.2 percent with the mother; 1.2 percent with the father) to 19.2 percent (17.6 percent with the mother; 1.6 percent with the father). Although this living arrangement is only temporary for most children in these families, clearly it is a significant experience.

Most children living in one-parent families are there because of divorce. The proportions of children living with a divorced parent more than doubled in the 1970s; and the proportion living with a never-married mother tripled. Moreover, 13 percent of the children under eighteen living with two parents in 1977 were living with a stepparent (8 percent) or were born to their current parents after one or both had remarried (5 percent).[14]

Living arrangements for children under eighteen in the United States in 1979 as summed up by the Census Bureau are shown in Table 1; the contrasts for very young children and for blacks underscore both variability and trends.

While more American children live with at least one natural parent than ever before (social disruption not yet having equalled the upheavals of

TABLE 1
Living Arrangements of Children under Age Eighteen in the United States, 1979

Living arrangements	% for all children under 18	% for all black children under 18	% for all children under 6	% change for all children under 18, 1970–1979
2 parents	77.4	43.4	78.9	− 18.1
1 parent	18.5	44.0	15.7	40.6
mother only	16.9	41.9	14.7	41.3
father only	1.6	2.1	0	33.5
Neither parent	4.1	12.5	5.4	10.6
TOTAL NO.	62,389,000	9,285,000	18,584,000	− 11.5

Source: Based on U.S. Bureau of the Census, "Marital Status and Living Arrangements, March 1979," *Current Population Reports*, Series P-20, no. 349 (Washington, D.C.: U.S. Government Printing Office, 1979), Table 4, and "Marital Status and Family Status, March 1979," *Current Population Reports*, Series P-20, no. 198 (Washington, D.C.: U.S. Government Printing Office, 1979), Table 4.

disease and shorter life spans in an earlier day), the experience of family break-up is common—as is the likelihood of living with stepparents and stepsiblings.

Despite the fact that men and women are marrying later, and having children later, in 1977 the median age for marriage was twenty-four for men and nearly twenty-two for women. Nearly half the women under twenty-five (45 percent) were not married in 1977, a significant increase over previous years; however, it is still presumed that close to 95 percent will marry, a figure that should assure all concerned that marriage is still in favor.[15]

What of the aged? Some 11 percent of all Americans were sixty-five years of age in 1980. Of these, 38 percent were over seventy-five. Sixty percent of the aged were female. In 1979, most older men were married (77 percent); most older women were widows (52 percent). Eighty percent of older men but only a little over half the older women lived in family settings. Forty percent of the older women lived alone.

On the basis of this brief review, we can emphasize the following about the American family:

Marriage continues to be an integral part of the lives of almost all adults, as is marriage and childbearing for almost all adult women.

Simultaneous child rearing and employment are becoming increasingly characteristic of adult women, as more than half today are now coping with both sets of responsibilities. Moreover, although data are not available for labor force participation of men by the ages of their children, it is increasingly likely that married men with young children have wives who are working too. Thus, in addition to the long-standing pattern of the single mother who works, a new family life style is emerging—the two-parent family in which both parents work.

Adults are increasingly likely to experience divorce, and, of particular importance, close to half the children born in recent years will spend at least some time in a one-parent family while growing up.[16] It is almost as likely that they will spend a portion of their lives in a reconstituted family, living with a stepparent.

Most of the critical family life cycle events still occur (as they have previously) within a fairly narrow range. Thus, between their mid-twenties and early fifties, adults are likely to marry, have their children, experience divorce, remarry, be stepparents, and see their youngest child leave home. And all these occur during those years when labor force participation rates for adults are at their peak (ages 25–54).

For the aged or aging there are special problems and issues, especially for the older woman, likely to be a widow and likely to live alone.

These are critical events, with important consequences for the adults experiencing them, for their spouses and significant other adults, and for their children. Do these events present problems for families and family members? If so, what kinds, and where do they turn for help? Before we explore in more detail the kinds of help they seek and use, however, we need to look at the problems families have.

Family Problems

There are some annual figures available on family problems—not all of the same validity, overlapping in unknown ways, and signifying different things: 320,000 families seen briefly and 230,000 seen more intensively in family service agencies; almost 2 million people served in community mental health centers; 5–15 million participants in various forms of self-help; several thousand clients in pastoral counselling programs that report totals; an estimated 1–2 million clients of private psychotherapy, including individual, marital, and family counselling and therapy; tens of thousands of participants in marriage encounter groups; 500,000 children in the child welfare service network; uncounted millions of readers of self-help books, magazines, articles, and newspaper columns. Are these figures significant? Accurate? Enough? Of high salience? The picture is relatively incomplete. Yet if we turn from social bookkeeping to epidemiology, demography, and survey research, we find that knowledge there is also incomplete and is not always focused on the questions we are concerned with here. Still, what information there is does give us a better idea of how Americans view their personal and social problems, where people go for help with these problems, and how and why different people use different kinds of help.[17] (Readers who are impatient with research summaries may prefer to move at once to the services picture in the next chapter.)

The Existence and Perception of Problems

Comprehensive information on these issues—and all the issues addressed in this review—is scarce. The classic study, by Gerald Gurin, Joseph Veroff, and Sheila Feld, was *Americans View Their Mental Health*.[18] But this study collected its data in the late 1950s. Since then, there has been no research as thorough or as direct in covering both problems and help-seeking behavior. Now, Veroff, with a number of colleagues, has replicated *Americans View Their Mental Health* with data from 1976. Thus far, there are available for review only papers with preliminary analyses of these data, including one focusing on definitions of problems in the American population and one on help-seeking perceptions and behavior. We will lean heavily on this information in our review, comparing other research with the findings from this study.[19]

In 1977, the Gallup organization asked a representative sample of 1,516 adults in the United States to report the most important problem facing their families at that time. The most frequent response (this information is not broken down by demographic groups)[20] was "economic and financial problems" such as making ends meet, inflation, the high cost of living, and high taxes. The second most frequently reported problem was unemployment. Third was illness. Fourth was problems in educating children, followed by plans for retirement, concern over children's futures, maintaining harmony within the house, the energy shortage, relocation due to job change, and loneliness.[21] Economic concerns were the predominant problems reported by the population as a whole at this time, as at earlier times. When similar questions were repeated in 1980, the only problems receiving large numbers of responses were "the high cost of living" (81 percent of those interviewed), "energy costs" (53 percent), and "decline in religious and moral standards" (23 percent). All other items, including job-family conflict and "communicating with children," received responses by 11 percent or fewer of the interviewees (there were multiple responses). It should be noted, however, that the pollsters offered interviewees few personal problem categories to choose from and many relating to economic needs. It is also of interest that sexual, racial, and marital status variables, while significant in relation to economic and social concerns, were not important differentials on the few personal concern items listed. The main exception was the tendency of separated and divorced people to be somewhat more concerned than others about "conflict between job and family responsibilities."[22]

In their 1976 research, on the other hand, Veroff, Helen Melnick, and Richard Kulka found that their respondents named family, not economic, problems as most prevalent.[23] In a sample of 2,264 representative American adults who were asked about their perceptions of problems in marriage, parenthood, and work, most frequently reported problems were problems with children: 70 percent of the men and 76 percent of the women indicated parent-child difficulties. Marital problems were second in frequency, reported by 59 percent of the men and 64 percent of the women. Third in prevalence were work problems (41 percent of the men and 28 percent of the women).[24] This ranking of problems—parental, then marital, then work—holds for both men and women across age and education groups.[25] The only exception was among grade-school-educated men, who reported marital problems more often than they did parent-child problems.

The variation between the Gallup findings and the Veroff, Melnick, and Kulka results, of course, may be due in part to the ways in which the questions were asked in each study. In the Veroff, Melnick, and Kulka research, people were asked about their individual problems—about what problems they had personally in any area of their lives. The Gallup poll, on the other hand, asked about problems experienced by the respondent's family. This may have directed the respondent's attention away from the family itself as possibly problematic—assuming it to be a unit—toward the more contextual societal problems it was facing.

In looking at problems within each life area (family, work, and personal welfare), two types of research seem most valuable for our purposes—that which allows open-ended self-definitions of problems and that which focuses on particular pre-defined problems in each area. For more open-ended information, we have further results from the Veroff, Melnick, and Kulka research. Respondents were asked to what source they attributed their problems, and those responses were then categorized as "self-attribution," "another," "situational," "interpersonal," and "general." Within the area of marital problems (reported, as we noted, by 59 percent of males and 64 percent of females), men most often reported situational problems (36 percent)—having too many debts, having problems with children, or having their job interfere with their marriage by infringing on time. Nearly as many men (32 percent) complained of interpersonal problems, predominantly problems of conflict in the marriage, of understanding, of getting used to each other. (These relative frequencies hold for men within each age and education group except grade-school-educated younger and older men, who most often reported general problems—"lots of little things," or "everything.") It is interesting that, as Veroff, Melnick, and Kulka note, in 1957 husbands with less than a college education were more likely than more-educated husbands to explain marital problems with situational attributions (approximately 35 percent versus 25 percent, respectively), whereas highly educated husbands more often gave situational attributions in 1976 (approximately 23 percent versus 42 percent).

For women, the dominant explanations of problems in marriage were similar, except that interpersonal problems were reported somewhat more frequently (32 percent) than situational ones (30 percent). This also holds for women in different age and education groups, except among grade-school-educated young and middle-aged women, who reported problems somewhat more often in terms of self- and general attributions, respectively. These findings also represent a change from the earlier study: women in 1957 more often attributed problems to their husbands (27 percent versus 20 percent in 1976) and, among the cohort of college women, to themselves (12 percent among young college women in 1957 versus 2 percent among middle-aged college women in 1976).

There were other types of attributions for marital problems in 1976. Twelve percent of the men and 7 percent of the women overall gave self-attributions, saying that they drank too much, were not considerate enough, or were too stubborn. Eight percent of the men and 20 percent of the women blamed another—the spouse drinks too much, is inconsiderate, is unreliable. The percentages of general attributions were 12 percent among men and 11 percent among women.

Parenting problems, as we noted, were reported by 70 percent of the men and 76 percent of the women. When men specified such problems, interpersonal types predominated—getting children to listen, getting them interested in school, fights between parents and children. Forty-five percent of the men reported this type of problem. (The exceptions were among grade-school-educated middle-aged and older men and among high-school-educated older men, all of whom reported more situational, primarily financial, problems in relation to children.) For women, both interpersonal (33 percent) and "another" (32 percent) attributions of problems predominated. ("Another" attributions refer mainly to a child's being ill, to the child's getting into trouble, or to the child's being too emotional or unhappy.) The only exceptions to these types of attributions were among grade-school-educated middle-aged and older women, who reported more situational-financial problems. In fact, Veroff, Melnick, and Kulka note a general increase over time in the percentage among the less-educated cohorts of both men and women reporting situational-financial types of parenting problems. The other types of problems reported in 1976 under the parenting label were those of self-attribution—knowing the right thing to do, trying to understand the child (reported by 3 percent of men and of women)—and general attribution—everyday problems, just a lot of little things, difficulty with physical care (reported by 7 percent of both men and women). In addition, 26 percent of the men attributed their problems to another, and 19 percent of the men and 25 percent of the women complained of situational problems.

Finally, in Veroff, Melnick, and Kulka's third area—work—41 percent of the men and 28 percent of the women admitted difficulty. Both men and women most frequently reported self-attribution problems (43 percent for men and 35 percent for women). These problems include being "mixed up" about what work to do, being sick and unable to work, and doing poorly at work. However, men reported these problems more often and more consistently than women. For men, in each age and education group—with the exception of young grade-school-educated men, who reported more general problems, like not being able to find work, "a lot of little things," "didn't get along"—self-attribution problems greatly predominate. Veroff,

Melnick, and Kulka do report, however, that in 1976 younger men and the college-educated cohort of middle-aged men were less likely to attribute work problems to themselves than were men in these age and education groups in 1957, while the cohort of older men increased in percentages of self-attributions. For women, situational attributions, such as the hours or working conditions being bad, the kind of work not being right, or the factory shutting down, were also common (27 percent), in particular among college-educated young and middle-aged women and among grade-school-educated older women. (Since women were not asked about work in the original study, comparisons cannot be made with 1957.) For the other types of work problems in 1976, 10 percent of the men and 9 percent of the women attributed their problems to another, generally their supervisors. Nine percent of the men and 19 percent of the women reported interpersonal problems—not liking the people they had to work with, fighting with their boss, and not getting along with their supervisor. Fifteen percent of the men and 10 percent of the women gave general attributions; 23 percent of the men gave situational attributions.

This summary is based on self-reported problems within three different life areas for men and women. As we have mentioned, however, our information is still incomplete. We have no information on demographic characteristics besides age and education, nor on problems in other areas such as social relations (friendships, for example) or physical or more traditional forms of psychiatric health and disorder problems. Within the areas of marriage, parent-child relations, and work, however, we can see patterns of predominant problems. In relation to problems with both spouses and children, most people identified aspects of interpersonal relationships as major points of difficulty, while problems related to themselves predominated in the work area. These findings did not vary systematically by age or by class for marital or for work problems, but there is evidence of a class difference in relation to parenting problems, which, as will be recalled, is the area most frequently reported as problematic. Among younger and more highly educated groups, interpersonal problems did dominate. Among older and less-educated groups, however, taking these as indicators of lower social class, situational, particularly financial, difficulties were most frequently reported. Thus, we might suggest, at least in relation to the family, that at lower class levels, economic problems are most important and most often offered in response to queries. Perhaps when economic stability is assured, other issues such as interpersonal or situational difficulties become salient.

This may help us re-evaluate the conflicting evidence on what problems are "most important" to American families. In the Gallup poll data, as we noted, economic issues were reported as most problematic; in the Veroff,

Melnick, and Kulka data, on the other hand, parenting problems were the most important. But we see here that the nature of parenting problems depends, at least in part, on the social class of the individual. And even when economic issues are defined as most problematic, they are reported in the context of the family—either by the way the question is asked (in the Gallup poll) or by self-definition (as in relation to raising children in Veroff, Melnick, and Kulka).

Although few open-ended studies have been carried out on individuals' perceptions of problems, many studies have been concerned with socially pre-defined social or personal problems. For example, studies have been carried out in the marital area on the rate and distribution of marital instability in the population. Also, research has focused on child deviance problems and on violence against children. Many studies have concentrated on rate of unemployment and some on under-employment, others on poverty, and others on work dissatisfaction. Finally in relation to personal welfare, much research has attended to both physical illness and the prevalence and distribution of psychiatric disorders. It is this research to which we now turn.

Marital Instability

As we saw above, the divorce rate among American families and the number of children involved in divorces have risen drastically over the last decade. Marital violence is also high. A national survey conducted in 1975 found that 6 percent of all husbands and wives used serious forms of violence on one another one or more times.[26] And this figure does not include less serious, unreported violence.

Several studies have examined marital instability—including rates of both divorce and separation—by basic demographic characteristics in the population.[27] Separation and divorce have been found to be related to social class, to unemployment, race, age, housing, and geographic region. Among economic indicators, income seems to be of particular importance.[28] Paul Glick and Arthur Norton, for example, find that income is more important than education. Lee Rainwater claims that only income, among socioeconomic status variables, is a predictor of instability rates. Other research finds occupational status also to be a differentiating factor. Frank Furstenberg cites studies showing the rates of marital instability to be about twice as high among lower-status occupations as among high-status professional groups. Despite reports of consistent relationships with income and less consistent relationships with education and occupation, however, the general association between marital instability and social class seems to be diminishing.[29]

Marital instability rates are also associated with recent unemployment, according to research reported by Isabel Sawhill.[30] Greta Miao found, however, that this relationship only held for the 1950s, disappearing in the 1960s.[31] She suggests that the relationship between marital instability and unemployment may exist only in times of relative economic prosperity.

The evidence for the association of rates of divorce and separation with race is contradictory. Furstenberg reports higher rates for blacks within each occupational group; Farley reports blacks having higher rates, but finds this due to employment and income differences; Robert Hampton finds no differences in rates by race; and Norton and Glick only find lower-class blacks to have higher rates. However, Furstenberg and Farley focus on the rates at an earlier time period (1960s) than do Hampton (late 1960s into 1970s) and Norton and Glick.[32] Thus, it is possible that, like social class differences, differences between blacks and whites in rates of separation and divorce are also diminishing.

Age at marriage seems to be one of the most important variables in predicting marital instability; indeed, Larry Bumpass and James Sweet found it to be *the* most important.[33] Individuals who are younger at marriage, particularly women under twenty, have a much higher probability of separation and divorce than do those who marry later. In divorces before middle age, the spouses were married an average of two years younger than those whose marriages remained intact to middle age.

Finally, two other factors have been found to be associated with rates of marital instability. One is the quality of housing—including type of housing, ownership, defects, value of housing, type of other housing in the neighborhood, and distance to the nearest city—which James Morgan found to be one of the most powerful predictors of separation and divorce.[34] (Housing, we note, could be a surrogate for a more basic unidentified variable.) Interestingly, the association between housing and marital instability holds even when income is controlled. The other factor is geographic region.[35] Bumpass and Sweet found that rates of divorce and separation are lower in farm areas than in other regions of the country, although this is hardly surprising in view of the importance of cultural and religious contexts to marital permanence.

Parenting Problems

Parenting problems for which data exist fall into two groups: problems of children themselves and problem behavior of parents in relation to children, particularly child abuse.

The top priority among children seems to be substance abuse. The Gallup Youth Survey found that most teenagers regard drug abuse as the most important problem facing their generation.[36] In a related study, 1,500 parents also gave drug use, as well as smoking and alcohol use, as the

problem with their children for which they would most want further education.[37] This finding held for parents across both economic and social class groups.

Recently, the problem behaviors of parents most reported have been child neglect and child abuse. The true prevalence of either is not known. Public initiatives and funding from the federal level have increased reporting in all states, but abuse and neglect are often undifferentiated, or are differentiated in inconsistent ways, and distinctions are often not made (perhaps cannot be made) between reported and validated cases. Nonetheless, the flurry of federal activity and the large industry created by new funding has heightened awareness of neglect and abuse and has generated many new formal and informal helping programs.

Murray Straus, Richard Gelles, and their colleagues, in their basic epidemiological research, have focused on a particular form of behavior, family violence, that is not synonymous either with abuse or with neglect as statutorily defined. Their national survey of such violence in a cross section of American families, conducted in 1975, found that in the course of the year 1.7 million children out of 46 million between the ages of three and seventeen were kicked, bitten, punched, beaten up, or threatened with a gun or knife. Most of these behaviors (except the gun and knife threats) generally occurred more than once during the year. Three or 4 percent of all parents were involved. These data refer to relatively severe violence. Abuse and neglect legislation and family court statutes may or could result in public action in the instance of much milder physical attacks or threats. On the other hand, the totals of cases reported into the public intervention networks are smaller than the violence totals in the surveys available.[38]

Work Problems

Research into employment problems has been focused on unemployment, on poverty, and on work dissatisfaction.[39] Such studies have consistently reported unemployment levels to be highest among lower-class workers, in particular blacks, Spanish-speaking persons, and workers from "slum neighborhoods"—apart from the ever higher rates of youth unemployment.[40] Unemployment is also more serious among workers with low-wage jobs and with low occupational status in general. Rates are also higher among those with low education; high-school dropouts, for example, suffer twice as much unemployment as do high-school graduates.

Many other studies have focused on the distribution of low income or poverty itself as the dependent variable, examining its variations with other social factors. Among individuals giving self-reports of financial hardship, the percentage reporting their financial situation to be poor (as opposed to excellent, good, and only fair) is highest among blacks (approx-

imately 26 percent versus 9 percent for whites), low-income groups (particularly under $5,000—approximately 30 percent versus approximately 8 percent for higher income groups), low-status occupational groups (clerical and sales, manual workers—approximately 11 percent versus approximately 4 percent for professional and business occupations), and low-education groups (grade-school-educated—approximately 17 percent versus approximately 9 percent for more highly educated).[41] When respondents were asked about their satisfaction with their standard of living, in contrast to their financial situation only, the percentage dissatisfied was higher among blacks (50 percent versus 24 percent for whites), low-income groups (approximately 40 percent for below $5,000 versus approximately 23 percent for above $5,000), low-status occupational groups (approximately 32 percent for clerical, sales, and manual workers versus 19 percent for professional and business groups), and, to a lesser extent, low-education groups (33 percent for grade-school-educated versus approximately 25 percent for more highly educated).[42]

Differentials in wage rates and earning potentials are characteristic of various demographic groups. Women's salaries in the United States are about 60 percent of male rates, on the average. Moreover, female-headed households are much poorer than those with male heads, the median income in 1978 being $19,109 for male householders and $8,537 for females.[43] Black men earned about two-thirds as much as white men. Both a low level of father's education and low respondent educational status are significantly related to low wage rates.

Several studies have been concerned with identifying which groups have high or low levels of discontent with work. In comparing black and white workers, polls taken by Roper in 1975 and by Gallup in 1972 showed blacks to be much less satisfied than whites with their jobs.[44] Looking at other demographic variables in addition to race, Gallup found the highest discontent to be concentrated among blacks (34 percent versus 10 percent for whites) and among low-income groups in general (for example, approximately 17 percent for below $7,000 versus 7 percent for $15,000 and above).[45] Thus, a person "very dissatisfied" with his or her job is likely to be young and black, to have less than a college education, and to be employed in unskilled manual labor.[46]

The reasons for the high level of dissatisfaction are various. As Stanislav Kasl points out, job satisfaction seems to be related to job level mainly in terms of self-esteem, self-actualization, autonomy, and income, as opposed to factors such as working conditions or relationships with other workers.[47] Michael Piore found that in lower-class groups, where discontent was highest, lack of upward mobility was a major complaint.[48] Thomas Harris and Edwin Locke, in a small study that focused on different class groups,

found lower-class workers more often citing monetary concerns as sources of dissatisfaction.[49] And Gallup found poor wages to be a primary reason for job dissatisfaction in general.[50]

Physical Health and Psychiatric Disorders

In relation to physical health, men, blacks, and individuals with lower social status die younger and have higher age-adjusted mortality rates for many diseases.[51] Social status differences are greater for women than for men, for communicable than for chronic types of diseases.[52]

In relation to psychiatric disorder, rates of psychosis and of personality disorder have consistently been found, in true prevalence studies, to be higher in the lower class (the specific rates vary from study to study).[53] Rates of neuroses and affective psychoses have been found to be higher among women than men, and rates of personality disorder higher among men than women.[54] In summarizing results of studies using rating scales of overall mental health, Bruce Dohrenwend and his colleagues report that higher disorder rates have been found among women (33 percent versus 22 percent for men), among low social classes (38 percent for the lowest social class versus 11 percent for the highest), and among individuals in urban areas (25 percent versus 17 percent for rural areas).[55]

Families Seek Help

We have seen that American families have, and see themselves as having, problems. But once families identify themselves as "having a problem," what do they do about it? What solutions do they view as possible? Where (if anywhere) do they turn? How?

In examining these questions, we will draw upon our review of Veroff, Melnick, and Kulka's information on attributions of problems, since these attributions can be seen as indicators of perceived loci for solving problems.[56] We can interpret the types of attributions as ranging from internally based solutions (self-attribution) to externally based ones (interpersonal, another, and situational attributions). With respect to marital problems, as we have noted, both men and women see issues as predominantly interpersonal and situational. However, the ranking of these attributions differs. Men more often see their problems as situational, with interpersonal attributions second in frequency. Women more often see them as interpersonal, as being more internally located, perhaps because of individual adaptation or adjustment, than do men. For parenting problems, men and women both report interpersonal attributions predominantly, with women also frequently perceiving more externally based another-attributions (somewhat a reversal from marital problems). In work, however, both men and women most often attribute problems to themselves, implying the need for internally based solutions involving individual or personal change. This stands in marked contrast to the poll and survey findings of distributions of nearly every social or personal problem according to the stratification of social groups, which implies a structural rather than an individual basis for social and personal problems and the potential availability of an external, societal locus for change.

Focusing on whether respondents had ever gone for help for problems, whether they thought they could have used help in the past, and whether they thought they might ever need help in the future, Kulka and his colleagues constructed an index of readiness for self-referral. The index consisted of the following responses: has used help; could have used help; might need help; self-help (respondent cannot conceive of wanting professional help in the future, but no emphasis on self-help); and strong self-help (same as above but with an emphasis on self-help). Kulka and his associates found "a substantial increase in readiness for self-referral over the past 20 years. The proportion of the adult population reporting actual use of professional help has almost doubled (from 14 percent to 26 percent) and the proportion who feel that they could always handle problems by themselves has declined from 44 percent in 1957 to 35 percent in 1976."[57]

Furthermore, men and women who have lower incomes and less education are less likely to define their past problems as relevant for help. This difference also holds for occupational status for men: those with white-collar occupations are more likely than those with manual occupations to see problems as relevant for help. Both men and women in low income, education, and occupational groups more often adopt a self-help position—reporting that they would not want to go someplace for help—than do those in higher social groups. Thus, we see consistent differences in the perceptions of problems as needing professional help by socioeconomic status. The groups identified as having the highest rates of problems are the least likely to perceive their problems as relevant for outside help. By 1976, however, the relationship between education and having gone for help was far weaker than it had been in 1957, and income-related differences largely disappeared when education was comparable.

The actual use of professional services by individuals is still a separate issue. Many studies have focused on this issue, particularly on the use of medical and psychological services. In relation to the need for help, it is estimated from general surveys of health that only about one-third of the people who report symptoms actually go for treatment.[58] This is down from an earlier review that showed 60 percent of those with physiological problems receiving medical care.[59] Among those with psychiatric disorders, this same study found that 67 percent of the men and only 35 percent of the women most severely ill sought treatment. Almost 1.5 million children under age eighteen needed immediate professional help (criteria not specified), according to the Joint Commission on Mental Health of Children, and less than 30 percent got treatment.[60] In fact, from a large review of studies of mental disorder, Dohrenwend and his associates concluded that between 12 and 17 percent of the entire United States population was suffering from a clinically significant disorder (by psychiatrists' judgments and/or by rating-scale criteria) but had never received professional help.[61]

Thus, according to these studies, the discrepancy between the existence of problems and treatment-seeking behavior is large. Who, then, does and does not go for professional help (the only source usually considered as help in help-seeking behavior research), and why? To whom do individuals go when they do seek help? How "serious" are the problems, and what does "serious" in this sense mean? In discussing these questions, we should recall the distribution of problems in different social groups reported above, comparing this to the distribution in demographic groups of help-seeking behavior.

We can summarize this comparison by stating that, as in the case of perceiving problems as relevant for help, help-seeking behavior per se is less frequent among the groups for which the rates of problems are the highest.[62] In attempting to understand the reasons for the inverse relationships between socioeconomic status and illness behavior, we can look at several models or sets of variables. Income differences alone—the ability to pay for services—have been proposed as the explanation, but, as John McKinlay points out, even when cost barriers are removed, wide variations among income groups and some ethnic groups still remain.[63] Others have suggested more social-psychological explanations. For example, James Anderson and David Bartkus find differences in need (existence of illness), symptom sensitivity (perception of symptoms as serious enough to consult a physician), and personal evaluation of services (as positive or negative) as determinants of social class differences in help-seeking behavior.[64] Another type of reasoning takes a more sociocultural approach (McKinlay's categorization). This approach includes several models of illness behavior. For example, Edward Suchman predicts the use of medical services from how cosmopolitan or parochial and how medically oriented the social group is.[65] McKinlay suggests and uses a social network explanation (patterns of relationships with kin and friends) congruent with Eliot Freidson's lay referral system concept for utilization behavior, distinguishing between utilizers and under-utilizers of medical services on the basis of the relative closeness of the kin and friendship networks.[66] He finds that utilizers are not as close to or dependent on relatives and have more differentiated friendship networks (on the basis of proximity, frequency of interaction, and age of friends) than under-utilizers. Allan Horowitz takes a similar approach in relation to psychiatric services, reporting social networks to be a stronger predictor of time of entry into treatment than social class.[67] Individuals without strong kin networks and open friendship networks (friends who do not know each other) tend to enter treatment early and for less severe problems, while those with strong kin relationships and closed friendship networks tend to delay treatment and present problems that are relatively more serious.

The fact that lower socioeconomic status groups make less use of services may be due to a correlation with the way people perceive their own problems and/or the way they evaluate professional help, which may incline them toward obtaining treatment or not. Individuals with lower socioeconomic status perceive their problems as relevant for professional help less often than do higher-social-class individuals.[68] The importance of the differential perceptions of problems by social class in utilization behavior is further underscored by the fact that, once a problem has been defined as relevant or appropriate for professional help, the class differences in utilization behavior disappear. There is no relationship between use of services and income, education, or occupational status. As a result, Kulka and his colleagues conclude that the association between socioeconomic status and utilization of services is due to the definition of the problem by individuals (the first stage of decision making) rather than to whether services are used or not once the problem is defined (the second stage).

Noting that this is a change from their 1957 data, they suggest that the general relationship between socioeconomic status—in particular, income and education—and utilization behavior has decreased over time.[69] In 1957, more highly educated individuals were more likely to go for help (70 percent among college graduates versus 47 percent for grade-school-educated respondents). In 1976, there was almost no difference by education (73 percent for college graduates, 80 percent for grade-school-educated). The same results are found for income: 69 percent of high-income versus 51 percent of low-income individuals went for help in 1957, whereas 70 percent of high-income and 74 percent of low-income individuals went for help in 1976. Kulka and his associates attribute this reduction in class differences to fewer barriers to services—in terms of both availability and attitudes—among lower-class people and emphasize that the remaining class differences in utilization behavior are due to differences in the perception and definition of problems.

Although class differences in whether professional help is sought or not disappear once a problem has been defined as relevant for help, class differences do remain in the selection of the particular help source. In asking those respondents who did use professional help where they had gone, Kulka and his colleagues reported the major sources for 1976 as follows: clergymen (39 percent), doctors (21 percent), psychiatrists or psychologists (29 percent), marriage counsellors (8 percent), other mental health practitioners or agencies (18 percent), social service agencies for handling non-psychological (for example, financial) problems (4 percent), lawyers (2 percent), and others (5 percent). In comparing help sources used in the 1950s with the 1976 data, they found that the use of clergymen (who had been the most frequent help source in 1957) and doctors declined over time, and the use of psychiatrists, marriage counsellors, and other mental health sources increased. In the 1970s almost half of those who had sought help went to a mental health professional, either an individual or an agency. There are differences by social class, however, in the use of these professionals. More highly educated individuals use psychiatrists and psychologists more often than those with less education (11 percent of college-educated respondents versus 3 percent of grade-school-educated respondents). A difference by income in the use of psychiatrists and psychologists is also noted, but, in further analyses, this was found to be explained by education. Lower-income individuals, however, are found to use social service workers and agencies more often than those at higher income levels.

A recent Gallup survey prepared for the White House Conference on Families repeats the finding that people turn to "professional counsellors" far less often than to clergy, doctors, the Bible, and "other books." Some 11 percent of respondents indicate that they have turned to such counsellors for "advice, assistance—or encouragement on family matters." (Kulka and his colleagues reported 14 percent of all respondents using professional sources.) Nonetheless (individuals gave multiple responses), the overall totals are not small. An age, geographic, income, education, racial, occupational, and marital-status analysis shows modest yet significant differentiation in counsellor use by education, region, age, income, occupation, and marital status. The "divorced-separated" status defines by far the highest use category (24 percent).[70] (See Table 2.)

As we have seen, then, almost all the people queried in public opinion surveys between 1974 and 1980 indicate that things are going "very well" or "fairly well" for them and their families.[71] Nonetheless, many people have encountered problems in daily living, and many of them see these problems as residing in or as affecting their family lives. Indeed, many people locate their problems within themselves and their family relations even where a broader analytic approach would attribute responsibility to economic and other general societal forces. Of those who are troubled,

TABLE 2
Sources of Help on Family Matters, 1980

Respondent characteristics	Other family members (%)	Friends (%)	Clergy (%)	Professional counsellors (%)	Family doctor (%)	Family lawyer (%)	Bible (%)	Other books (%)	No opinion (%)
National	49	40	22	11	18	9	32	17	23
Sex									
Men	43	35	21	10	14	9	28	14	27
Women	54	44	22	11	22	10	35	20	20
Race									
White	49	40	22	11	18	10	30	18	23
Non-white	46	37	21	9	17	6	42	8	24
Education									
College	60	53	28	14	21	10	27	29	17
High school	48	38	20	10	18	11	32	15	24
Grade school	31	23	16	5	13	5	40	4	31
Region									
East	50	40	18	7	16	7	20	13	28
Midwest	54	41	28	12	22	10	34	21	18
South	44	36	20	9	16	11	40	14	22
West	47	44	22	16	18	10	32	24	27
Age									
18–34 years	62	53	19	11	16	8	25	19	16
35–49 years	52	45	28	16	22	12	36	21	21
50 and older	33	22	21	7	17	10	35	12	33

Income									
$15,000 and over	53	44	23	12	18	10	30	21	22
Under $15,000	44	35	21	9	18	9	34	13	25
Occupation									
White collar	58	51	25	13	21	12	28	29	19
Blue collar	49	39	21	10	16	8	33	12	23
City size									
Central city	51	41	22	9	18	9	26	15	23
Suburbs	49	44	20	13	20	11	28	19	26
Non-metro	47	36	22	10	17	9	38	17	23
Marital status									
Married	47	35	23	9	19	9	35	16	25
Single	57	57	17	12	14	8	22	21	19
Widowed	38	25	23	5	15	10	34	9	31
Divorced/separated	55	56	26	24	23	23	29	22	16
Assessment of family life									
Satisfied	48	39	21	9	17	9	31	17	24
Dissatisfied	52	51	29	25	26	15	36	21	19

Note: Totals add to more than 100 percent due to multiple responses.

Source: Gallup Organization, "American Families 1980: A Summary of Findings" (processed; Princeton, N.J.: The Organization, 1980), pp. 50–51. Based on responses to the question: "From which of the following sources, if any, have you sought advice, assistance, or encouragement on family matters?" (q. 28).

many turn outside the family for help, yet others do not see outside help as appropriate or do not seek to utilize anything but their own personal resources in coping. Apparently whether a person defines a problem as requiring help is the key determinant of whether he or she turns to available resources; and the economic, educational, ethnic, and class differences shape the problem definition.

Helping Services for Families: Our Focus

The statistics on the frequency and extent with which families identify themselves as having problems have led some observers to describe the situation as the death throes of the American family as an institution. More moderate observers simply say that the family is no longer crucial to the American culture. Yet because the family is our major source of socialization, support, intimacy, emotional satisfaction, and informal help, it also inevitably becomes the major vehicle for more formal helping of its members and those in its extended network. Indeed, as we shall note in Chapter 7, society continues to regard the family as so critical that it is the appropriate object for buttressing and help when there is trouble.

We concur with those who remain convinced of the family's continued importance. In contrast to the position of some others, however, we do not view acknowledgment of the family as a key institution as contradicting an equally firm belief that families have changed, as has the society in which families live. As part of these changes, families now have new and different kinds of needs and wants, many of which require extra-familial service and help. Therefore, a special concern of ours is: To what extent are families seeking new kinds of help in addition to more traditional types (and why)? And to what extent are they finding such help, where, and who is providing it?

As will soon be noted, we arbitrarily do not discuss the needs of the aged, except from the perspective of adult children and their families who want to plan with or for their older parents. The remainder of the field of services to the aging, particularly the older aging (75 +) deals largely with the needs of individuals in relation to income-housing-medical service and their connections with social services. We have written about this subject elsewhere, and it is too large and too different a field to encompass in a discussion meant to focus on younger adults and the children with whom they live. Similarly, as now is clear, it may be useful in this first exploration to put aside questions of unattached youth and societal response to their needs.

We have described, albeit briefly, what families look like today, what kinds of problems they have (or say they have), and where they go for help (if and when they go). We have summarized research findings and data to provide a systematic picture. We turn now to the heart of our book, a picture of the kinds of help available. Here, no systematic data are available. We surveyed an astonishing diversity of helping services and discovered quite early in our exploration that what was most difficult to determine was the boundary of "help for families."

The pattern of helping services is complex and diversified: professional help or self-help, public or private, profit or non-profit, sectarian or non-sectarian, individual or group, therapeutic or practical assistance, didactic or participatory, medical or non-medical, social work or psychology or psychiatry or clergy or education or sociology. Families are rarely helped as units, although such help is available at times, for some. More frequently, parents request and receive help with or without their children. Children receive help as children, or with their parents, sometimes even with siblings. Most help is provided to individuals, often family members, but not always, and not necessarily.

Faced with a dilemma regarding what to include and what to exclude, some of our choices may seem arbitrary, although we tried to follow a consistent principle. We decided to focus on services that were explicitly described as being "for families" or family members (that is, individuals in their family roles, such as parents, siblings, mothers, fathers, wives, husbands) and services that family members or individuals specifically requested as being needed, wanted, or desirable for family-related reasons. Where the service was, or is, individually initiated or oriented, it may be discussed here as well if a significant body of professional opinion urges that it be somehow family related in its execution. This too will require further clarification.

Moreover, as indicated, our particular concern was with help for average families, families in ordinary circumstances, not severely disorganized families in pathological situations. We tried to focus here on "normal" problems, on life milestones and family and individual life cycle transitions, on the crises we all must cope with if we are to survive each day, not on extremely severe, crippling disorders. In short, our goal has been to seek out the diversity of ways in which help is now being provided to buttress average family life in the modern world. This is the sense in which we conceptualize a support service.

The picture is not comprehensive because the parameters are not firm nor the domain clearly defined. Our review is not rigorous for the same reasons. Moreover, even in the most salient areas, data are limited and soft. We view what follows as an exercise in cartography. We are attempting to map a new and as yet unexplored domain. Our goal is to launch an exploratory journey in order to clarify new directions, issues, and questions.

The conventional view of "helping services" has always focused on aid provided by religious institutions, private charity and voluntary service agencies, public beneficence and public social (personal) services. While we look at all of these, we deliberately go beyond these services here to underscore how the concepts of "service" or "help" and the types of help sought are changing, as families and the society change.

Thus, we begin first with the most disparate domain, the one least likely in conventional studies to be assessed for its provision of help—the marketplace. We elected to begin our explorations here for just that reason. The market, after all, reflects what some people want, seek, and use in the way of help when they have the money to purchase such assistance. What better place to look for new developments, or indications of change? Obviously the marketplace closes some people out; it may also reflect values that are anathema to many. And its failures make public and private non-profit provision essential as well. In contrast, therefore, the four helping systems we look at subsequently are all in the non-profit sector, although each has market relationships, spin-offs, and fee-charging components. From the market, we turn to the public sector: What is already a public responsibility in this field? Public personal social services and community mental health centers are most relevant. Next, in the private, non-profit sector, we differentiate family service agencies from the diversity of therapeutic, counselling, self-help, and educational programs that began with church initiatives. We also look at family ministry and pastoral counselling activities carried out or sponsored by religious organizations.

Family life education is discussed in several of these contexts but featured as part of family service agency programs. Self-help programs are looked at in a separate chapter. We conclude with a review of what is known about how and why the family is important and what we have learned from our explorations of the help now available to American families, and with some reflections and some conjectures about possibilities for the future.

2   Families Buy Help

Historically, the marketplace has been viewed as the source of innovation, whether in new products or new services. A recurring criticism of social programs has been that "need" is a subjective measure and that the potential dimensions of social needs are infinite. In contrast, "demand," an economic concept, is finite, and can be measured by the extent to which individuals exercise their preference for goods and services in the marketplace by paying for what they want. Given this view of the market, one way to begin an exploration of how the society is responding to family and related social change is to survey what is available in the way of services for sale or for a fee because people have been willing to expend their resources for such services.

Obviously if the market were a perfect barometer of need for services, mixed economy societies like ours would have no need for private nonprofit or public programs. Our society devotes some 25 percent of its gross national product to social welfare programs—goods, benefits, and services to which there is entitlement by other than marketplace criteria—and for good reason. We therefore shall also consider the limitations of market services. First, however, there is an exciting and instructive story about public programs now discovered as being so valuable as to merit marketplace replication ("reprivatization") and market innovation that identifies valuable services to which access should not be limited to those with funds.

A Smorgasbord of Services

The categories may have different labels. The classification schemes may vary. The numbers of subcategories may be limited in suburban newspapers or special newsletters. In some parts of the country, the "Yellow Pages" are the only information source. Despite the lack of consistency, the number and range of personal services—at a price, for a fee—now available to meet the new and changing needs and wants of Americans as individuals and as family members seem to have grown exponentially during the 1970s. A comprehensive picture is impossible at this time. What follows is illustrative and selective.

Besides such traditional personal services as personal financial management, budgeting, investment advice, and tax counselling, the classified ads in *Los Angeles*, a regular feature in this popular monthly, contain over two dozen listings of special catering and party planning services including one that offers "breakfast in bed," a second for "vegetarian French cuisine," and innumerable listings for cooking, bartending, waitressing, and flower-arranging services.

Other clusters of ads include listings for hypnosis, acupuncture, and "stress control," for psychics, astrologists, and palmists, and one for "The Future Shapers." This last offers "a comprehensive list of complete psychic services and personal development programs" including daily psychic counselling, ESP development, pet counselling, yoga and movement therapy, acupuncture, astrology, hypnosis, and nutrition counselling.

One category includes a special "shop at home" service for the busy working woman: "experienced wardrobe consultant will provide personal attention"—review your current wardrobe, analyze your life and work styles, advise you on the most appropriate and attractive styles for you, and go out and shop for you, bringing the "right clothes" directly to your home. An experienced exercise teacher will come to your home to analyze your body and your exercise needs and develop a daily routine to keep you in shape.

Another category, called "time savers," lists half a dozen services like the following:

"Do you need that 25th hour/8 day week?"
You name it; we do it.
WE'RE HEAVEN SENT
Services for Busy People

BIPROXY
Time Saving Services including gift-buying, errands, shopping.
Business or Personal

THE CREATIVE ORGANIZER
Feeling overwhelmed? Always missing deadlines or appointments?
We will organize your home or your personal life.

A long list of self-improvement services can be summed up by the following ad:

If your life isn't what you think it should be, call me . . .
Counsellor and therapist

Many major cities such as Washington, D.C., San Francisco, and Chicago have magazines offering similar advertisements. Among the most comprehensive is that in *New York* magazine. The categories may be different: entertainment/singles; gourmet services; instruction; counselling; personal improvement; personal services. They are not, however, discrete; some advertisements are listed under two or three headings. Specific ads are revealing. A selection that appeared in this weekly over a period of a month, directed specifically at family-related needs and concerns, includes:

Divorced, Widowed Persons—Learn how to socialize again. Six-week course on meeting people and establishing effective male-female relationships. Taught by licensed psychologists.

Two days-nights that can change your life. The Worldwide Marriage Encounter Weekend; an enriching joyful, memorable experience offered to married couples.

Problems? Qualified, moderate cost, counselling or psychotherapy for individuals, couples, families.

Is your child hyperactive? Behavior Modification Therapy without medication is available. Parents are trained to improve their child's behavior.

Transactional analysis: Ongoing group and couple counselling.

Women's Psychotherapy Network—consultation, referral, treatment.

Religion can help . . .

Bioenergetic-Gestalt therapy—Individuals, groups; couples a specialty.

Sexual problems in your marriage? . . .

Psychotherapies Selection Service—Helping the "consumer" make informed choices. Orientation films of major therapies; Explorations; Meet and choose among therapists. Only licensed therapists.

Change your image, change your clothes. I'll help any woman put together a tasteful wardrobe, inexpensively.

Baby Sitting Service—Reliable, competent, trustworthy, 30 years experience meeting the child care needs of parents.

Help for working women, working couples—Fabulous service providing bartenders, cooks, waitresses, movers, painters, repairmen, cleaning people, personal secretaries, errands . . .

Contemplating Divorce? . . . Experienced law specialists can help you to obtain a divorce with less trauma and conflict. We are sensitive to the emotional problems of divorce and offer understanding and sound advice on its legal problems.

Relocating? Moving? Our national network located in all major cities
will provide you with up-to-date information on residential areas,
price range of houses, schools . . .

Feeling Tied Down? Someone you care for needs help? Certified
social workers will plan, monitor, care, visit, counsel. Special vacation
services . . .[1]

In addition, of course, is the long list of specialized and individualized
self-improvement services. These include career counselling, résumé
writing, training for public speaking, assertiveness training for women, and
dozens of ads by psychotherapists and counsellors offering individual and
group therapy as well as marriage, couple, and family therapy.

A selection of ads from other regional or local magazines includes these:

Are you having problems with your spouse-partner-roommate-friend?
Qualified, moderate cost, individual-group-family counselling or
psychotherapy available.

Having difficulty in satisfying your partner sexually? Other kinds
of sexual problems? We offer sex therapy and sex counselling to
couples . . .

Parents! Learn how to communicate with your teenagers and end the
constant fighting and rebellion—or the "no talking" syndrome . . .

Hypnotherapy . . . Bio-energetic gestalt therapy . . . psychoanalytic
therapy . . . available through our group practice . . .

For women trying out new roles, balancing home and job need not be
a high wire act. Join the Women's Network—Women Helping Other
Women (WHOW!)

Do you miss the excitement of the early years of marriage? Participate
in one of our Communication Workshops for Couples. One weekend
will lead to a renewal of romance, intimacy, trust, and caring . . .

Worried about your widowed mother alone in Florida for the first
time? No time to visit her? She sounds depressed on the telephone?
We can be your extended family.

As this potpourri shows, an enormous variety of help for families can be
found in the private marketplace. We are well beyond the "help with
problems" as described in the research in Chapter 1. The domain is family
functioning—everyday life and household events—and the services that
meet needs in a changing social environment in which people do less for
themselves and purchase more. It may be that their own time is spent in
new ways and that they seek out services as a substitute; or, that new forms
of help are available, and, therefore, individual and family time can be

spent differently. But some of the services deal with intimate personal problems, with severe trouble, with disorder and illness as well as with efforts at self improvement. What kinds of help do families seek and use when they have the money to pay for help? Are there unique kinds of help available in the market, new social inventions that cannot be found elsewhere? What kinds of families and family members use these marketplace services as contrasted with those who use services in the other sectors? And finally, what, if anything distinguishes what is available in the marketplace and paid for at full market value from what is available in the public or private not-for-profit sectors?

Help with Personal Problems: Marriage and Family Therapy

Clearly, help with marital, child, and family problems is an important part of what is provided in the marketplace, just as it is an important part of the help families seek and use in the non-market sector. (For some examples, see the Appendix.) Indeed, the range of "help" available today itself suggests the wares of a marketplace. "We'd like you to think of marriage counselling, indeed the field of therapy, as a marketplace," say the authors of a book on marriage and family therapy written for a general readership. "The marketplace was once a small one with only a few versions of two basic products":

> One product was psychoanalysis—a long, costly process of delving into one's past in order to free the individual of growth-stunting neuroses. The success of analysis depended upon the special one-to-one relationship between patient and analyst, a relationship from which spouse and children were excluded except as they appeared through the words and feelings of the patient.
> The other product was adjustment therapy—a comparatively inexpensive, short-term process of talking about marital problems in order to have the husband and wife come to a better understanding of each other. The success of this kind of marriage counselling depended upon the couple, particularly the wife, realizing that with some concessions from the other, both could live together, and in any case, the adjusting was better than admitting failure and getting a divorce.
> But look at the marketplace now. It has changed and expanded to such an extent that a couple hoping to find a cure for an ailing marriage may not even know the name brands—Gestalt, Transactional Analysis, Bioenergetics, Psychodrama, Behavior Modification, Encounter Groups, Family Therapy, Sex Clinics, Pastoral Counselling, Marriage Encounter, Feminist Therapy—to mention a few.[2]

Regardless of the type of therapy employed, when the focus is on interpersonal or interactional problems with a spouse, a child, a parent, or within the family generally, the helping process is increasingly described as family therapy, or marriage and family therapy. The field of practice as well as the numbers of practitioners has grown enormously in the last ten years.

What Is Marriage and Family Therapy?

Marriage and family therapy began initially as two separate therapeutic approaches. Marriage counselling as a specialized field of counselling, usually for middle-class couples, began first in the 1930s.[3] Practitioners first formalized their identification in 1942, when a small group organized the American Association of Marriage Counselors (AAMC) in order to facilitate the development of the profession. In 1970, the AAMC expanded its focus by officially changing its name to the American Association of Marriage and Family Counselors (AAMFC) in order to include family therapists, who had previously had no national organization with which to identify.[4] In 1979, in part as an indication of the changing image and ideology of the profession, the organization underwent still another name change, to the American Association for Marriage and Family Therapy (AAMFT). In many ways, the organization is a microcosm of the field.

The field of family therapy is more recent, but has experienced an extraordinarily rapid growth, clearly outdistancing or, more appropriately, encompassing the older field. Beginning in the early and middle 1950s, family therapy grew out of an effort to find more effective methods for treating very severe emotional problems, especially schizophrenia or severe psychosis, especially when the individual with a problem was a severely disturbed child or young person in a family.[5] Among the pioneers and leaders in the family therapy field were Nathan Ackerman, Murray Bowen, Jay Haley, Don Jackson, Salvador Minuchin, and Virginia Satir.

Initially, marital therapists premised their counselling on the theoretical work of family sociology and clinical psychology while family therapists tended to use psychodynamic formulations, communications theory, general systems theory, and/or specific theories or concepts espoused by eminent family therapists. During the last decade, however, the two strains have increasingly converged, as family therapists began to focus on treating the marital couple as well as the whole family and marriage counsellors came to involve children, too, in their work with parents. Indeed, it would appear that most professionals treating children, couples, or families today describe themselves as family therapists on the assumption that all such problems have their primary locus in the family system.

Perhaps the most important thing to note in distinguishing family therapy as a field from psychoanalysis as such, or from any other kind of individual psychotherapy, is that family therapy experts define or describe as family therapy any intervention focused on the family system rather than the persons in it. Given this general framework, some family therapists see only couples; some see whole families—parent(s) and children; some see extended kin networks. Most use a diversity of therapeutic techniques and interventive strategies. For family therapists, the family is "the patient"; the individual member is more a symptom of a sick system. The therapeutic focus is on the family as a system and the changes that can be made in that system. All approaches to doing family therapy accept this basic notion: that the locus of pathology is not the individual person but the system, although the concept of system may mean the nuclear family for some and a much wider social network for others.

Thus, what distinguishes family therapy from all other therapies is not the kind of intervention made but the locus of pathology. "Any approach therefore in which the therapist sees pathology as residing in the system or interaction can be called family therapy. This is true even if at a given session only the marital dyad is seen or quite possibly only one member of the family. It is not the number of members present that constitutes family therapy but the conception of the therapist."[6]

Who Are Marriage and Family Therapists?

There is no way at present to assess the numbers of practicing marriage and family therapists, or to know what proportion among them are in private practice (paid a fee for service) as contrasted to those who are working for a public or private social agency or clinic and being paid a salary. Only six states (California, Michigan, Nevada, New Jersey, North Carolina, and Utah) license marriage and family therapists. Given current public attitudes toward government regulations, it is unlikely that more than three or four more states at most will institute licensing or certification over the next five years.[7] Since family therapy, almost by definition, is a multidisciplinary field, including professionals whose basic training is in psychiatry, psychology, social work, pastoral counselling, nursing, family sociology, human sexuality, and marriage counselling, professional or disciplinary affiliation does not clarify the situation either. Nor does membership in a national organization, although one clearly dominates the field.

The major national professional organization for marriage and family therapists has long been the organization now named the American Association for Marriage and Family Therapy (AAMFT). Other organizations that include marriage and family therapists in their membership are the Academy of Psychologists in Marital and Family Therapy, the Marriage and Family Therapy Sections of the American Group Psychotherapy Association, the American Orthopsychiatric Association, and the Groves Conference on Marriage and the Family. AAMFT remains, however, the major national organization exclusively for marriage and family therapists regardless of disciplinary affiliation.

Founded in 1942 in the northeastern part of the country as a small elitist organization, members of the AAMFT were limited initially to those holding Ph.D.s or the equivalent and having extensive specialized training and experience. It remained small (about one hundred members) until the late 1960s; the real explosion in membership did not occur until the mid-1970s. In the intervening years, the organization moved its headquarters to a California location and extended its membership throughout the country as well as to Canada, becoming in fact a national professional organization.

In 1964, California passed the first law licensing marriage and family counselling as a profession, limiting eligibility to those with approved training at the master's degree level. Because California was licensing a large number of counsellors who were not eligible for membership in the existing national professional organization, an independent state organization was developed. AAMFT was concerned with the quality of training these newly licensed counsellors were receiving and, at least as important, with the growth of a competing organization that might subsequently move toward a national membership. To assure itself the legitimacy and the constituency of the leading professional group, the AAMFT board realized it would have to expand its membership base and therefore change its standards.

In 1967, AAMFT changed its criteria for membership to include qualified holders of master's degrees in a behavioral science, marriage and family counselling, or a related professional degree (social work), plus supervised work experience. The organization anticipated a very rapid expansion in membership, although this did not occur until the middle of the next decade. The organization's change of name in 1970 was part of this deliberate attempt at planned growth and professional leadership.

In 1972, AAMFT (then AAMFC) had a membership of 1,200 individuals (a small fraction of those practicing marriage and family counselling nationally) and an annual budget of $60,000 and it hired a full-time executive director, C. Ray Fowler, Ph.D., who still holds that post today. In 1977, its membership was slightly under 5,300, its annual budget was $400,00 (all from membership dues), and the projected growth rate for membership was 25 percent. By 1980, its membership was over 8,000 and its budget more than $1,000,000. California, Texas, New York, and Illinois had the largest number of members, although the recent growth in membership had come mainly from the midwest.

About half the membership today identify themselves as "family therapists." Most others describe themselves as marriage and family therapists. Only a small group continue to view themselves as marital therapists solely or even primarily. Clearly, this broader view of family practice has emerged as dominant, another recent and significant development along with the truly extraordinary growth in the organization's size and membership.

One insight into the size and character of the field generally can be gained by comparing the membership of the national organization, based in California, with that of the parallel, independent California Association of Marriage and Family Therapists. The latter has a membership of 3,000 state-licensed counsellors while the national organization has about 1,200 members from California, most of whom belong to both the state and the national organizations. There are close to 20,000 licensed marriage and family therapists in the six states that license such therapists today. (If this proportion held up nationally, it would suggest that there might be about 250,000 qualified marriage and family therapists in the United States now.) Although some state licensees may feel national affiliation unnecessary, the existence of so many who are not members of the more prestigious national organization raises at least some questions about the qualifications of some practitioners. Since only six states require licensing, this discrepancy clearly reveals the problem in estimating the total number of practitioners as well as the problems of assessing the quality of training, preparation, and practice. In effect, licensing establishes only a minimum standard. The absence of licensing in the vast majority of states places the primary burden for monitoring quality on the national organization members themselves (voluntary self-regulation) and on consumers.

As the official accrediting organization for specialized graduate and post-graduate educational and training programs, the AAMFT has a direct impact on professional practice. Its standards for membership require approved training, supervised experience, a certain number of hours of continuing professional education annually, as well as adherence to a code of professional ethics. However, its membership still reflects only a fraction of those practicing marriage and family therapy and calling themselves marriage and family therapists. The organization is now planning a major effort at public education, convinced that more formal regulation (state licensing or certification) is unlikely to occur in the next few years. Since most marriage and family therapy is indeed a private marketplace enterprise, the responsibility for informed choice lies with the consumer. Voluntary self-regulation by practitioners is necessary but clearly not sufficient, by itself, to protect consumers against the consequences of unqualified practitioners. Current and growing stress by the national organization on consumer education is premised on the assumption that ultimately it is the consumer who seeks help, who must be knowledgeable and discriminating in choosing among the competent, experienced, highly qualified practitioners, on the one hand, and the many inexperienced practitioners, on the other hand, or, even worse, the outright charlatans and quacks who prey on gullible and troubled couples.

AAMFT membership is predominantly made up of psychologists and social workers, who between them constitute about two thirds of the members in roughly equal proportions. Another 15 percent are pastoral counsellors, while the remaining 15 to 20 percent includes psychiatrists, psychiatric nurses, and clinical sociologists. About 60 percent of the members hold master's degrees; the other 40 percent hold doctorates. The membership is largely white; ethnic and racial minorities constitute about 10 percent of the membership.

A 1978 membership survey underscored the private market nature of marriage and family therapy. Responses to one question confirmed the fact that by far most members are in private practice and derive all or a significant portion of their income from that practice. About 40 percent of the respondents stated that they are in full-time private practice. Only 25 percent work full time for social agencies or clinics. The remaining 35 percent divide their time in varying amounts between private practice and agency- or clinic-based work or teaching. This combination often requires twenty or twenty-five hours per week in private practice. All members of the National Board of Directors of AAMFT are heavily engaged in private practice, although about half have university, social agency, or clinic affiliations also.

In discussing his views on some of the most important trends for his organization, Ray Fowler, the executive director of the AAMFT, stressed three that would seem to have particular significance for the field generally. One is the decline in formal regulation and standard setting (the slowdown in state licensing), which clearly implies problems for consumers when choosing among private therapists, as we have already mentioned. Another is the enormous growth in the family therapy field. The third, which we will discuss later, is the growing interest of private industry in this field.

For AAMFT, the immediate issue is the tremendous increase in membership, which for the past five years has expanded at a rate of about 25 percent a year and is projected to continue at this rate for at least the next few years. Parallelling the growth in membership has been the increased training, experience, and identification of members with family therapy as contrasted with marital therapy alone. It would seem that family therapy is increasingly viewed as subsuming marital therapy. In that respect, we are convinced that AAMFT reflects broader developments in the country at large.

Nationally, family therapy, as defined broadly, seems to be expanding enormously. More and more professionals describe themselves as "family therapists." More professionals describe their practice as "family therapy." More agencies and clinics include "family therapy" as an important part of what they offer in the way of helping families. More popular magazines include articles on the subject, informing the general reader that this is an available kind of help. Moreover, not only are these articles appearing in the women's magazines that have always been interested in the topic (*Ladies' Home Journal, Redbook, Working Women*) but even in business magazines with a very different audience.[8] Most important, from all reports, more individual family members are seeking, using, and finding marriage and family therapy helpful. Indeed, the astonishing growth in this field, as evidenced primarily in the marketplace, is a phenomenon that has received inadequate attention thus far. Few of these private practitioners qualify for third-party reimbursement—that is, payment out of health insurance and government-sponsored medical programs like Medicare and Medicaid—even though, where licensing applies, some private insurance programs do include coverage for licensed marital and family therapists. This increase in numbers of people paying personally and directly for the service is a clear demonstration of growth in effective demand, an interesting indicator of changes in social and personal attitudes toward the use of such help. Whether or not there is any firm evidence that all or most of this kind of help is effective, consumers certainly view it as such. If the marketplace is an indication of demand, clearly this kind of help is viewed as important, needed, and worthwhile. However they describe it, experts around the country seem convinced that a belief in the value and efficacy of professional help in solving marital and family problems, often in ways other than divorce, is "an idea whose time has come." And even among those seeking help who conclude, subsequently, that divorce is the only viable alternative, there is a growing recognition that professional help and therapy may attenuate some of the pain of divorce or enable people to deal with the inevitable problems more effectively.

Family Therapists at Work

Keeping this background in mind, we turn to a more detailed picture of what is involved in the private practice of marital and family therapy. What do family therapists do, and what, if anything, do they view as distinguishing private practice from the practice of family therapy in a social agency or clinic? A few examples will clarify the picture.

Mrs. A has a master's degree in social work and over twenty years experience in a family service agency. For ten of those years, she worked as a therapist in a family therapy clinic headed by one of the pioneers in the field and received specialized training as well as supervised experience under him. During the next ten years, she worked half time at the clinic and half time at her own private practice. Now she combines private practice with clinical consultation to one of the leading family and children's service agencies and teaches family therapy at a nearby university. Her office is in her home.

At present, Mrs. A is seeing fifteen families, each once a week for about an hour and a half. This is a fairly typical pattern in her practice, which usually averages twenty-five to thirty "patient hours" a week. A typical case lasts about two years. In addition to such cases, she usually sees one or two families for very brief periods—four or five sessions—around an immediate crisis, a specific time-limited problem, a recurrence of an earlier problem, or a new problem in a family seen previously in long-term treatment. Her present caseload includes five families where she sees both parents and children, two single-parent families where she sees the mother and the children, eight families where she sees the husband and wife only, and three individual patients. Most of Mrs. A's work is with couples or with marital problems and their consequences for children. Almost all her patients are referred to her by previous patients, the families of former patients, psychiatrists she knows who are treating individuals and feel their families should be involved in treatment, colleagues and friends who are in the field, or current and former students. She does not advertise, viewing advertising as "unprofessional."

An approach she uses frequently in her practice is to begin with several sessions in which she sees the whole family, then to work with the couple for an extended period of time, and finally to return to several sessions with the entire family to conclude the treatment. One case illustrating this pattern is that of an affluent, successful, interracial couple, both professionals. The man was white, the woman black. They had three children: an eighteen-year-old girl, a fifteen-year-old boy, and a twelve-year-old boy. The children were all attractive, articulate, and clearly able, yet all were underachieving at school. The girl, just entering college, was unclear about what she wanted to do and what kinds of occupational choices were available to her. The older boy had similar problems; moreover, he was constantly described as unreliable and undependable. The youngest had no friends and was acting up at home and in school, increasingly revealing an uncontrollable temper and tantrums.

The parents came for help because they were concerned about their children. During the first interview they denied the existence of any problems between the two of them and disclaimed any insight into their children's difficulties. They insisted that their marriage was perfect; there were no problems as a consequence of their racial differences; they had plenty of friends, both blacks and whites. Despite their denials, in the course of the first interview it became increasingly clear that there was enormous tension between the two. The husband was implicitly encouraging his daughter to disobey her mother, while the wife was supporting the older boy in similarly disruptive behavior; the youngest was caught in the middle. All their conflicts were expressed through their children, since neither parent was able to confront the other directly where there was disagreement.

Mrs. A saw the family as a unit for one year. By the end of this year, both the parents and the children were able to recognize and acknowledge that the problems were the parents' problems, not the children's. She then saw the parents alone, as a couple, for almost another year in order to help them learn to deal with their marital problems. Finally, the family was seen all together for four more sessions before treatment was concluded.

Dr. B, another family therapist, also began her training as a social worker and subsequently received a doctorate in social work at a major eastern university. She, too, had extensive experience in a family service agency and was trained and supervised by one of the leaders in the family therapy field. She combines teaching master's and doctoral degree social work students with a private practice in family therapy. Her caseload, too, averages about fifteen families weekly and about twenty-five to thirty patient hours per week. Although a typical family session is one and a half hours and she sees most families once a week for about two years, she generally sees couples for only one hour. She also uses intensive full-day treatment sessions on a Saturday or Sunday and weekend "marathon" sessions. Her patients come to her in the same way Mrs. A's do, a pattern that is fairly typical for qualified marital and family therapists throughout the country.

Dr. B works only with family units. When someone calls to ask for help and tries to make an appointment to see her the first time, her immediate question is, "With whom do you live?" She begins with this question even before asking the caller how she or he feels about the problem. No matter what the problem is, her approach is to place it in a family context. She says that the typical problems people bring who are seeking help are: "My child has a problem" (or "My child's teacher says he/she has a problem"); "My wife/husband is depressed;" "I/my spouse thinks there is something wrong with our marriage."

The first two or three sessions with a family are viewed as "consultative," and for these she insists on having every member of the family present. Although Dr. B views this as a tentative, diagnostic phase, 90 percent of all those seen in this phase continue in treatment subsequently. She places great stress on the first telephone call and the first few sessions. She views this "family intake" phase as significant for pointing direction and establishing an implicit contract with the family regarding work to be done and possible goals. Although she works only with families, the whole family does not have to be present at every session after the initial diagnostic phase is completed. She may work with subgroups within the family—with the marital couple, one parent and a child, even an individual—periodically seeing the whole family for feedback or for further problem delineation.

A typical short-term case began five weeks before Christmas with a phone call from a young woman who had been referred by her boyfriend, a former student of Dr. B's. The caller was divorced, a professional, originally from the west but now living in the east near three of her siblings. She called for help for her whole family because, as Christmas approached, she found herself becoming more and more apprehensive about what she described as an annual crisis. Every Christmas her mother came east, from her home in Seattle, to spend the holidays with her children. Each visit brought tension and fighting. The last few years since her father's death had been even worse, according to the girl. Now that Christmas was near and it was definite that her mother was coming, she found herself in a panic, dreading the visit, incapable of saying no to her mother, yet unable to deal with the inevitable crisis.

The "treatment" lasted four sessions. One session was held before the mother arrived. Two were held with her, and a fourth, a follow-up, after she went home. Before the first session, Dr. B requested each family member to send her a written statement on how they viewed their family and two charts or diagrams of their relationships with other family members. One chart was to describe family relationships before their father's death and the other after. During the first interview, it became apparent that the request for treatment had been initiated by the mother, not the daughter who called. In speaking to each of her children about the forthcoming visit, she had indicated her own anxiety and expressed some interest in whether there was not some kind of "help" that could be obtained to make the visit a more pleasant occasion for them all. Also, during this interview, it became clear that the one brother, the only man in the family, was the current family scapegoat. When he arrived five minutes late for the first session, his three sisters all pounced on him for being late, describing his behavior as "typically selfish" and "irresponsible." The family charts suggested that this young man was now the recipient of much of the resentment that earlier had been directed toward the father. His sisters were especially resentful of the fact that he had married and moved away from home soon after his father's death. Among other things that emerged during the sessions when the mother was present was the fact that she really wanted to stay with her son and his wife when she came east but could not deal with what she thought would be her daughters' jealousy if she chose a daughter-in-law in preference to them.

One result of these sessions was that when the mother returned home, she entered a group therapy program there, to deal with a growing problem of alcoholism that she had been trying to hide from her daughters. In addition, she began to explore how to communicate more effectively with her daughters, trying out telephone conversations with them in advance, in order to avoid the kind of stimulus-reaction patterns that constantly resulted in a fight or some other crisis.

Dr. B emphasized that there are no easy answers to family problems and family conflict. The major result of therapy may be the resolution of an immediate conflict and some recognition of how the crisis emerged—and how another might be avoided, perhaps, another time. In this case, the therapist relieved the mother and the family of a noxious situation in which the mother could not explain what was wrong and therefore kept escalating crises in order to gain attention from her children and recognition of the fact that there was a problem, even if the problem they identified was not the problem of real significance.

Group counselling, led by male-female therapy teams, often husband and wife teams, offers another new approach to the practice of marriage and family therapy. In a group of five or six couples, each couple provides support for the others. The presence of a couple as co-leaders also provides a different kind of leadership and catalyst, although this approach can be effective only if both team members have equally strong skills, with neither needing to—or tending to—dominate the other. The presence of a male-female team in a leadership role tends to offset the occasionally skewed result that occurs when one therapist, regardless of sex, is leading a group of couples. The therapists become role models as well as leaders in such situations. This approach can be particularly effective in working with dual-career couples. Sometimes these couples become so obsessed with their careers that they lose track of their personal lives. With a dual-career couple as group leaders and co-therapists, a new perspective can be introduced, with group members feeling that their life styles are understood and shared in a way that no therapist working alone could convey.

One therapist described the work he and his wife did together with low-income, working-class couples. Bringing together five or six such couples for a weekend at their house in the country, these therapists ran multiple family therapy groups, acting as co-therapists, and often as surrogate parents, for working-class couples seeking help with their problems and unlikely to use more conventional therapeutic approaches. These weekend, "marathon session," multi-family therapy groups became a kind of surrogate family or extended family network. In an informal, relatively unstructured, quasi-social setting, under the warm and supportive leadership of the husband and wife team, couples aired their problems, spoke freely to one another, and became open to new insights.

Several therapists discussed the increase in marital couples coming for help together. One suggested that the growth in requests for marital therapy should be viewed as a positive development: "Instead of immediately assuming that divorce is the only solution, more and more couples are coming for help with their marriages, with their relationships with each other. Often, with a little help, in particular in understanding how the behavior of each contributes to the couple's problems, a marriage can be very much improved."

Another, commenting on the same trend, said, "After all, many people marry for the wrong reasons and even after long years of marriage still don't understand why they married and, therefore, why there is conflict. Some come for help in resolving conflict, or, they say, to improve their marriage. Often, however, the real reason is to get strong enough themselves so that they are no longer dependent on one another and they can live separately. Sometimes this takes years. Marital problems frequently reach a crisis when other kinds of developmental changes occur in a family, such as when children leave home."

All the therapists we interviewed talked about the enormous increase in the numbers of reconstituted ("blended") families now coming for help. Some stated that by definition a reconstituted family is always in need of help. The major problem these families face is the need to deal with the past while trying to cope with a new family system in the present and work on tasks for the future. Whatever the current situation is, and the problems presented by "his children, her children, and our children," often a concomitant prior problem is the unfinished business of the marital couple, who may still be dealing with the unresolved problems of their first marriages, even in the reconstituted family. In effect, the couple's tasks include solving problems of their previous marriages, their present marriage, and, frequently, the children of all three marriages.

Sometimes a couple comes for help before getting married, saying, "We are very much in love and want to get married, but our respective children object, and we don't know what to do." Other couples come with a plaintive announcement, "We got married too quickly, and our kids are giving us difficulty. We never anticipated this, and we don't know what to do. We need help." Sometimes the problem is assigned to the children, but sometimes a couple asserts, "We know we have a problem. It's clearly affecting the kids. We're sure it has nothing to do with them. It's our problem and we need help in handling it before it gets worse and the kids really do have a problem too."

In describing how he works with a typical reconstituted family, one therapist talked about a couple, both of whom had been married before, who had considered their current marriage successful until recently. The man's first wife had died a year before, and he now had living with them the ten-year-old son of his first marriage, who had previously been in his wife's custody. His second wife, a clinical psychologist and therapist herself, had children who were all grown, either away at school or working and living on their own. Until the boy arrived, theirs had been the perfect companionate marriage. Both were professionals in the same field (he was a psychiatrist), and they were free to come and go as they wished, sharing professional as well as various other interests. Suddenly, there was a young child in the home, and he was not even hers. Moreover, her husband adored his son and also felt guilty about the boy's having experienced the trauma of his parents' divorce, first, and then the death of his mother.

"I feel like the wicked stepmother," his wife cried out in the middle of one session. "I know that what I am doing is wrong, yet I'm so angry at the two of them—my husband and the boy—and I'm consumed with guilt because of it." The boy kept manipulating the situation in order to remain close to his father and to keep his stepmother away. The father, caught by his love for his son and his guilt regarding what the boy had experienced, permitted himself to be manipulated. And his wife resented it all, yet, too, felt guilty about the boy. In effect, this was a prototypical problem for a reconstituted family. In this case, as in many others, the dilemma is that, the more the child makes an adjustment to the new family, the more he feels disloyal to his own mother.

Dr. C, the therapist, discussed how, with such families, one must support both parents and attempt to develop a greater equilibrium in the family. In the case described above, it was important for the father to become more of a disciplinarian and the mother to be more of a pleasure seeker. The first and most important step, however, was to get the parents united. "Love," Dr. C said authoritatively, "is not the issue in the relationship between the stepparent and the child. If you get love, you're just plain lucky, and you should realize it." And then, somewhat reflectively, he added, "The only issue of importance between stepparent and child is fairness. In fact, it's a mistake, even inappropriate, to aspire to love."

Role conflicts continue to be a reason many couples come for help. For some years, there was a recurring problem as women, after ten or fifteen years of marriage and full-time motherhood and housewifery, found themselves restless and resentful, knowing full well that the choice to remain at home had been their own, yet now wondering if it had been a mistake. Ambivalent about leaving the security of a clearly defined and approved role, resentful of what they now viewed as having been a socially determined choice, these women often took their anger out on unsuspecting husbands who did not understand why they were being blamed for choices made by their wives, with which they may have concurred but which they surely did not consciously impose.

Such situations are increasingly less likely to occur today, when more women are already in the labor force or are seeking to enter it after a much briefer hiatus. The role conflicts presented today for family or marital therapy are more likely to involve young, newly married couples in their twenties and thirties. Before marriage, the woman may have announced firmly that she expected a fully equal status in her marriage. Unclear what this meant, let alone what behavior it implied for him, the man agreed. Surely he believed in equality between men and women in marriage, at least in theory. Once a couple is married, however, there are still the details to be worked out: Who cooks? Who cleans? Who markets? Do they have a child—and when? Who takes time off to care for the child? Who is responsible for arranging for care, and for being available in case the child care person fails to arrive or gets sick? These are the grounds on which the equality issue gets played out, and often it is around such conflicts that the couple comes for help. If they are lucky, the crisis occurs before they have children. When asked whether most couples today do not work out these details before marriage, we were told by one therapist, "The ones I see are the ones who haven't worked it out yet." Another therapist offered a more insightful comment: "It doesn't matter what they work out in advance. Marriage creates a different reality. And even more important, there is no way of assessing how two people will react once they are well launched on their respective careers and decide to have a baby. All the pre-child discussions about equality and sharing occur in a vacuum. Then the reality occurs—the baby arrives. And the trouble with babies is that they don't go away. You can't change your mind about having them once they arrive." Many young couples today are deciding to delay having children until they feel secure in their jobs or careers. Some are having them, sharing responsibilities for care and rearing, but electing to have only one child, or two at the most.

All these family therapists described their family patients as "the healthy sick" (as did those who described families who came for help to a family service agency). "By and large, the families who come to me for help are functioning," said one family therapist. "They work; they make a decent living; they are concerned spouses and reasonably adequate parents. Most of their problems have to do with interpersonal relationships, sometimes with anxiety and/or depression."

The major difference between private practice and working for an agency, according to those who have experienced both, has to do with socioeconomic class. Private patients can spend more money on treatment—for getting help—and can invest more time (and more money too) in obtaining help. Problems of poverty, illness, inadequate housing, and unemployment are less likely to be present, although under-employment is often an issue, as are problems of money, health, age, personal space. The patient population seen by private family therapists is also more homogeneous than that seen in social agencies and clinics, not only because of class but also because the clients are more likely to be urban, young or middle-aged, articulate, and fairly well educated. Although these are the characteristics of many family agency clients too, they are far more likely to describe those seen in private practice.

Two other differences were cited by therapists as significant, and suggested some of the "costs" to practitioners of private practice (and also why so many practitioners combine their private practice with teaching, or with an agency, clinic, hospital, or research institute affiliation). One therapist spoke of how she missed the availability of videotape equipment for treatment supervision and training. Several spoke of the absence of opportunity for group or peer supervision, for co-therapy, or for other opportunities for using multiple therapy techniques under one aegis. As one therapist said, "If I think one family member needs individual treatment, I have to refer him or her elsewhere and chance losing control of the case. In the clinic, all the therapists involved continue to meet and stay related to what is happening in a case." Most stressed the lack of opportunity for collegial stimulation and sharing, complaining of the inevitable professional and personal isolation incumbent on private practice. Indeed, several insisted that no competent private practitioner could remain in private practice only, especially if that practice were family therapy. "The need to keep up with new therapeutic techniques, to share ideas with others working in the field, to have a sounding board and occasionally check out conclusions with others you respect, makes some kind of contrasting experience where colleagues are present and available on other than an informal social basis essential."

Private practice offers the opportunity for family therapists to earn substantially more in fees than an agency or clinic can provide in salary. Sometimes, these fees are used to supplement a secure basic salary from a "regular job." At the same time, private practice by definition implies a kind of isolation that must be offset by compensating professional activities. Private practice offers consumers maximum opportunity for choice but no assurance of at least some minimum standards of practice, which an agency or clinic can guarantee. In the marketplace, the burden of making an informed choice regarding quality of treatment is on the consumer.

Help with Personal Problems: Private Industry

Besides the direct help offered by private counsellors and therapists in the marketplace, there is a new trend in the marriage and family field noted by Ray Fowler, the director of the AAMFT, and confirmed, independently, by Keith Daugherty, executive director of the Family Service Association of America (FSAA), in regard to family services. This trend has to do with the growth in counselling services provided by private industry and the increased interest of business executives in providing such help for their employees and their families.

According to Fowler, the number of AAMFT members currently describing themselves as employees of private industry, or providing services under contract to industry, or "working closely with a particular company on a direct referral basis," has increased tenfold over the past five years. He is convinced that the major new trend in marriage and family therapy will be a closer tie to industry with these services increasingly provided as a fringe benefit entitling employees to purchase services from any therapist who meets the company's requirements for approved service, as an on-site service provided by a counsellor employed by the company, or as a referral service with access through the company's personnel or medical officer, or arranged by means of a special contractual agreement.

Most of these services began as, and still may be labelled as, counselling services for alcoholics and their families. Now, increasingly, the services are being provided by fully trained professional clinicians, often family therapists. For example, Dr. Dan Lanier, director of a company-wide treatment program at General Motors established to deal with the problem of alcoholism, was himself trained as a family therapist and had extensive experience in the field before going to General Motors. He operates a program that is described by others as a first-class company-based family therapy program in all but name. The program is highly touted by leaders in the field.

General Motors is not alone. Kennecott Copper, United States Steel, Standard Oil of Ohio, the Polaroid Corporation, and CNA Insurance are among the major corporations operating counselling programs. FSAA has recently signed a contract with Xerox to provide off-site counselling for employees. Edward D. McLaughlin, special assistant to Keith Daugherty, and coordinator for FSAA's new Xerox Employee Assistance Program, commented on some distinctive aspects of the model developed as part of this program.

The Xerox model is an off-site counselling service providing employees, as a fringe benefit, with an initial diagnostic and assessment service at a family service agency near the employee's residence or workplace. It was developed in response to a study of employee problems that confirmed that alcoholism was a significant problem at Xerox and recommended the establishment of an employee-assistance program to provide some needed help. Instead of establishing a narrowly focused alcoholism program, however, the company elected to develop an alternative model, one usually described as a "broad brush" program designed to address any problems experienced by employees (or their dependents) that might affect job performance.

The first two interviews, described as a "diagnostic and assessment service," are paid for in full by Xerox. The assumption is that in these interviews some determination of the nature of the problem can be made, as well as an assessment of the type of treatment needed and the appropriate locus for help. Employees will then either be referred elsewhere or encouraged to continue in counselling at the agency.

Who pays for subsequent help will be determined by the nature of the problem. If the problem is an alcohol or drug problem, the employee's normal medical insurance benefit plan comes into effect. If the problem is neither alcohol nor drugs, then responsibility for payment is the employee's.

McLaughlin suggested that this focus on alcoholism and drugs is fairly standard for employee assistance programs when they are first launched. Many such programs subsequently broaden the type of problems dealt with. Some evidence of a broader perspective is already emerging at Xerox, beginning with current plans to develop a family life education program for employees with workshops on "Pre-Retirement Counselling" and "Stress Management." Given the growing interest in employee assistance programs, FSAA may offer this contractual model for providing off-site counselling to other companies, once the Xerox program is fully operational and a proven success.

This model is not original with Xerox, although the FSAA-Xerox program is, apparently, the first such attempt to "go national." A similar model was established in 1974 by Family Counselling of Greater New Haven, one of the country's oldest family service agencies. Its Industrial Counselling Program provides counselling and related services to the New Haven business and industrial community on a contractual basis, and includes both on- and off-site service provision. Other agencies may be involved, also, where there are special needs that cannot be met by the agency. In an alternative approach, corporations may contract directly with private social work consulting firms for provision of counselling services.[9]

The development is not yet extensive and the reports thus far only anecdotal. We illustrate this point further with several approaches reported in a survey by General Mills.

Other Employee Assistance Programs (EAP)

International Paper's EAP. This program has two goals: first, to help employees find their way out of both serious and relatively minor problems and, second, to manage human resources effectively and keep valued employees through caring, awareness, and action.

At each U.S. International Paper location, a company representative is available to assist an employee in getting the help needed, and to do it in total confidence. Contact happens three ways: request by the employee, supervisor referral, or the urging of co-workers or union representatives.

EAP then works in a systematic way to help the employee recognize, control, and solve the problem. It has worked with such serious, life-disrupting problems as alcohol and drug abuse, severe depression with suicidal intent, marital break-ups, compulsive gambling, or a death in the family. Less serious but still real and preoccupying problems with which EAP has assisted include: adjustment to new locations, concerns with children and aging parents, interpersonal relationships, single parenthood stresses, and weight control.

The program also works for prevention by conducting educational programs to help employees avoid job-draining problems, such as stress originating at home. In existence since 1975, EAP has assisted hundreds of employees and is fast proving its merit as an investment.

The Evaluation and Referral Center: Contracting Employee Assistance Programs. The Evaluation and Referral Center Employee Assistance Program was funded in 1976 in Fort Worth by the Texas Commission for Funding through the Tarrant Council on Alcoholism and Drug Abuse. Not a treatment facility, the Center's focus is on education, prevention, information, and referral. Participating employer organizations contract for the service on a fee basis.

The Employee Assistance Program has one objective: to offer help to the employee who has a personal problem affecting job performance. Recognizing that problems within the family often adversely affect the employee, the program is also open to family members.

Features of the program include: training supervisors in program use, confrontation methods, and referral procedures; orienting all employees to the program; maintaining a high level of program visibility through the use of newsletters, bulletin board posters, and program brochures; using follow-up mechanisms; around-the-clock availability; professional staff members; client confidentiality.

In the past four years, the Employee Assistance Program has served over 2,000 clients, and the community has been most responsive. Although the Center has not solicited clients, seven organizations contacted it for service in the past year, bringing the Center's total number of business clients to twenty-seven. Several organizations have used the Center's assistance in establishing their own "in-house" programs, and the Center has also served as a referral agency for some labor union programs.

Mead Packaging's Program of Stress Management: Primary Prevention in an Occupational Setting. This effort at primary prevention serves as a special training extension of the company's Employee Assistance Program. Termed Employee Personal Services, this in-house, full-time counselling and referral program has serviced over one-third of Mead's Atlanta-based workforce since its inception in mid-1975. Recognizing that more could be done in the area of prevention, the program expanded in 1977 to include workshops on the management of occupational stress.

The stress management series of seminars has been extremely popular among Mead's salaried employees since its development. These seminars have not only served to promote positive mental and physical health practices but have also encouraged early self-identification of problems and subsequent use of the individual counselling program. The program is taught by the Director of Employee Personal Services and focuses on such themes as the productive use of stress, optimizing the use of one's personal energies, physical fitness, relaxation, and effective cognitive practices.

Recognizing that stress is an inevitable facet of working life, the program does not advocate either its elimination or total control of its effects. Rather, it encourages participants to use its positive qualities to good advantage. Should stress-related problems develop (either physical or psychological), employees are better equipped to recognize such symptoms in the early stages and are ready to use their newly acquired coping skills as a means to better life management.

ACTWU Social Services: Helping troubled workers and their families. Established in 1972, the Social Services Department of the Amalgamated Clothing and Textile Workers Union has developed a program that focuses closely on local needs. It is a network that links workers to community resources through social services committees in local unions. Built on a model of group dynamics, a key program component in making information accessible to members at their place of work, and in neutralizing the stigma of using help, is peer support.

The professional is seen as a team member providing training, information, and back-up support to social service committees that (1) work with community resources getting information on what services are available and how they work, (2) determine the nature of individual or family need and what kind of help is available, (3) make referrals to local agencies, and (4) follow-up on their referrals.

Programs for retired members similarly reflect local interest and concerns. These programs are established to maintain ties with the union, and provide social, emotional, and economic support. Other special projects are also established on the local level with technical assistance from the Social Service Department. These include child care, credit unions, legal panels, health education, alcoholic rehabilitation, consumer education, humanities programs, and programs for women workers.

The staff of the Social Service Department consists of four professionals, three administrative assistants, and two second-year MSW students, plus eleven field representatives.

An important overall objective is improving the quality of life beyond the plant gate for working people. Helping ACTWU members to become more aware of benefits and services available through the union has contributed to a preventive approach in meeting individual and family needs and expanding their choices in the community.

Polaroid's On-Site Counseling Program. Polaroid's basic belief in the necessity for industry to respond to the needs of individuals was essential in establishing and maintaining its Counseling Department. The Department began in 1958 and now includes five social workers with degrees and a counselling assistant who is a recovering alcoholic. It has two main objectives: (1) to assist Polaroid employees in solving problems that tend to lend imbalance to their individual well-being and restrict their ability to function and develop, and (2) to assist the Corporation in sensing human and organizational stresses and to join in corrective efforts.

The functions of the Counseling Department include individual counselling and consultation (always provided in strict confidence), the sensing of stress in the environment, group facilitation, special programs, and research.

The kinds of problems presented tend to fall into three major areas of life involvement: problems related to work, those related to self, and those related to others, especially the family.

After many years of working with individual problems associated with alcohol, the Department identified a need to become active in this concern. To this end, a program of education and consultation was developed by personnel people, line supervisors and managers, the employees' committee, and those directly affected by alcoholism.

Several articles have appeared recently in business publications confirming this general trend. Included among these is an article that appeared in the *Wall Street Journal* and is representative of several articles in other journals:

> The executive was distraught. His schizophrenic adult son repeatedly visited his father in the office and threw wild temper tantrums. He would calm down only after his father gave him money.
>
> To break this blackmailing habit and give the son a firm message, Dr. Harry Brownlee first had the family obtain a court order barring the young man from the office. Then, because his son frequently skipped his antischizophrenia medication, Dr. Brownlee arranged for medicine that needed to be taken only every couple of weeks. After several weeks the young man went to work as a clerk, the first job he had held in eight years, and his father was freed from the office tantrums.
>
> Surprisingly enough, unusual assistance like the executive received has become an employee benefit at many companies. Dr. Brownlee is director of New York's Brownlee, Dolan, Stein Association, one of several organizations that counsel employees and help them do everything from saving their marriage to quitting drinking to buying a used car.

"Broad Brush" Programs

Counselling has become big business. Using outside consultants or their own staff members, at least 2,500 employers operate alcoholism programs alone, four times the figure in 1973, the National Council on Alcoholism says. But employee counselling no longer focuses overwhelmingly on alcoholism while handling other problems peripherally: the "broad-brush" programs that try to handle practically all personal problems of employees are "probably in the majority now," says William S. Dunkin, a National Council official.

To some these "employee assistance programs" represent insidious Big Brotherly meddling in employees' private lives. To others, they are yet another management fad and waste of money. And clearly, many of the programs are next to worthless, for reasons ranging from haphazard administration to employee doubts about their confidentiality. "Fewer than two dozen programs achieve their real potential," Mr. Dunkin contends.

But whatever the programs' value, hundreds of employees now make use of them.[10]

Where this development will go remains to be seen. One place it seems to be going is into graduate schools of social work. A new area for social work expertise, called "industrial social welfare," has emerged during the last decade. Among the leaders in the field are Dr. Sheila Akabas, director of the Industrial Social Welfare Center at Columbia University's School of Social Work, and Dr. Paul Kurzman of the Hunter College School of Social Work, City University of New York. The emphasis in these programs is on case finding and referral as well as on program development skills, in both industrial and union settings.

Clearly, help provided at or through the workplace could offer another option to American families seeking help. The business sector, thus, also could be a significant funding source.

Since the development is new and experimental, many questions will need to be explored and many issues debated. For example, are counselling services more appropriately provided on-site (at the workplace by counsellors employed by the company), off-site, on a contractual basis as a fringe benefit whereby any licensed counsellor or therapist can provide a reimbursable service to an employee, or independently but linked with the company through a referral service? Here questions of confidentiality, possible conflict of interest, and paternalism, all arise and are not easily answered.

Another question is: Does there need to be consistency in the use of on- or off-site provision for educational as well as counselling services? One might, for example, argue for on-site provision for one and off-site for the other. Or, one could argue for case finding and referral on-site rather than intensive treatment.

From another perspective, there may be implications for the equity of resource allocation too, as one group in the society (employees of companies with good benefit programs) receive more and more tax-free benefits, paid for in part by the dollars of taxpayers generally, most of whom are not receiving any such benefit.

These questions connect to a larger issue: what should be the role of industry in providing what Richard Titmuss once described as "occupational welfare" and how should this be related to the "welfare" (social security, education, and so forth) provided citizens as a universal right by the society at large?

Alternatives to Direct Help:
Some Other Technologies

Some people seek out more limited kinds of help. They may not want to expose their problems to "a stranger," or they may not be prepared to form a more intimate relationship. Or they may simply want to educate themselves about what options are available, and are convinced about their own capacity to use whatever knowledge is available.

Books

As we saw in Table 2 (Chapter 1), many people turn to books to answer their needs. We can get some sense of the range and quantity of self-help books now available by looking at a partial listing of book titles in two sections of a New York City bookstore. First, in the section called "Personal Help": *I'm O.K., You're O.K.; The Sensuous Man; Total Living; Born to Win* (gestalt therapy); *Self Rescue; The Facts of Life; Hey, God, What Should I Do Now?; I Ain't Much, Baby, but I'm All I've Got; Things People Play; What Do You Say after You Say Hello?; Your Erroneous Zones; Pulling Your Own Strings; The Marriage Art; Be the Person You Were Meant to Be; Cutting Loose* (how adolescents separate from their parents); *I've Done So Well, Why Do I Feel So Bad?; How to Get Control of Your Time and Your Life; Creative Divorce; The Secret of Happiness; Scripts People Live; Loving—Free; EST—Sixty Hours That Transform Your Life.*

A second section offers books dealing with parenting and child-rearing: *Signals: What Your Child Is Really Telling You; Is My Baby Alright?; Part-Time Father; Toilet Training in Less Than a Day; How to Raise a Brighter Child; Six Practical Lessons for an Easier Child Birth; Moving through Pregnancy; Having a Baby after Thirty; The First Twelve Months of Life* and *The Second Twelve Months of Life; Understanding Your Child from Birth to Three; Black Child Care; Mother Care; Dare to Discipline; How to Father; How to Parent; How to Discipline with Love; Hand Book for New Parents; The Complete Book of Breast Feeding; Liberated Parents, Liberated Children; Every Child's Birthright; The ABC of Child Care; The Boys and Girls Book about Divorce; Between Parent and Child; Between Parent and Teenager; Help: A Handbook for Working Mothers; Raising the Only Child; The Single Parent Experience.*

Self-help books of various sorts have been high on the best-seller lists in recent years. The most popular have tended to fall into one of two categories. The first is self-improvement books—how to be more successful, lose weight, stop smoking—as contrasted with the perennially popular how-to-do-it books, designed to enable readers to provide their own expertise in carpentry, plumbing, sewing, or others of the increasingly expensive and often unavailable practical services. The second is books designed to help readers improve interpersonal relationships or roles, which are directed at helping people enhance their marriages, friendships, collegial ties, parenting roles. Each of these categories of books suggests one other way people use the marketplace to find help for their personal and family-related problems.

To underscore the significance of books and articles, we would note, for example, that Dr. Spock's *The Common Sense Book of Baby and Child Care* has sold more than 28 million copies.[11] Average annual sales for books on child care were estimated at 44,000 during the period 1970–1975. Twenty-three million copies of books on child rearing have been sold. In addition, the circulation of journals and magazines regularly featuring such articles is over 26 million. The Government Printing Office publication issued by the Children's Bureau, *Infant Care*, has reached an extraordinary 35 million families. Needless to say, these figures are not cumulative. Many individuals read more than one book. Many journals are read by more than one person. Not every book purchased is read. Not every book read is helpful or even influential. Nonetheless, books and articles are clearly an important form in which "help," be it information, advice, or instruction, is sought and reaches individuals with family-role concerns and problems and with family responsibilities.

A related category of books includes those designed to help adults improve their relationships with one another—as spouse, lover, friend—rather than focusing on parent-child relationships. A few illustrations will clarify this category.

In response to the growing concern among some young couples regarding how to adjust to changes in male and female roles, there has been a spate of books advising men on how to be "the new male." One such book, written by a psychologist who apparently does individual and group psychotherapy and conducts encounter groups, is premised on the assumption that the changes now occurring in the world and among women mean that men must change too.[12] The author offers his analysis of the problems facing men and gives what he claims is practical advice for those men who want to avoid unnecessary conflict and pain.

The book is heavily anecdotal, based on cases from the author's private practice, newspaper stories, and so forth. The general theme is that men are socialized into a "compulsive masculinity" that is unnecessary and self-destructive. As a consequence, men grow up to be rigid, work compulsively, and participate in sex compulsively; they do not know how to relate naturally to their children, and in general are pretty horrible. Women, on the other hand, have been playing the counterpart role. The combination of the two traditional male and female roles have led to bad results for all of society.

The author argues that, now that the women's movement has led to a redefinition of women's roles, it is urgent that men undertake a countershift. More flexibility in roles would lead to a more humane society, which in turn would find such androgynous roles more attractive. Men would become pliant and more expressive, able to reveal dependency and vulnerability, and therefore more capable of intimacy. Men would also become more independent in certain areas of self-care (preparing meals for themselves, for example) and would be able to develop more mutually satisfying relationships. "It is time for the man, therefore, to reject the role demands on him to play superman: the unneeding, fearless, unemotional, independent, all-around-strong-man. Liberation for him would mean a reentry into the world of playfulness, intimacy, trusting relationships, emotions, and caring, and a fulfillment of *his* needs and *his* growth."[13]

In effect, without any data on which to base his conclusions, the author makes a series of positive assertions and oversimplified sweeping generalizations. His conclusions suggest at least as much stereotyping of "new" male and female roles as the traditional stereotypes he rejects. Moreover, even if his assessment is accurate, and his advice regarding change valid, there are many who would question whether men could actually make use of his advice. Indeed, the author himself raises questions about this when, in one of the final chapters, he says that men and women who want to change may require a "support system composed of other men and caring women."[14] Nowhere does he explain how such a support system should be created, supported, and operated—much less found by those needing it.

Who would not pay a great deal to learn *How to Get Whatever You Want Out of Life?*[15] For $9.95, Dr. Joyce Brothers, psychologist and well-known television and radio personality, will tell you. Although her focus is on individual achievement, primarily occupational success, money, power, and prestige, she also includes instruction and advice on how to achieve success in personal relationships, both sex and love.

The theme of the book is that anyone can succeed if he or she really wants to. Using the tools of the psychology of human behavior, Brothers stresses the need to define your goal clearly in advance and then concentrate totally on achieving it, to the exclusion of all else, by developing a rational, goal-specific plan of action.

Clearly written, drawing heavily on anecdotes and case material, the book combines a popularized research review (not always accurately reported, not always appropriately qualified, and frequently outdated) and a miscellany of information and common sense to suggest possible game plans. Her style is informal, chatty, and authoritative. Her discussion of sexual problems is as explicit as her discussion of career problems, and her advice is not too dissimilar.

For the supremely rational individual who is clear about what it is he or she wants—and implicitly clear about what his or her values are and able to choose among conflicting values where they exist—such a book may be useful. We would guess that those who would be able to follow her advice are already doing so. For other readers, those for whom problems are more complicated and choices not so clear cut, with each choice having costs and benefits and thus each choice presenting dilemmas, there may be a problem in finding her advice either helpful or useful.

In a similar vein is the enormously successful *Your Erroneous Zones*, by the psychologist Dr. Wayne W. Dyer, who followed this success with another variation on the theme, *Pulling Your Own Strings*.[16] The theme of both these books is that life can be beautiful as long as you are in control of what happens ("pulling your own strings"), assuming you choose to be happy. By placing your happiness first, becoming more aware of the choices open to you, you can learn to avoid self-defeating behavior (the erroneous zones). Change is difficult, but if you really want to, you can do it. "This book outlines a pleasant approach to achieving happiness—an approach that relies on responsibility for a commitment to yourself, plus an appetite for living and a desire to be all that you choose to at this moment. . . . You don't need a professional background . . . to understand the principles of effective living. . . . You learn them by being committed to your own happiness and by doing something about it. This is something [to] work on every day."[17]

Each chapter of *Your Erroneous Zones* is written as if it were a counselling session, with the author-therapist acting as counsellor (and counsellee) throughout. The book's conclusion is that the individual who has eliminated his or her erroneous zones is happy, independent, does not need any one else's approval (including spouse, parent, child, sibling), and has achieved a kind of personal nirvana.

Included among some of the other books in this genre are those directed at helping individuals become "more assertive"[18] and those designed to improve one's personal relationships in marriage or with one's lover, or, perhaps more important, to help people develop loving relationships. Merle Shain's *When Lovers Are Friends* is one such book.[19] The theme of the book is that the greatest emotional dilemma of our time is the "fear of intimacy and commitment, and our seemingly contradictory fear of loneliness." Only through real self-acceptance ("If I am not for myself, who will be for me?" is the title of one chapter) can the individual begin to trust others, and only through trusting others can he or she be open to love.

Taking a different tack is Nathanial Lande's *Emotional Maintenance Manual*:

> Each of us has experienced anxiety and depression. They are completely normal reactions. . . . Yet the 1970s were characterized earlier in the decade as the Age of Anxiety and then as the Age of Depression. Does this mean our coping mechanisms have blown a fuse? Are we subjected to so much stress that our emotions have run rampant?

This recognition of the immobilizing aspects of anxiety and depression is evident in the abundance of self-help books that have entered the market in recent years. There are books designed to make their readers happy, confident, powerful; teach them to overcome feelings of inferiority; straighten out their sagging psyches and knotted personal relationships—in short, to chart a thousand and one better ways to be. The books don't always work.[20]

The author focuses here on providing a "maintenance manual, not a repair manual," "a new, scientific, and revolutionary three-day preventative program," "a break-through in psychotherapy." In effect, like some of the famous crash diets popularized through similar self-help books over the last decade, this book provides a three-day crash program and an eight-point tune-up for those desirous of maintaining psychological fitness by themselves. The book includes a "distillation of over 70 psychoanalytical schools," including Freud, Sullivan, Jung, Adler, Horney, Maslow, Gestalt, transactional analysis, behavioral modification, crisis intervention, family therapy, as well as quasi-religious cults, novel pyschotherapies, wisdom schools including ARICA, EST, encounter groups, TM, Yoga, Zen, and so forth.

Lande provides a general introduction in which he summarizes everything that is wrong with all other self-help books, reviews various alternatives for providing help, and implies that almost everyone who wants to can really help himself. He follows this by a "test" for the reader's current state of mind and then proposes a three-day crash program to help readers "change directions." This program includes recommendations for diet, exercise, "insight," and practice in behavioral modification. Once the reader is in shape as a consequence of following the three-day crash program, the proposal for a "life-long maintenance program" follows. Anyone who cannot follow this program, according to the author, is either not interested in being helped or has such serious problems that he or she clearly needs professional help.

In contrast to those books offering advice and information on parenting (*Infant Care, Working Mothers*), the self-help books discussed here are clearly focused on individual needs and concerns and less on family-related problems. Taking a somewhat universalized approach (everyone feels anxious, depressed, inadequate . . .), authors emphasize how the readers can help themselves if they really want to. Offering a few superficial insights, suggesting a little behavioral modification, they focus on the reader's motivation in achieving occupational or relationship "success," however defined. At best, we would hope that such books do no harm to vulnerable readers who find themselves unable to follow through on the proffered "advice" or, even when they do so, incapable of realizing goals that may be inappropriate, unwise, or unrealistic where they are concerned.

Telephones and Tapes

Telephone "hotlines" or "help lines" are now a well-established service provided by a variety of voluntary agencies, self-help groups, and volunteers. Usually they are for emergency or crisis services: people who are suicidal, rape victims, people in crisis. Many provide general or specialized information and referral services.

Some new "help lines," however, have been established recently to provide ordinary people with help around ordinary problems, usually with family-related problems. One such service, "The Family Phone," was begun by the Nassau County Mental Health Association to respond to such family problems as concern about marital conflicts, divorce, parent and child tensions, sibling relationships, as well as illness and death. The executive director of the mental health association administering this program was quoted in an interview as saying, "Today, with family life so complex, there are external pressures and intergenerational conflicts of all kinds. With nowhere to turn, there is a great need for a support system."[21]

Another "technology" that has been getting increasing attention is the use of cassettes to increase knowledge or, more important for us, to help in self-development and in dealing with everyday personal and family problems.[22] One "series," for example, includes: "Marriage Therapy," which offers information about marriage therapy and advice about selecting qualified therapists; "Step-parenting," which discusses the typical problems experienced by step-parents and offers advice on how to cope with "live-in and visiting step-children, new mates, and ex-spouses"; and "Working Mothers," which offers advice by a child development specialist on how such women can solve the problems they are likely to experience as wife, mother, and working woman. Still another such cassette in a group of twenty-six listed in one advertisement is "Changing Your Children's Behavior," in which two educational psychologists advise parents on how they can encourage positive traits in their children and discourage negative behavior. This particular series of cassettes is available by subscription, renewed annually, just like a book club, or can be purchased as individual titles.

Combining the telephone "help line" and the information and advice-providing cassettes is still another new service: a telephone information service provided by cassettes. In one such service, seventy-six different topics are listed and published in a daily newspaper for the information of readers who may wish to telephone and request the information and advice of their choice. Among its listings are: "Things to Consider in Looking for a

Mate," "Positive Communication and Sexual Fulfillment in a Marriage," "Fair Fighting in Marriage," "Common Marital Problems and How to Handle Them," "Preplanning for Children," "Parenting Skills," "Divorce: It Could Happen to Us," "How To Deal with the Realities of a Divorce," "The Death of a Marriage," "If Your Parents Are Divorcing," "Dual Career Couples," and so forth.

One series is described as being designed for "psychologically healthy people who are wrestling with common, day-to-day problems." It claims to provide "positive help. . . . Listening to a tape isn't going to solve anything by itself, but the information gives you more resources for managing and effectively dealing with issues. . . . [These] tapes are for people who want to learn, who want to increase their interpersonal and intrapersonal skills in living . . . for people who want to live a fuller life, who aren't afraid to ask for information, who want to know more about themselves and how to manage their personal relationships better."

Neither the telephone services nor the cassettes nor the combined service are a substitute for direct personal help or treatment. Rather, they provide an informational resource or a bridge for those people seeking something but not quite ready to come in person for more extensive aid. For some, the limited help, be it a book, a tape, or a brief impersonal contact on the telephone, may be enough. For others, the feeling of learning new information, of gaining some knowledge about a problem, may suffice. But for still others, such help can only be temporary or an illusion.

Evaluation of such services or resources is difficult: they are self-selected and their impact is almost impossible to measure. Those controlled experiments that have been completed show that mothers of newborn children who received educational letters or brochures felt that they were useful. Otherwise we simply know that there is a demand—that people buy books and tapes, and call the hot line numbers. Where there is relative consensus about the advice to be given, or even certainty at a given moment, the public or non-profit private agency may meet the need—as was done in publishing the Children's Bureau's successive editions of *Infant Care* and *Child Care*, for example. But here there are diverse styles and needs— some people find it easier to buy a paperback in a supermarket or drugstore than to go to a government agency or write to one for a pamphlet. The market offers access, diversity, and useful experimentation in its books and tapes, ranging from Dr. Spock to Joyce Brothers. The "price" appears to be the publication of a lot of books and tapes that simplify, divert, offer false reassurance, and delay useful help. A society must pay this price for pluralism and free speech. Sensitive monitoring of the market could warn people off and pick up cues as to what might be made accessible to those who depend on government or nonprofit initiatives and who simply cannot afford too many wasted leads.

Practical Helping Services

Another category of services for sale is the practical helping services. The boundaries are especially unclear in this category as to which are services for families and which are for individuals. There is also the question of whether, indeed, there is a clear distinction between the two. What is clear is that there are a large number of products and services now coming onto the market designed to meet the changing needs of today's families, and of individuals experiencing similar changes.

In one suburban neighborhood, for example, a new service is advertised in the local paper:

For Women Who Don't Want to Go to Work—after Coming Home from Work

One of a growing number of catering services, this one offers several alternative dinner menus each week, and gives a user the option of picking up the meal (which includes soup, a meat or fish dish, and vegetable) in person or having it delivered after work.

In a similar vein are the growing numbers of people offering specialized services designed to provide expertise, save time, or assure access to other services. Many of these services have been around for a while, used by those with enough money to avail themselves of extra, special help. There are, for example, architects to design the house of your choice, and often to carry out the arduous tasks of supervising those involved in the actual construction. There are interior decorators to suggest furniture, fabrics, the general decor, and then to shop for each item, assuming responsibility for coordinating production, delivery, and the ultimate "look" of the house. There are investment and related financial counsellors to advise the consumer on how to save, invest, and often budget and spend his or her income. There are travel agents offering specialized advice on personalizing vacation plans: where to go, when, how, and what it will cost.

New types of services, not too dissimilar from the ones above, are directed toward providing a still wider array of help, often geared more to a middle- and working-class consumer than to the earlier affluent service users. Included here are household cleaning services, which provide a bonded staff to work by the day or hour, as a substitute for the almost obsolete domestic servant, once the mainstay of large or working families. These services provide everything from window cleaners and men who can do heavy cleaning and floor waxing to waitresses, cooks, and bartenders for more elaborate occasions. The same range is now emerging among the catering services. Once a luxury service for the affluent few, these services are now becoming available at relatively low prices, sometimes even as an adjunct to neighborhood restaurants. Related to this, of course, has been the growth of fast food stores and the increase in prepared meals sold at supermarkets, either at specialty food counters or, more routinely, as pre-frozen, complete packaged dinners.[23]

Certain other types of services previously available only to the wealthy are also becoming available at a more moderate cost (and sometimes even free to those with low incomes) as the rationale for their need and significance grows. Just as low-cost legal services for the poor or the elderly have become an important service, we now see signs of other services for special groups, like tax counselling for the elderly, emerging in the marketplace.

The market is also picking up on services previously performed only by the families themselves. One such service is directed by two professional social workers in Florida, who found themselves spending more and more time giving information and advice about services for the elderly to friends (and friends of friends) living out of state who had elderly relatives in Florida. As a result, they decided to open a private consultation service.[24] People with elderly parents or relatives in Florida can now call from all over the country for information and advice—or, later, to take advantage of the special visiting and supervision services these geriatric consultants offer. These special services begin with a home visit, where the consultants have an opportunity to talk with the elderly person and explore his or her situation and needs. Subsequently, the consultant telephones the son or daughter with recommendations. The service may make referrals to a local private for-profit or non-profit facility. Specific factual information may be given and recommendations for other kinds of help made. The service offers ongoing supervision and regular weekly or monthly visits, if desired. There are fees set for an initial assessment only, for follow-up phone calls, or for regular visits.

In another service, an explicit family role is professionalized. Several years ago a group of California pediatricians added a "professional grandmother" to their staff because they found that few of those whom they served had extended families to advise them about child care. The help provided by this service includes: pre-birth classes for expectant parents, taught by a woman who herself has raised four children and is the grandmother of four; hospital visits to new mothers within the first two days after childbirth; and at-home visits to mother and infant, shortly after they return home. The help provided is mostly information and reassurance. In answering the questions of new parents, most of what is offered is basic information about feeding and bathing the infant and about normal infant behavior and development. In addition to such information, this "grandmother" provides reassurance to mothers who have never cared for a baby before. She allays their fears about minor problems, assures them that certain behavior is "normal" and will disappear in a matter of a few days (or a few hours), and tries to convince them that they will not make any dreadful mistakes if they use their common sense.[25]

In addition to the help mentioned above, the professional grandmother service provides a telephone information and advice service to answer parents' questions about breast feeding, sleeping and eating behavior, sibling rivalry, and other aspects of their child's development. A limited baby-sitter referral service is also available. Women with older children may call for advice on how to respond to their older child's resentment when a new baby arrives. Fathers call, too. Indeed, over one-quarter of the calls reported during the first three years of operation were from fathers.

In an article printed in the *New York Times*, the pediatrician who initiated the service said:

> I started the service . . . because I found that so many parents of newborns were tense and nervous. . . . Although well-educated, many of the couples had little knowledge of child care because they had never been around young children. They had lots of questions but were reluctant to "bother" us doctors because they didn't want to appear stupid. In the past they would have gone to grandmother for answers, but in mobile California it seems that nobody has an extended family living nearby.[26]

The traditional "matchmaker" service is also proliferating—now buttressed by computers, discotheques, large-scale advertising, and goals that often offer alternatives to a marriage: companionship, intimacy, multiple brief relationships, easier access to sexual partners. No two are alike in ambiance, clientele, or objectives, and many enjoy large responses. Evening gatherings, group excursions, and summer vacation arrangements are common. Such services are even franchised. One northeastern franchise, called Turning Point, is sponsored by a franchise holding company with a leading place in the fast food industry. Charging $295 annually for its services, it rates all participants on a scale of 1 to 10 in accordance with a variety of criteria relating to age, appearance, education, and social and economic status. Members are "matched" only with others of similar ranking. The fee guarantees three introductions each month; trips, events, and excursions as occasions for meeting; and occasional "rap" sessions, which are optional.

Shopping centers and supermarkets are also expanding into the personal service field, including services for families. "Baby Parking"—child care services provided for a few hours while parents shop—is becoming increasingly available in suburban areas. One such service, located in a large shopping center, is open twelve hours a day, six days a week, to care for children aged two and a half to eight, for from one to three hours, while parents are shopping or going to a movie. The aim of this service is to provide care as well as a focused short-term learning experience for the children. Several of the stores pay a portion of the fee if parents make a purchase. The staff consists of professionally trained teachers who have specialized in early childhood education. The program is designed so that children may come at any time, work and play independently or in groups, and have an opportunity to do things (woodworking, for example) they may not be able to do at home because of lack of space and facilities. The children enjoy themselves, and the parents can relax in the knowledge that their children are well cared for while they pursue other activities.

In a much less elaborate form, many supermarkets now provide a similar service while parents are shopping. In their search for more customers and higher profits, supermarkets have moved in two different directions. One has been the growth of "no frill" stores offering a limited selection of commonly used items at much lower prices than in conventional stores. A second, contrasting approach, of particular interest to us here, has been the growth in the number of stores providing a wide complement of special services.

According to a recent article, "It is service, rather than price, that has been luring buyers to what industry people call megamarkets. These triple-sized supermarkets are latter day bazaars with thousands of items and dozens of services under one roof."[27] Some of these stores offer dental and legal services, opticians, travel agencies, wine cellars, and restaurants, as well as child care services. Others are winning customers with education services and programs. One New York chain puts out a newsletter for its customers, giving shopping tips on food and kitchen equipment, recipes, and nutritional advice on everything from how to make baby food at home to how to prepare tasteful yet safe meals for diabetics, cardiac patients, and others on special diets.

The head of a major supermarket chain, who was interviewed at some length about how social change is affecting the food and supermarket industry and how, in turn, the industry is looking for new ways to respond, remarked that "the goal is to hold, if not to increase, the numbers of customers, to increase the dollar volume of sales, and to keep costs to a level that make it possible to generate a reasonable profit." He identified three major changes affecting supermarkets: the increased number of households, the declining size of families and households, and the enormous growth in the numbers of working women. As a consequence of the first two factors, stores are selling far more single-portion, small-portion, or small-size items. The growth in the numbers of working women, he said, has two other consequences. First is a growing tendency for supermarkets to increase their sales hours to seven days a week, often twenty-four hours a day, in order to assure store access to the majority of adults who are now working during the usual daytime, mid-week hours. Second is the expansion of the product lines the stores carry to include general merchandise, health and beauty aids, prescriptions, fast-moving clothing items, and many types of ethnic foods, items previously purchased in separate locations or prepared at home.

With more women at jobs rather than at home, he pointed out, the demand for one-stop shopping to save time and effort has increased significantly. Many stores have established "catering" and specialty food departments for prepared take-out foods in response to the demands of consumers who have less time to shop and prepare meals at home and will purchase these items at some slight increase in cost to save the preparation time. The housewife–wage earner of today wants her chicken cut up and ready to fry, her spinach chopped and frozen, some of her meat precooked and either prepared or ready to prepare, her rolls ready to pop into the oven, and her orange juice squeezed. She also demands a variety of prepared mixes that will instantly and effortlessly yield everything from cookies and cakes to mashed potatoes and puddings. She wants to shop for these products in the quickest and most accessible manner.

Another problem facing the industry is the changed attitude of consumers toward supermarkets and shopping. When these large markets were first established after World War II, they were a novelty. The plethora of items available seemed like something out of a fabulous bazaar. Today, the novelty has worn off. With most adults working, they have less time to shop, less energy for shopping, and less interest in doing so. For most, shopping has become a chore. Consequently, one problem of the industry is how to make shopping attractive enough to lure customers in, or easy enough so that the business continues even if customers spend less time at it. Given increased costs, due not only to higher food costs but, more important, to high labor costs and higher energy costs, the industry is faced with a dilemma: higher costs at the same time that consumer interest is declining.

Supermarket operations do not lend themselves particularly well to automation or mechanization through significant capital investment. The consumer's desire for lower prices, easier accessibility, time saving, and service makes labor costs the largest operating expense, and results in significant increases in operating costs within the present structure of the industry. Ultimately (and not even in the too distant future), as our consultant pointed out, the industry may find it easier to eliminate the high-cost retail store operations—the traditional supermarkets as they are known today—with high rents, high energy costs, and high labor costs and replace them with a new form of shopping utilizing lower-cost warehouse locations, some mechanization, and lower cost of labor. In such a system, customers could order by phone, perhaps selecting from items shown on closed-circuit TV, and deliveries could be made from a less costly, centrally located warehouse direct to the customer's home, at a time convenient to the shopper.

Two other services provide some radically contrasting perspectives on what might be ahead of us in the way of "help" available for purchase. One is a highly specialized, controversial, personalized, and expensive service with limited marketability and very limited supply. The second is a very basic service, with an enormous potential demand, and a rapidly increasing supply, one that may yet emerge as a new and major service industry.

The first, described as "Pregnancy by Proxy," is surrogate motherhood by artificial insemination of a fertile woman by a biological father whose wife cannot bear a child. In effect, this service is "babymaking" for childless couples who want the baby they cannot have themselves and who are prepared to pay fertile women who are willing to have their children for them. At a time when healthy, normal, adoptable children are almost totally unavailable, this service places a premium on "child production" in the open market.[28]

The second service is child care. Proprietary child care centers in particular experienced an extraordinary growth in the 1970s in response to the demand for child care services to care for the growing numbers of children of working mothers. The call for increased public subsidies to support such services was countered by the response of political conservatives that there was no real "demand," that only feminists and child care professionals were pressing for publicly funded and operated day care, and that indeed most parents viewed this as inappropriate government interference in families. To quote the famous Nixon veto message of the comprehensive child care service legislation, government-funded child care centers would represent an effort by government to support "communal child rearing."

During these same years, in contrast to the politicians who chose to ignore radically changing social realities, business entrepreneurs correctly saw the promise of a burgeoning market. Child care, for the children of middle-class families, has turned into big business: ten major chains operate about one thousand child care centers, collecting about $100 million annually. According to a *Business Week* article, "although the chains account for only 5 percent of the country's 19,000 licensed child care centers—and all licensed centers account for only $2.3 billion of the estimated $7.5 billion spent annually on child care—they are by far the fastest growing segment of the market."[29] In 1980, the total was probably closer to $9 billion, and the individual consumer accounts for over $6 billion of this.[30]

Some chains have experimented with developing corporation-based child care centers; however, the consensus is that the future of child care services lies in residential neighborhoods, whether paid for by parents, by government, or by employers. Most proprietary centers, like most public and non-profit centers, are located in residential areas to meet the preferences of mothers who would rather have their children cared for near home than at work. For the proprietary child care centers, the greatest current growth is in middle-class suburban neighborhoods, where female labor force participation has outstripped the rates of all other areas, where alternative publicly subsidized services are not available, and where parents can readily afford the fees.

Private industry is also expanding its support of the child care service needs of its employees, by experimenting with a variety of alternatives in addition to the oft-discussed though not preferred mode of work-site care, a mode that in actual fact is thus far very limited in the United States. Among the other options now being tried are support (by one or several companies) of off-site child care services in centers located near where employees live, purchasing slots or places in existing child care centers that are already used by employees, providing a cash benefit to pay part of an employee's child care costs, and developing a child care information and referral service covering the neighborhoods where employees live.

Despite the discussion, there is little in the way of work-site child care services as yet. A comprehensive survey of employer-sponsored day care in 1978 documents its rarity: nine day care centers sponsored by industry, seven sponsored by labor unions with funds from employers of its members, fourteen sponsored by government agencies, and seventy-five sponsored by hospitals. In addition, there were two hundred centers sponsored by the military. The limited involvement of private industry is notable. In fact, the number of industry-sponsored centers declined in the 1970s. However, there is currently much increased interest.[31]

Insights and Cautions from the Marketplace

Those who go to marriage and family therapists are not asking for help to improve or enhance their marriages. They are coming because they have a problem—a dysfunctional condition—and it is causing them pain. They are seeking help because they think their problem or condition is serious enough to warrant serious and perhaps sustained treatment. They choose a private practitioner because they are convinced that the greatest opportunity for choice of treatment and quality is in the marketplace. They have confidence in their ability to select a competent therapist, and they have the money to pay for it.

Those who go for counselling through their place of employment may go for similar reasons, or, more likely, because their problems are so impeding their functioning at work that they are under pressure from their employers to seek help.

Those who buy books or tapes, or use a telephone service—for whatever reasons—are not necessarily at this stage. Nor are those others whom we did not describe here who use such "helping" services as newspaper advice columns like "Ann Landers," radio information and advice services like that of Bernard Meltzer, television information and advice like the talk shows of Dr. Joyce Brothers, and others. These people either define their problems as more limited, or they do not feel themselves to be ready to ask for or truly avail themselves of more sustained help. For many, this limited approach may be adequate. Others may decide, subsequently, to seek another kind of help.

For many others, the problems they are concerned with are not problems of relationships, roles, or personal adequacy. Instead, their concerns are with changes in the society that suggest the need for more information and for special skills, or that impose new demands for time and expertise at a time when older supports are no longer available. For these people, the search for help involves a desire for practical assistance in matters of daily living: assistance with child care when parents are working away from home during the day and/or grandparents and relatives are not available to provide such help; assistance with household maintenance (cleaning, laundry, cooking) when cheap domestic help is no longer available and all adults in the household are in the labor market; information and advice about products and services as the variety available multiplies and the possibility for having sufficient knowledge and expertise to make an informed choice becomes more and more difficult; information and advice about normal life cycle developments and transitions as these stages and phases become more diverse and individuals search for help when experiencing new situations and new patterns; time and energy savers when there is only one adult in a family trying to cope with the myriad of tasks two adults may find trying, or when both parents are trying to manage the dual responsibilities of home and job; and assistance with management skills as services increase and become more specialized and organizational help and assistance, as well as coordination tasks, require greater expertise than ordinary users possess.

One way of assessing the extent and impact of social change in the United States has been to monitor developments in the marketplace. We have noted elsewhere that in the United States, in contrast to Europe, it is often the private for-profit sector that plays the innovator role in service provision as in product development.[32] The range of choices in the marketplace is truly astonishing, and our perception is that the market is only just beginning to reflect the major social changes emerging in family life styles.

We have ranged over a very broad territory and, before closing this phase of the discussion, wish to call attention to three things: the market exploration suggests a very broad view of helping services; the market has serious limitations as a guarantor of helping services; and it is particularly difficult to sustain the concept of a family service as contrasted with an individual service.

The Range of Helping Services

Our interest is in what supports family functioning, what makes it possible for adults and children to go about their daily business and to get along harmoniously as an intimate living unit. Obviously, most of what is required is spontaneous, voluntary, learned while one is growing up, and informal. Society does not need to help families live as families in most respects; it would not want to; it has no right to. It is therefore instructive when people choose to purchase information, maintenance, time-saving, child care, or food services. The marketplace is a very good environment for encouraging innovation and we would do well to monitor it. The emphasis on practical services—aids relevant to the lives of average families; resources that see the user as consumer rather than as patient or as client—is also instructive. Should not public and private agencies also consider whether they too might give more attention to practical supports—beyond child care programs, modest homemaker–home health aid, and house repair services for the elderly? Clearly family service is not just counselling and substitute care. We do not mean to underplay counselling in its many forms, however. It is in the nature of modern society that people want and need advice, information, emotional support, understanding, and insight about themselves, their families, their behavior, and their relationships. When they can afford to do so, they purchase help. Some of it seems to be strange and questionable to the rest of us, but they seek it freely. What is more, sophisticated employers find it increasingly worthwhile to provide or pay for personal help for employees. At the very least this suggests that public investment in helping services for other people—whether the poor, the elderly, veterans, the handicapped, or others who may even be prepared to pay fees for good public service—can also be respected and need not stigmatize. It is part of an increasingly common provision in the modern world where social services are an ongoing need of all population elements.

The Limitations of the Market

There are limitations and problems, however, when the marketplace carries the major role in responding to the changed realities for families. As large as the numbers of people affected by marketplace developments are, the response is inevitably episodic and sporadic. Indeed, there is no way for a coherent response to emerge in the market. Certain services will be found only in large metropolitan areas or heavily populated suburban communities because a market response requires a sufficiently large demand. Families in rural areas or in middle-sized cities may have similar needs or wants, yet service provision may not be economically viable. Services that may be worth providing on one scale may be unprofitable at another. Services may be viewed as desirable if available at one price, but not at another. Yet the consequence of not having them may be costly to the society at large, as well as to individuals. Standards and program quality may fall victim to market pressures. Nor can or does the market always respond rapidly enough when the pace of social change accelerates.

More important, access to market services is limited, by definition, to those who can pay. As a consequence, availability, coverage, and use of such help is restricted to the more or, sometimes, to the most affluent. The changes in families and in family life styles that we have identified are not limited to any one sector of the society. Indeed, they pervade all sectors, as do the problems, needs, and wants we have discussed.

There may be ways to get around some of these limitations by the use of demand or consumption subsidies that make it possible for those with less income to exercise their preferences in the market. However, such an approach assumes, among other things, sufficient elasticity in the market to respond to increased demand quickly, without a concomitant increase in price, sufficient knowledge to make an informed choice, and a consistent pattern of demand in all communities. Whether such a device is a good idea and would work is debatable. The current reality is that there are limitations in the market's provision of help to families: limitations in access, availability, coverage, and quantity.

Market provision has other limitations as well. Sometimes a community defines a service as too important to be restricted to those willing to pay for it. This may be the case with family life and adult education courses. It is certainly the case for kindergartens (and in some states, pre-kindergartens). Some provision—if successful—must take the form of a public good that cannot be restricted to those who do (or do not) pay. An example would be a public television program that instructs about family relationships or allows viewer "call-ins."

Those who offer market services do so because, among other things, they earn profits in the process. Because of this, there are temptations to cut corners, not to worry about quality, to short-cut the process. Where the service person is a professional, the assumption is that professional ethics, licensing requirements, and monitoring by professional associations protect consumers. The premise may or may not be valid at all times. It is also assumed that consumers watch for quality and walk away from poor service. But here there are problems: service is often not visible (what goes on in a day care center when the parents are away?), quality is often impossible for the consumer to judge (how does the client judge a competent therapist?), and clients may be especially disadvantaged in the marketplace while under severe stress (the deserted wife who needs to make an immediate decision about next steps in her life). There are those who argue, therefore, that in arenas in which professionalism is not adequate protection, public regulation should be strong. The alternative of non-profit (public or private) services is preferred by some; however, the distinctions among these are not as clear as was once thought.

Family or Individual

A psychiatrist may decide that he is most successful if his service has a family orientation. A child care worker may regard it as essential to relate the child's group experience to his at-home life. This is more difficult to sustain as a perspective in relation to many of the practical services mentioned: management, food, maintenance, books, tapes, casual education. These are useful to families, or might be. They cannot be limited to families.

In short, our exploration is apparently leading to the notion that some services must be—or are more beneficial if—offered to family units. Illustrations might be family therapy or "marriage enrichment." Some would appear to be more effective—except where clearly inappropriate for individual reasons—if carried out with alertness to and consciousness of the primary family group as a unit as in the case of counselling and child care. Some programs offer services that, although very useful to families as supports, need not be family related and are useful to single people too. They are still an integral part of family support services as well.

To conclude, we have identified some emerging trends and some social innovations in the types of help offered and the ways in which the offer is made. We have uncovered a large, and what seems to be a rapidly growing if loosely defined, domain of help, one that has clearly emerged as more than a response to pathology and inadequacy. Here we see "help" in all its diversity: in response to traditional problems and changing definitions of problems, but also in response to new realities in the way ordinary, average families live.

We turn now to explore what kinds of help can be found in the non-market sectors. Are there other differences between the services provided in the market and those available elsewhere?

3   A Public Service System?

If there are some people who cannot find or afford help in the marketplace, and if the market does not offer range and access for all needed services or fully protect quality, does public responsibility take over? Do public services fill the gaps? Do they initiate where clearly they have the lead?

We are at the "intake" desk of a general social service office in a big-city public social welfare department. The social worker takes a phone call. It requires very few questions for her to get the story and settle on a course of action—the case is one in a continually repeating category: A frail elderly man in his eighties lives alone in a basement in a low-income neighborhood. The telephone call is from his neighbor. The man has a bad heart but gets little medical attention. Neighbors drop in from time to time to help with household chores and shopping, since he appears to have no relatives at all. Now he needs more regular medical help, which he cannot afford, and he probably needs some kind of home support service as well. Because he has managed on his Social Security income and has not applied for Supplemental Security Income (SSI), he has not been a Medicaid recipient. The neighbor is sure he is eligible for Medicaid, and the telephone description makes it seem likely he will be.

This "case" will be handled by assignment of a caseworker for a home visit within seventy-two hours. (It will take longer than it should because of a backlog.) The likely outcome after social work and medical assignment? A Medicaid card, the ticket to needed care, and a home attendant, who will visit for personal care (bathing, dressing) to prolong the man's ability to manage in the community.

Three kinds of home service are available through a department in this office for income-eligible families or elderly people living alone. Home attendants offer personal care and dressing. Housekeepers, whose maximum is four hours a day, help with cleaning and related chores if the help will keep an elderly or disabled person in the community. Homemakers provide substitute child care in the home during an emergency—a mother's hospitalization, for example—so that the children's routines are continued and their placement elsewhere avoided. (The medical system also offers home health aides who assist the homebound with medical routines not requiring hospitalization.)

The next request comes in the form of an in-person interview. A very young-looking sixteen-year-old woman has come in with her baby. It is summertime: the child is in Pampers and a shirt, the mother in jeans and a T-shirt with sandals. She answers questions, but volunteers little after the first response to "What can we do for you?" She is depressed and inarticulate; her speech pattern is poor and she sounds uneducated. The request again is familiar: she needs a place to stay, her own apartment, her own welfare check. She and her baby have been living with her parents in a four-room apartment in a six-story building in a rundown but respectable area. Both of her parents work. Her mother told her to clean the apartment and the girl resented the request: "The baby is enough work. . . . Why should they take advantage?" There was an argument. Now her parents have put her and the baby out. Such cases are common in this office.

The social worker tells us what two other staff members also repeat. The request for an independent public assistance budget is usually refused, and the girls usually return to their parents' home. Parents are legally responsible for care and support until the daughter's twenty-first birthday, and the social workers make this clear. If the parents are on a public assistance budget, the baby can be added to it. If the applicant is actually out of the household and has been for some time, she may be classified as an "emancipated minor" at age eighteen and have her own assistance budget. But first she must be assessed in a social work study as capable of living alone and responsibly caring for herself and the child.

This general social service office devotes most of its time to cases like these: frail, elderly people needing home services or Medicaid cards; teenage mothers who want financial help and their own apartments. This also is the entry point for referral to public assistance offices and poverty programs for those who are eligible for winter fuel assistance or for home improvement services that make it possible for the elderly and the handicapped to continue living at home. Others need help and guidance in finding or applying for public housing or housing assistance.

Now we join the social service worker in the public assistance intake office. People are applying for Aid to Families with Dependent Children (AFDC) or for local Home Relief, the cash assistance for those not eligible for AFDC or SSI. This social worker, one of two constantly available all day, is assigned to the assistance office by the general social service office. When people complete their applications for financial aid, they find on the last page of the application form a checklist asking whether they need help with personal or family problems. The list is comprehensive and clear:

stretching the budget dollar; finding a better place to live; getting or keeping a job; dealing with difficulties with the children; getting along with one's spouse; dealing with a family member's alcoholism or drug addiction; obtaining guidance and supplies for family planning; obtaining Medicaid or psychiatric treatment for oneself, a child, or another relative. Those who check the list are channelled to the assigned general social service worker for advice, information, or referral.

A woman in her late twenties has been referred to the welfare office by the Emergency Shelter, where she came with her two children. She is unmarried. She lives with her two grandparents in an atmosphere of constant conflict. They have insisted that she get out within two weeks, a fact verified by the Emergency Shelter social worker. Now she has applied for assistance. She is told how to seek an apartment and what the rental limits are, on the assumption that her assistance application will be approved. Because she has checked that she wants help "in getting and keeping a job," she is interviewed by the social worker.

The applicant is impressive: though poor, she is neatly dressed and appropriate in her manner. She speaks clearly and well. She has a sense of purpose and direction; she wants help with finding an apartment, enrolling in a training program, and getting a stipend until she finds a job. She takes information about how and where to apply for the training and is a good prospect. The social worker describes child care resources, too (without exploring the possibility that the grandparents might help at this level).

These social services desks in the office devoted to cash assistance are largely channelling points for information and referral. The processing of the checkmarks indicating interest in help is no more individualized than the checkmarks themselves. The aides behind the desk give information about rules and procedures, but make no effort to individualize or assess. People are treated with respect. The services are presented as a right. But there is no attempt at providing a personalized service. Little more than general channelling is provided, at best. If the situation is anything beyond a routine matter, a social worker from the general social service office will be asked to make a home visit for a more individualized assessment. There are occasional cases of child dependency, possibly abuse and neglect; these are referred to a specialized Social Services for Children, a public child welfare program working in close relationship with voluntary child welfare agencies. Cases of the elderly or the disabled will be referred to the specialized Adult Services Department if the clients have service needs requiring more than assessment of eligibility for home care services.

Some people who are not eligible for cash assistance are seen in the general social service intake. By definition, those seen in the assistance office are the welfare poor. Even though some service could be given to those above the poverty line, under public social service policy, the channelling system makes it unlikely—except for possible cases of child abuse, child neglect, and elderly home care. The other major exception is public day care: the eligibility levels do include the non-welfare, working, low-income families and in some cities there is an access system that encourages them to apply.

Both office and field staff meet some clients who clearly need ongoing attention, counselling, and treatment. They make regular use of the treatment "teams" in the services available at two local hospitals, staffed for intensive counselling and therapy.

Clearly, some of these cases are in the general category of problems in daily living. Others reflect severe pathology and deprivation. Some call for resources (money and/or food stamps), access to service (medical care), or substitute living arrangements (foster care or adoption). Others express need for information, advice, reassurance, or counselling—or for intensive residential or community-based therapeutic intervention.

The particular city described above separates its general social service, child welfare, day care, and adult social service offices. Elsewhere, public departments may combine these units in various ways. Everywhere the public sector is the largest funding source for social services that are therapeutic and remedial or that offer substitute care for children, the aged, and others requiring special living and protective arrangements. Public social service departments sponsor many of these publicly financed services themselves, but also pay for a substantial portion of services available through voluntary non-profit agencies (Chapter 4) and church-related agencies (Chapter 5). As we have seen, through demand-subsidies (vouchers, fees for service, etc.) public funds even pay for some of the costs of therapeutic, counselling, and helping programs found in the market-place. Of the national public social service primary caseload of some 7 million in 1978, at least half of the cases that were publicly paid for received service in the private sector. The public delivery system is often fragmented, stigmatized, avoided by people who have other options, or inaccessible as a matter of policy to all but the welfare poor, children, and aged needing "protection."

Exploring the public agency's service delivery in a typical American city, one finds a number of locally based or centrally located public social service offices. If not identified by an acronym (HELP, AID, COMMUNITY ACT, etc.) they may be called by any one of many formal names: Social Service Department, Human Resource (or Service) Center, Neighborhood Service Office, Public Welfare Office, Family and Child Services Center, Court Welfare Office, County Family and Child Welfare Office. Programs for the aging and the handicapped are often operated under other names, if not integrated in general multi-purpose centers or family and child social service programs.

These programs often share office space and administrative auspice with the public assistance unit delivering Aid to Families with Dependent Children (AFDC) and local general assistance operations, but the staff and operations for service delivery are generally separated. In some places, however, the "service" is a responsibility of the social workers who deal with financial eligibility for public assistance, Medicaid, and food stamps as well.

There are centers with well-decorated and comfortable waiting rooms, new and conveniently located buildings, offices allowing for privacy and relaxation, play areas for children, a coffee urn and doughnuts. Generally, however, the offices are unattractive, crowded, not comfortable. The reception area on a typical morning is full of poorly dressed and unhappy-looking people: the old and physically disabled, sometimes accompanied by escorts or helpers; mothers carrying infants or wheeling strollers; pregnant women; sullen adolescents in jeans and T-shirts; silent men of various ages in rumpled clothing and worn shoes. Depending upon the city or neighborhood, the representation in the waiting room could be heavily or exclusively black, Hispanic, or (far more rarely) Oriental. Almost everywhere it is largely a poverty population, with some sprinkling of working-class and occasional lower-middle-class people. Foster care, adoption, child protection, special needs of the aged, and problems arising from addictions may take one well above the poverty line.

Most of the "business" relates to or grows out of a dozen types of cases: financial need; child abuse; spouse abuse; need for "protection" of the aged; applications for child care; applications for homemaker or home health aid service; foster care placement, replacement, termination, or, in some cases, adoption; applications for Medicaid; need for emergency or special assistance grants (or shelter) growing out of emergencies (fire, theft, imprisonment or hospitalization, desertion, utility cut-off for non-payment of bills); loss of "cards" for assistance or Medicaid; housing-related problems (rent non-payment, rent increases, housing condemnation, applications for public housing or other housing assistance); applications for food stamps.

In short, the problems here are largely in the category of need for money, service referral, protection, or therapeutic and rehabilitative intervention. Some of the most complex of personal and social problems requiring long-term and deep interventions are found in these offices daily. Some cases, however, do reflect the more typical need for service to support daily living, life transitions, or the recurrent "crises" or requirements of "normal" individual or family experiences. They are problems not necessarily associated either with poverty or with deep pathology. The public social service offices vary in all of this because both states and localities exercise many options in requesting and deploying available social services funds.

Some thirty or thirty-five states have "combined state human service agencies."[1] Others have public social service departments with somewhat narrower mandates. All states administer or supervise locally operated programs run by such agencies. As noted, these agencies or their local counterparts are sometimes called social service departments. They most often incorporate family and child welfare programs, or child welfare programs that stress a "family orientation." Programs for the aged are generally encompassed by such agencies too. Not infrequently, however, they carry responsibility as well for work training, care for the retarded, veteran aid, alcoholism and drug programs, community mental health, delinquency and correctional efforts, many types of institutions, parent locator and support programs, rehabilitation and other programs for the handicapped, as well as several public assistance programs.[2]

Nor is this all. Across the country some six hundred community mental health centers, while concentrating on the mentally disordered, are also providing preventive, crisis, educational, consultative, and counselling services for hundreds of thousands of people who are not severely ill in the psychiatric sense.[3] Indeed, a significant amount of what is done in such centers overlaps with public and private "human services" or "personal social services." In some states, community mental health is administered by the "combined state human service agencies"; some of it may be financed by social service funds (Title XX programs, for example).

Is this, then, the needed general source of family help? Or, if not, is it a prototype for the development of such a resource? Or is it completely irrelevant? A historical and organizational overview will prepare us not only for answering these questions but for the examination in later chapters of activities in the voluntary non-profit sector as well.

From Poor Law to Modern Social Services

The idea that government might operate or finance services to buttress the family is foreign to either a mercantilist or a laissez-faire industrial society. Family, church, and neighborhood were primary institutions and they were expected to support one another. Family and neighborhood solidarity, mutual aid, and Christian (or Jewish or Moslem) charity were taken for granted. Advice, food, money, and guidance came through such sources and were seldom formalized. To the extent that the help went beyond mutual aid and routine family interchange, it was the fortunate and the successful who were helping, guiding, and controlling those in difficulty.

As cities grew and economic needs could no longer be managed informally, it became necessary to arrange for public provision, or at least for relatively formal voluntary agencies, if not a combination of both. Voluntary charities, poor law authorities, and, later, public assistance officials auctioned off the labor of those who were not self-supporting, indentured their children, offered some cash for at-home relief to those not deemed employable—or placed many categories of dependents in mixed almshouses or workhouses if more economical for the locality or more congruent with policy at the time. The three motives were (1) deterrence: they did not want to create a work disincentive, (2) economy: helping to keep the financial burden down, and (3) humane response: offering help to victims of "acts of God" but controlling those whose conduct could threaten the system. Since these motives required both differentiations among people in need and attempts to reform or correct them, the practical help came together with advice and instruction. A popular formulation was: "Not alms, but a friend." The home visitors and evaluators were volunteers until late in the nineteenth century, and then members of the emerging social work profession were deemed "professional altruists."

Parallelling all this was the work, on the one hand, of priests and nuns, and of those who administered public and private institutions, on the other. As the special needs of various deprived and handicapped groups were identified, the religiously motivated, more secular humanitarians, and practical public officials began to separate the care of these groups from the care of the "undesirable" poor law residue. Varying with the handicap and the place, special provision was made for dependent and neglected children, physically handicapped children, the mentally ill, and even some delinquents. Soon, there were helpers who tried to arrange foster care and adoption, to instruct, and to assist.

For the most part, the system was, in its impact, cruel and ultimately punitive as it affected people early in this century. There were some admirable, humane, specialized institutions—orphanages and schools for some of the physically handicapped, for example—but the outstanding places were few, met only a small part of the need, and were exclusively for special groups (for instance, orphans of sea-battle victims), making up a fortunate minority. There was a fundamental strain in the ethic that stressed self-reliance and that blamed victims for their fate. People claimed credit for their own successes and distrusted the characters and motives of most of those who were dependent. Though everyone could recognize that famine, fire, illness, accident, or bad luck might strike even the most resourceful family, most policy was still premised on individual self-determination and the likelihood that the unfortunate, had they been good, moral, and motivated, might have managed otherwise.

Thus, people were needed who could distinguish the worthy from the unworthy, the motivated and the helpable from the hopeless—as understood and defined in that time. And staff was also needed to guide, aid, support, and counsel those believed capable of managing on their own after receiving aid. Moreover, the helpless needed to be dealt with in agencies and organizations specially geared to do the work.

American attitudes gradually changed as Social Darwinism and strict Puritanism were challenged in the Progressive era. From the 1890s to World War I, social science redefined some of the causal dynamics and problem specifics: individual and dynamic psychology, some of the others. Economic realities were better observed and described. The ethic became more tolerant of the troubled and the troublesome, and the helping repertoire was broadened. Economic determinist and medical-illness models were applied to many needs and problems, so that the counsellor did not always assume the client's inferiority, moral culpability, or hopelessness. Yet the attitudinal residues were strong, and most users were still members of the social underclass. Thus, insensitivity, control, stereotyping, and blaming of the victim were often in command, while service reformers sought to enhance respect for clients, clients' self-determination, and sophisticated individualizing as a basis for helping. Service and treatment were meant to be good enough for anyone, but had not yet achieved this status, in the view of most citizens.

By the third decade of this century, there was a fairly extensive counselling, advice, guidance, and information network, but it was almost always connected with the giving of cash assistance, food, medical service, residential care, or as a component of work in courts, schools, prisons, hospitals, clinics, or welfare offices. Often called social work and identified as social casework, it usually dealt with the poor, though it occasionally rose above the poverty line, since some problems clearly affected those who were better off. But the bulk of the public and private social service provision belonged in three systems: it was associated with giving cash assistance, with dealing with child welfare problems, or with establishing the right to charity for medical care. Settlement houses also were numerous and important as multi-program community centers and resources, and they sometimes contained counselling, clinic, and educational programs. The evolution from this base since the passage of the Social Security Act in 1935 is relevant to our effort to define a future locus for family services.

Given the present proliferation of counselling, self-help, and private therapy programs, it is difficult to envision the "social service" repertoire of earlier periods. Psychiatric illness began to have some primitive medical attention as early as the time of the American Revolution, even though the first significant reform wave did not begin until the 1840s, and the beginning of a more scientific approach to the problem occurred in the 1890s. But this was a medical, not a social service, activity.

"Casework" above the poverty line began with Red Cross home services in World War I, where there were family-related problems to be dealt with apart from economic aid. The same was true of Travelers Aid and some sectarian programs. The social service work with refugees from Nazi-controlled countries during the 1930s focused on settlement, housing, job adjustment, and coping with past experience, as well as short-term financial problems.

The child guidance movement began just before World War I but became significant in the 1920s, some of it based in schools and health clinics, some in juvenile courts. Here, too, professional personnel did some counselling not tied to the giving of financial aid. The same was true of medical social work departments in leading hospitals, where it was understood that personal help in response to both practical and emotional consequences of illness and hospitalization could be of considerable benefit to patients and their families. Veterans Administration social service programs shaped a broader view of the mission too, but mostly after World War II, when VA outpatient psychiatric clinics proliferated.

Yet, for all this, there was no extensive public or private service, family life educational or counselling program, prepared in the 1930s to deal on a significant scale with problems of family functioning, milestones, transitions, interrelationships, and problems of development. All the beginnings were in place (as were private models, prototypes, and small programs in family service agencies, churches, settlement houses, child welfare agencies, and community centers). A theory of social casework had developed. Journal articles were written and read. There were schools for the training of social workers. But in both public and private sectors, the giving of money and of guidance and personal help were intertwined and, therefore, the clients were largely what are now described as the welfare poor.

The critical elements in the tradition were "poor law" and "charity organization." If people had economic need, they might require financial aid, but it had to come with advice, guidance, and direction, because the "adequate" would make it on their own. The best prospects ("worthy," "helpable" victims of short-run external forces) were the special province of private charity organization societies (earlier, "societies for the prevention of pauperism" or "associations for the improvement of conditions of the poor"; later, "family service agencies"). The others were the responsibility of the public authorities, who became increasingly accountable for financial aid where they were once only in charge of the almshouse or workhouse, oriented to minimizing costs, referring to, or giving public work, and who were not a source of much personal help.

The enactment of the Social Security Act in 1935 started a process of change that was not fully delineated until the 1960s and was not formalized until 1974, when Title XX of the Social Security Act, a social services title, was passed. The 1935 act had provided for modest funds to the states to create child welfare services (largely foster care, adoption, and institutional programs) and special maternal and child health programs. Beyond this, however, there was no explicit social service provision, although the "public assistance" titles of the Social Security Act provided for 50 percent reimbursement to the states for administrative costs. The Washington leadership, in shaping the implementation of the eligibility procedures relating to the administration of assistance, chose a model like that of the charity organization society: a social worker would determine eligibility for financial aid, "diagnose" the problems occasioning need, and offer case-work help in dealing with those problems. State and local government would be reimbursed for 50 percent of the costs of this service under the heading of "administration."

Thus, in a roundabout way, a form of public social services for poor families, elderly persons, the blind, and the disabled began to develop in the United States, though to different degrees in different regions. It was legitimated in 1956, when Congress distinguished "service" from "administration" more formally. The federal reimbursement level was raised to 75 percent in 1962 to expand the availability of services on what proved to be the mistaken assumption that expanded service would decrease the need for financial assistance. Since "former" and "potential" public assistance recipients as well as "current" recipients could be served, however, the mandate was large. Nor were the service specifics stated. Service staffs and budgets grew. By 1967, state and local social service departments, in addition to providing services, were permitted by the law to contract for services with public and private service agencies.

The transformation of the social services into an autonomous activity under the Social Security Act was completed by the 1974 amendments, and implemented in 1975.[4] The political problems and social objectives behind the shift are documented, but are not relevant to our purposes. What was important was the recognition that "service" and "cash assistance" are two separate things, that state planning for services is critical, and that such planning, in turn, requires considerable public participation and political visibility. Title XX, the service title of the Social Security Act, accounted for $2.5 billion and, later, $2.9 billion in federal funds, the largest non-categorical funding stream for general social services. The successes and problems of the planning process and the opportunities it offers for social service reform are under constant discussion in the relevant professional and public affairs literature and in official reports. Title XX is important for us insofar as we must answer the question: Are family-oriented social services guaranteed under Title XX, or could they be?*

Service Delivery: Public Programming

We must defer a characterization of what is included under public programming until we have summarized those other post-1935 developments relevant to public social services for families. The late 1940s launched the federal community mental health initiative, but it was 1963 legislation that supported a national expansion of community mental health centers. Since this time, these centers have not only concentrated on serving the moderately ill and those with ordinary problems of living by prevention, education, and consultation, but have also focused, especially in recent years, on the severely disturbed, through inpatient, outpatient, and emergency services, and on supporting deinstitutionalization campaigns. Thus, under the rubric of "prevention," some community mental health programs, either publicly operated or under private auspices but supported with public subsidies and grants, may offer the kinds of family services we are focusing on here, but, for most, this is not the central activity.

The Great Society programs of the 1960s were enacted in the context of a series of social policy initiatives so extensive as to rival the New Deal. But the relevance to family service programs was marginal: The Older Americans Act launched planning and coordination efforts and supported a variety of individual and group projects and service efforts for senior citizens. All of these were and are, however, categorically separated, and practically none serve the family problems and interests highlighted here. If anything, there is a failure to integrate service for the aged and general family programs. Various hospital and health programs, both comprehensive and categorical, have recognized the need for social service support and linkage, but almost all focus on social service buttressing of a medical rehabilitation, psychiatric, or educational effort, rather than on creation of a coverage network or even a significant number of service outlets to meet family needs, per se, or to treat family problems. The community action agencies of the poverty program and their almost one thousand local service outlets feature access and advocacy efforts, child care, and job programs. Whatever counselling they offer is peripheral rather than inten-

---

*As we go to press, state options are increased, federal requirements minimized, and funds cut under Reagan administrative initiatives.

sive, and not ongoing. Educational programs, too, have expanded services, but none have supported comprehensive family initiatives, except for family life education, as we will see.

There have been other programs enacted to deal with foster care, child abuse and neglect, delinquency, runaway youth, adolescent pregnancy, and more recently marital violence, but they were enacted in response to "problems" and feature categorically narrow responses. Each may see the relevance of family. Many call for planning and linkage with other categorical systems so as to ensure integrated or comprehensive service systems. The law, however, offers no sanctions; local agencies are not specified. The constituencies that have initiated categorical responses tend to join forces with congressional supporters and bureaucrats who administer programs to ensure that delivery systems remain fully—or at least some-what—categorical, visible, and separate.

The history is one of categorical programming for problem groups; the orientation is toward intervention with individuals. While the value system emphasizes families and the knowledge base calls for holistic approaches and service integration, the political and organizational dynamics create fragmentation, separatism, and an inability to shape comprehensive approaches to services that are family-oriented. Nonetheless, efforts have been made and there are possibilities. We shall make brief mention here of major innovations of the past fifteen years, some of them continuous with earlier initiatives: multi-service and one-stop centers; service integration programs; state umbrella agencies for the human services; and the various child and family development programs, derivative of Head Start, that serve low-income families as a means to offering successful compensatory experiences to their children. Finally, we shall focus on the proposals made for employing Title XX funding and sanctioning, and related public social service legislation, to create a free-standing, publicly based personal social service system. The basis for an overall assessment will thus be established.

Multi-Service and One-Stop Centers

From the mid-1950s, conscientious social welfare agencies and social work staffs sought to improve their impact and facilitate client access by means of locally invented and implemented efforts at coordination. Some were federally funded through various project initiatives. These efforts variously involved co-location, multi-problem outreach efforts, and case integration and management.

Co-location. Different human service programs or categorically organized social service agencies (employment, nursing, housing, public assistance, child welfare, and so forth) shared buildings, storefronts, or office clusters to facilitate client access and staff interchange. Sometimes there was a common information or doorway service as well. Where participants were enthusiastic, leadership strong, and the innovations visible, these programs often achieved useful results. Some still do; however, arrangements were often dependent on locally relevant and often transitory commitments to cooperate. Each of the categorical programs reported to its own funding source, was constrained by its own system of regulations, and was tied to its own orientation and priorities. Even given good will, the obstacles were and remain formidable. These initiatives, while often impressive and locally useful, are insufficient to change the overall picture. As we have summed up elsewhere: "Part of the problem is a failure to recognize the interdependence of federal-, state-, and local-level initiatives, the impossibility of success unless work is done at all levels. . . . The neighborhood service center . . . cannot adequately correct or undo program fragmentation at the federal or state level."[5]

Multi-problem outreach efforts. Special units, some based in one agency, some involving cooperation by several, have made all-out efforts to help those burdened with many disadvantages and problems. These units have often been expertly staffed and have managed to cut red tape and to achieve priority attention for those with whom they have worked. The efforts have generally been family-oriented. Most such initiatives were confined to the 1950s: staff caseloads had to be small, the work was expensive, and the method seemed most relevant where extreme pathology and deprivation came together.[6] Even though such work continues, it is not evident on any significant scale; it tended to be deprecated in favor of "institutional" approaches in the 1960s, and no new resources were made available in the 1970s.

Case integration and case management. Within co-location programs and various other multi-service, storefront, and integrated program efforts, there has been some emphasis on the meshing of simultaneous and sequential services to an individual or to several family members. A youth may move from a residential institution to a community-based school: should the counselling strategy not be consistent? A mother may be receiving help in a family agency, a daughter in a juvenile court probation department, the father in the veterans' hospital clinic, and a son at a settlement house: can the "system" ensure consistency and some mutual reinforcement? The methods have varied from a clerical type of case management, consisting of referral, coordination, and assigning service, to full professional accountability while drawing upon specialized services and personnel in other units or agencies, to professionally sophisticated case meshing while others provide most of the service. There is testimony and research to the effect that some of this case integration—both individual and family-oriented—is not needed for those able to coordinate and integrate for themselves, but it can have significant value in protective work, concerning, for example, at-risk children or the frail aged, aftercare in the community for the mentally ill or those who have been in children's institutions, and work with some categories of the handicapped.[7]

This approach offers a professional technique and an orientation toward accountability. It needs to be located in a delivery system and an ongoing structure for assured availability and impact. The personal social services delivery system, as described below, offers a possibility.

Services Integration Programs

During Richard Nixon's presidency, Secretary Elliot Richardson of the Department of Health, Education, and Welfare (HEW) was struck by the difficulty of creating a coherent delivery system out of the literally hundreds of federally funded programs within the scope of his department. He also was made aware of the consequences of fragmentation, duplication, lack of standardized access and categorical programming on costs, efficiency, and client well-being. His strategy for responding consisted of two elements: an effort to facilitate waivers by the states of program regulations and procedures that blocked coordinated and integrated programming; and support for management information systems, service delivery, and state-structural reforms through demonstration and research funding.

The effort to simplify federal regulation, facilitate waivers, and permit states to repackage federal efforts enjoyed modest success, although the major effort, an Allied Services Act, was not passed by the Congress. But Title XX did benefit from the several attempts at passage and the resulting public discussion. The research and demonstration grants created a variety of comprehensive and useful management information systems, supported some of the service delivery initiatives mentioned above (one-stop centers, multi-service programs, and so forth), and encouraged the creation of state umbrella agencies for administration. Interesting demonstrations and experimental projects came and went as funding availability fluctuated. None of it resulted in any basic reconceptualization of delivery strategies or reduction of categorical initiatives. The effort was in fact not especially family-related.[8]

Umbrella Agencies

Encouragement and federal financial support for state and local capacity-building (management and organizational capacity to deal with social service fragmentation) led some states to put all or many social welfare programs together for overall administration. Pressure for such organizational restructuring also derived from the reality that many of the programs were interdependent for funding purposes or required operational coordination if clients were to be well served: services to the aging, the mentally ill, the retarded, children, the handicapped, delinquents, veterans, alcoholics, and so forth. Indeed, because of legislative and administrative laxity and confusion, many of these programs were in part being paid for out of federal public service funds from the late 1960s until a congressional freeze in the early 1970s that ended with the enactment of Title XX of the Social Security Act in 1974.

States constantly organize and reorganize. A 1978 report shows thirty to thirty-five states with umbrella agencies, depending on definitions. The "core" programs are the old public assistance cash and service programs: Aid to Families with Dependent Children (AFDC), food stamps, general assistance, Medicaid, services to adults (really the social services and aid program to the aged and some related programs), services to families (of limited scope and scale, but included in almost all umbrella programs), child welfare, "work incentive" training and placement for AFDC clients, and child support enforcement. Beyond the core is great variation, but umbrella agencies often deal with vocational rehabilitation, mental retardation and mental health programs, public health generally, corrections, employment programs, and other social services as well. With the exception of a few pioneering states that have attempted extensive changes, most states with umbrella agencies use the device for overall budgeting, programming, and coordination, but retain all the categorical differentiations at the level of local service delivery, whether through state-administered local outlets or state supervision of local government operations. In short, a line from categorical subchiefs and supervisors extends from the state capital to the delivery unit. Service delivery is guided and shaped by categorical and program-specific regulations, guidelines, and professional traditions.[9]

The few states and counties that have sought to integrate at the delivery level have had to face the question of the scope of what can be combined (across what system or systems can one in fact integrate client-level service?) and the way in which such initiatives can be supported by reform of local delivery. These efforts are few, and will be discussed later. What is immediately relevant is that umbrella agencies have not produced an overall family orientation and they seldom, if ever, create a significant family-oriented social service network as a subcomponent within their delivery strategies. If anything, they may increase child welfare service resources and align themselves with the goals of avoiding child placement by encouraging family-oriented solutions to problems and choosing "least restrictive environment" (home and community) dispositions for general personal problems.

Early Childhood and Family Development Programs

Head Start, a compensatory child care program for children aged three to five, was initiated in 1965 during the "poverty war." For most, it was a half-day offering and thus did not meet the needs of most working mothers. Since it was defined initially as an attempt to remedy deficits in children's backgrounds that produced "cognitive" lags, it responded to needs quite different from those of traditional day care. Its philosophic and ideological orientation is "developmental," yet in a broader perspective it is a therapuetic and remedial child care program. Quite early the experience was seen to validate the importance of parental participation in a significant sense. To many of its adherents, participation was interpreted as administrative or policy "control." Strong linkage to or incorporation of related supportive services was deemed essential: nutrition, health, social services, and mental health. The program has been politically popular and has grown. In its first major expansion since 1968, Head Start was granted a $150 million budgetary increase for fiscal 1978, to bring the total to $625 million. It served over 400,000 children in the 1978 fiscal year and had shifted its emphasis from the cognitive to social-emotional growth. After earlier discouraging reports, follow-up research claimed significant gain for participants.

Relevant here are a number of programs that, are different from but based on the experience of Head Start. The experience yielded the conviction that optimum impact on families did not necessarily require the model of Head Start, a child care center program. After all, many of the "target" mothers are at home. They are the objects, too, and their children may gain more if they are the program implementors. Moreover, some families will gain more if they are served when children are infants and toddlers. Three sizable derivative demonstrations relevant here are Parent and Child Centers and Parent and Child Development Centers, Child and Family Resource Programs, and Home Start.[10]

Parent and Child Centers (PCC). Between 1968 and 1970, HEW (which became HHS, the Department of Health and Human Services, in May 1980) funded thirty-six parent and child centers, each designed to serve one hundred children under age three and their families. These multifunctional centers offered "comprehensive" health, education, social service, and participation programs to the very poor. In 1978 there were thirty-three centers serving four thousand children and three had become

Parent and Child Development Centers (PCDC). Early evaluations of PCC showed a diffuse program, many variations among units, management problems, and unclear focus. Nonetheless, HEW remained convinced of their value and they continue, with some management reforms.

The three PCDC's have attempted a more intensive focus and a research orientation since their launching in 1970. They offer parents information and guidance on child development and care, maternal and child health educational activity and service, help in using community resources, social services, and a diversity of educational activities for parents. A five-year research assessment documents gains in maternal attitudes, mother-child interactions, social-emotional child and mother development, and cognitive and language development in the children. To a considerable extent the "service" is staffed by other mothers who have themselves completed the program. A series of replications began in 1976 and are being evaluated.

Child and Family Resource Program (CFRP). Begun in 1973, the Child and Family Resource Program aims at children below the Head Start age. It begins with an assessment and designs responses to meet needs. As yet there is no standardized format. Some $130,000 is added to a local Head Start budget and at least eighty families must be reached. There are eleven locations; no expansion is planned. In general, parents are guided, educated, helped to deal more competently with their children and draw upon available resources. Their own roles are stressed. A longitudinal research design is to report results in 1985.

Home Start. The Home Start program began between 1972 and 1975 as a demonstration. Now it is an optional Head Start "component" serving over 17,000 children out of 325 programs (1976–1977). The theory is simple: as an alternative to the center-based child care program, resources are devoted to a periodic home visit (typically one and a half hours twice per month, per family). This is supplemented with monthly group activities for parents and children. The premise is that in counselling, advising, and teaching parents to deal with family, health, nutritional, and psychological-social needs and in how to play with children, one enriches the relationships involved and makes the most permanent impact on family strength and development. Six programs offer technical assistance and training to Home Start programs, whose sponsors regard them as effective.

In addition to these efforts under the leadership of the Administration for Children, Youth, and Families (ACYF) of HHS, a variety of similar efforts is carried out by the Appalachian Regional Commission and several states.

A recent, positive General Accounting Office assessment of efforts in this category called for expansion.[11] Nonetheless, it also revealed that, apart from Head Start, a child care program, these are basically small, compensatory demonstration programs, targeted for the very poor, generally operating on the premise that the mother is at home, and requiring a willingness to integrate health, mental health, nutrition, and social service programs so as to enrich the child's development. The substantive content and the interventions would be regarded as patronizing, unnecessary, and intrusive by those families who can usually manage, even if they are willing to use advice, information, and occasional help. While the program might be provided for a small group of the poor in a special effort, there is no likelihood that this could become a general pattern of social service or a widely attractive mode of service delivery.

Will Title XX Change Things?

The transformation of the social services was accelerated in 1974 with the enactment of the Social Security Act's first all-service title. While the Congress that voted on Title XX may have seen it as a compromise solution to the misuse of service funds by the states under the earlier public assistance provisions, as well as a way to move from open-ended expenditures to an appropriations ceiling, or as a further step toward "special revenue sharing," which gave more service options to state government, the legislation was so drafted as to permit additional interpretation. For the first time, a large funding stream that permitted, but did not require, states to develop a comprehensive, free-standing, universal system of personal social services that could aspire to "coverage" in all localities had been created.

It was argued that such a system could evolve only if certain necessary developments occurred, and in a mutually consistent fashion: federal legislative, administrative, and budgetary mandates to cope with categorization and fragmentation of programs; reorganization of support structures in the HEW, now HHS; state-level design and reorganization of human services; local experimentation to shape appropriate alternative delivery systems for the general-personal social services; and commitment to public operation of front-line services and public accountability for purchased services.

There, in short, was an opportunity for major new service initiatives, but legislative signals were mixed, the obstacles were large, and both the states and the voluntary sector agencies could decide to use the opportunity to solve financial problems without reorganizing. It was by no means clear whether Title XX would serve merely as a funding stream, even a publicly funded United Way, or would become the cornerstone of a new service program.

As a form of special revenue sharing, Title XX offered states and localities opportunities, but few mandates. In general, the act did not define services, did not require specific services (with some exceptions), did not require federal approval of the substance of state plans for the money expenditure, and did not mandate delivery systems. States would divide $2.5 billion on the basis of population size, and each state could have its share if it completed a visible, accountable planning process geared to assure public participation (in accord with published regulations). Broad, general goals were listed for the services, goals so broad and general as to offer few restrictions for service repertoires. Half of the funds allotted to each state were to be spent on the welfare poor. States were to charge income-related fees at levels they determined to those users above 80 percent of the state median income and could charge fees below that income level. Eligibility would end at 115 percent above the state median. In effect, this would mean that a legislative springboard for potential universalism had been created: states had options in fee size, and 115 percent above the median moves one well into the income distribution. Different fee levels were acceptable for each service.

Also mandated under Title XX are some services without regard to income: information and referral, protective services, family planning. In areas of high need and low income, eligibility may be determined on a group rather than an individual income-tested basis. These specifications, too, favor a general social services development.[12]

Shortly after the implementation of Title XX, HEW reorganized for greater functional efficiency and, in the process, unified to place both universal and selective (means-tested) programs in units with the potential for systematic general development to serve the public at large—"not for the poor alone" and "not only for those who have paid contributions." Thus:

The *Social Security Administration* now combined its "insurance" programs with the administration of Supplemental Security Income (SSI) and AFDC in one overhead organization (but keeping "insurance" and "assistance" separate at the lower tier).

The *Public Health Service*, concerned with health delivery, training, and prevention, was and remained concerned with all population groups.

The *Health Care Financing Administration* (HCFA) brought together Medicare ("insurance") and Medicaid ("means tested") for purposes of ensuring cost control and professional self-policing.

The *Office of Human Development Services* (OHDS) joined in one structure the unit implementing Title XX (Administration for Public Services) with units responsible for categorical service programs, most of which are not limited to the poor: the Administration for Children, Youth, and Families (ACYF), the Administration on Aging (AOA), the Administration for Native Americans, the Rehabilitation Services Administration (RSA).[13] With access to Title XX, OHDS has potential leverage with reference to almost half of all general social service funds expended in the United States. It has been stymied, thus far, in its initiatives by categorical interest groups, in Washington and the states, identified with one subprogram or category or another and not favorably inclined to federal cross-cutting initiatives.*

Evaluations and statistical reports indicate that the "promise" of Title XX and OHDS are thus far unrealized. Despite a Title XX call for coordination of social services, there is no specific mandate or specification of a lead agency. Planning requirements have created a participation process, but the outcome favors the better-organized categorical social service interest groups (day care, foster care, community services to the aging, and the like), and these, in turn, are dominated by service "providers." Citizen consumer interest rises and wanes and few lobbies call for expenditure balance. Among various subgroups of social service consumers, there are no significant lobbies for family services or for the public interest generally. "Family services," whether in ACYF or in the states, are really categorical programs like battered wives programs or teenage pregnancy initiatives. Nowhere in state Title XX programs are significant resources devoted to the daily concerns of average people, to life transition and milestone supports, to the home-work adjustment needs of working-class and middle-class families. This is no cause for surprise: within a short time the congressionally authorized ceiling expenditure, based on population size, had been reached in most states and there was a feeling in many places that resources were insufficient for high-priority "social problem" services like protective programs for children and the aged, emergency homemakers help, day care for children of single mothers and working mothers, or assistance during family and housing emergencies.[14]

While statistical tabulations are inexact and incomplete, there are data about how states expend most public social service funds, whether through direct operations or purchase of service, referring to Title XX, child welfare funds, or service connected to public assistance and work incentive programs. Although "counselling" is common, the term apparently refers to the interviews connected with applications, referral, and access to other services, not to intensive personal help. After such counselling, service

---

*As we go to press it is not possible to judge the success or consequences of President Reagan's block grant initiatives. Funding has been decreased as well, and many unrelated programs packaged together.

totals and expenditures are dominated by day care, family planning, health-related activity, protective services, and foster care. Major categories after this are homemaker, transportation, and case management services—in varying orders, depending on the quarter.

As might be expected, 44 percent of all users are assistance recipients and another 34 percent are income eligible, as per Title XX rules. Only about 18 percent are people above the Title XX income eligibility level. Protective programs, family planning, and information and referral dominate this "without regard to income" category. A similar analysis that adds public child welfare and work-incentive clients to the Title XX groups does not change the ratios much since Title XX pays for 6,527,000 of 7,142,000 primary recipients of public social services in the United States.[15]

"Needs assessments" are mandated in Title XX plans and are reported by all states regularly, but clearly the methodology is primitive and the activity largely ritualistic.[16] Established expenditure patterns remain in place, and by the third year most states had reached their authorization levels and were not prepared for major redeployment of funds. To a considerable extent Title XX was from the beginning regarded as a funding stream "solution," not as a delivery system challenge. By late 1979, up to 60 percent of the funds may have been contracted out to other public and private agencies (half to the private sector) and have not been used for operating a Title XX delivery system at all. Data are soft on this topic. There were great state variations not only in this but also in public versus private contracting. In general, private child welfare agencies are now overwhelmingly publicly funded in contrast to the situation a decade ago, and private family agencies have significant public funding, something that was not the case even five years ago.

A few efforts have been made to integrate statewide programs into delivery structures that are more coherent. While there are instances of excellent service and delivery reform on a small scale, the district service system in Florida, where one of the largest initiatives is taking place, has one manager at the delivery level, but actual service delivery remains largely categorical and legal roadblocks have interfered with other initiatives. Another state, Utah, is encouraging local reform of delivery and integration of services, but it is moving slowly at the local pace. Minnesota is experimenting with county "block grants" to encourage local personal social service planning.

Proponents of delivery reform to establish the personal social services as a free-standing, universal, publicly sponsored system that builds on Title XX have received support and endorsement from major standard-setting groups, but financial, legal, and organizational obstacles have precluded all but modest, local initiatives. The most ambitious designs promulgated call for: a publicly operated coverage system consisting of local personal social service offices; baseline services in such offices to offer information, advice, and referral, protective services for children and the aged, capacity for front-line counselling, and case integration and accountability capacity to serve identified categories of vulnerable citizens, especially the "deinstitutionalized" and multi-problem groups; and specialized services provided in the local offices, or in public and voluntary agencies that are organized for delivery of such services as shelter, detention, day treatment, center programs, and various specialized interventions paid for out of their own budgets or contracted through Title XX and other funding streams. These offices would feature family-oriented service delivery.

A variety of alternatives has been identified with reference to the frontline professional's role in the local offices, with most proponents favoring "advanced generalist" social workers who would span traditional case categories and stress holistic, supra-category services to individuals and families. Several alternatives have also been proposed for local unit governance and for managing the Title XX contract system to assure priority to service needs as identified in the course of service operations and to reflect assessments by consumers and local staff of the relevance, priority, and quality of contracts in the overall context.[17]

While the policy support of leadership groups in the professions has been and remains strong,[18] the relevant powerful interest groups and congressional committees have endorsed neither cross-cutting strategies nor delivery coherence, neither a minimum of public delivery capacity nor provision for holistic case-accountable emphases. "Integrated social service networks" remain attractive goals but are not now widespread policy objectives. Universalism—serving the needs of all income groups, not only of the poor—has many champions but is seldom fully implemented. A service system oriented to information, advice, socialization, education, and development—not only to protection, counselling, treatment, rehabilitation, and social control—is discussed but not implemented except episodically. Personal social services offer a rallying point but as yet lack political appeal and visibility.[19]

Could There Be a Public Family Service?

None of this signifies that a publicly initiated personal social service network will not emerge or that it is not a significant potential locus of family-oriented social services for all families. Thus far, as we have seen, progress has been modest. During all the campaigns for the development of reorganized service delivery through creation of such networks, the Congress and HHS have been coping with public concern for families. The administrative, legislative, and funding initiatives have been largely categorical:* programs for battered wives, teenage pregnancy, family planning; subsidized adoption, "permanence" for foster-care children, and "least" restrictive environment for treatment; runaway youth and youth employment programs; service networks for the aged; compensatory, family-oriented programs for the very poor, on a project basis, not offering coverage. Yet several factors suggest that there may be more movement.

For one thing, resource constraints are creating pressure for efficiency, integration, and the careful use of scarce public dollars. Some governors and state commissioners have come to favor integrated social service networks, local public outlets, public delivery of most Title XX services, and not mere contracting.

Second, some observers have come to recognize that the fact that categories rise and fall in popularity undermines categorical organization. Services are in "fashion" for brief periods and are then neglected.

Third, observers of Title XX needs assessment, public participation, and general planning have come to wonder whether any *process* mandate can protect the public interest. Should Congress not expand its policy initiatives and take more action with reference to the service system minimums?

Fourth, social and behavioral theory argues for holistic views of individuals and families; research into intervention speaks to the negative consequences of fragmentation and the need for case integration and case accountability devices; researchers and analysts report on the contradictions between categorical service organization and the scientifically—and morally—argued case for "normalization" and "mainstreaming."

Fifth, analysts of the social scene and of the efforts to reform care of the handicapped, the mentally ill, and the retarded, as well as child welfare and services to the aged, call increasingly for a family focus that is organic and not merely rhetorical.

Finally, there is strong sentiment in many parts of the country in favor of devolution to the state level of as many federal programs as possible, to encourage state "consolidation" efforts appropriate to local needs. Social services could fit into such initiatives.

One thus concludes that the public social service initiatives out of what was once called "public welfare programs" should not be discounted for all time as a source of family services. Little is offered at the moment except to the "welfare poor," the frail aged, children needing adoption and substi-

---

*Again we acknowledge the non-categorical block grant initiatives of the Reagan administration that are accompanied by budget-cutting. As we go to press their effects are unknown.

tute care, and those with the severest of personal problems and the greatest poverty of personal resources. And the services are symptom-, age-, or category-oriented. New initiatives of another sort could emerge in more places, as they already have in some. But public resources remain scarce and rationed. At the most, in the near future, one might expect a problem-oriented service that crosses categories, is family oriented, and features information, advice, and referral as well as protective services to neglected and abused children and the frail elderly. It would cope locally with both interpersonal and personal emergencies, including psychiatric problems, and would assure a continuity of community attention to the most endangered and vulnerable. It would offer or arrange for community social care of the frail, handicapped, and dependent. It would counsel, refer to specialists, and occasionally, relying on its experience, advocate and contribute to planning. It could in some places provide a locus for self-help initiatives and family life education.

In short, reasonable developments in the public personal social service system would be a useful step forward in helping America's families. As long as resources remain scarce and political obstacles are substantial, strong advocacy of a public personal social service network with a separate and independent office in each locality remains essential. The objective would have to be a high-quality, universal service, free for some users and charging fees for others, to ensure high-quality service and wide access. Ongoing specialized intensive service might perhaps be carried out variously in the public office or through private purchase and contracts, depending upon the local resource situation.

A realistic scenario suggests only gradual progress—if any—in such direction and therefore a scarcity of resources for at least some time. Public social service priority will need to go to the poor and disadvantaged while preserving the quality and attractiveness that justifies universality. Because it is not certain that a public personal social service network will be established and will thrive, or that if developed it will attract and hold all elements of the population, or that any monopoly could deliver the diversity of services required, alternative and parallel possibilities discussed in the earlier chapter and in the chapters that follow cannot be easily dismissed.

Community Mental Health Centers

Before we draw conclusions, however, we must take note of another relevant public program, usually called a community mental health center. The sign in front of the large edifice, the hospital wing, or the modest neighborhood storefront can carry such other titles as Family Center, Emergency Service Center, Outpatient Clinic and Day Hospital, or Psychiatric and Mental Health Service.

Few of the approximately 590 operational community mental health centers are cut on the same pattern. Nonetheless, these programs may be introduced by listening to an intake worker as clients arrive for service at one such center in a poor neighborhood in a metropolitan area. The interviewer could be a psychologist, a social worker, a psychiatrist, a psychiatric nurse, or a neighborhood paraprofessional aide. In this instance, she was a social worker:

"My son was in the county hospital for two weeks. The police took him there because I called when he threatened everyone in the family with a baseball bat. Now they've sent him home. No one told me he was coming or what to do. He is on drugs. He lies on his bed and mumbles. We are all afraid."

"Please do something to save my grandchild. That mother of hers will neglect her to death. My son works on the buses and can't stay home. When I visit, the kitchen is like a pigsty—and the bedroom too. The sheets are filthy. The baby isn't changed. There are roaches in the refrigerator. Yet she just watches TV and says I shouldn't bother her."

"I'm afraid to go to my job at the insurance company. I am a file clerk. But some of the guys don't like me. They play tricks. Last week they hid my lunch and my jacket. I heard them whisper that they should hide me. But my wife says I must work or we won't eat. How long do I work there? Five years. But I just began to realize what is going on."

"Must I keep on having sex with my husband? I hate it. We have three kids. I'm tired. I can't get enough energy together to shop and do the house things. I wish he would not come home. Can you get him to divorce me? Or could he be made to live elsewhere?"

"Something is wrong. My doctor can't help. The baby won't stop rocking or hitting his head on the crib. He is not growing as he should. And he lies there too quiet. Tell me, is he retarded or brain-damaged? Or will he become that? Did I do it? Is it heredity? What should I do? Is there a place to send him?"

"My father can't be at home any more. He is seventy-eight, and careless. Yesterday he wandered away and my mother called frantically. He was out walking somewhere for four hours. When he got back, he was filthy and mumbling. She's too sick to go with him. He doesn't wash or dress right any more. He forgets. It's senility. Can you arrange a nursing home?"

"This is Frank Q from the ABC Family Agency. I am referring a very depressed woman. Her kids are grown and away. Now her husband has walked out. We think she could be suicidal. Here are some facts. . . ."

"I need some medicine. I can't sleep. I dream terrible dreams. I can't rest. How will I work? I have a rash all over. Medicine is what I need." "Can you go out on a visit? A black man in my parish lives alone. He's in his twenties. Ambulances have come twice in three weeks. He collapses from overdoses of drugs. I think he drinks, too. I have visited and he tells me he will stop. He'll kill himself. He was in a mental hospital last year."

If public welfare programs (services to poor families, to the aged, and to children in need) have been dominated historically by the cash assistance delivery system, services to the mentally ill have been shaped until recent times by the control of the severely disturbed in large mental hospitals, most of them operated by state government. Since the early 1960s, however, care of the mentally ill and disturbed has increasingly been assigned to community mental health centers. And such centers, emphasizing secondary prevention as well as education and consultation, have taken on a good deal of the types of counselling, family life education, and related programs that are associated with general family helping services. There is virtually no form of family therapy, family life education, personal and marital counselling, parent-child treatment, or general advice about the exigencies and contingencies in daily living—carried out in private family service agencies, marketplace counselling and therapy, schools, settlement houses and community centers, churches and pastoral counselling centers, public personal social service centers—also not offered in some mental health centers under similar or different names. Thus the question is whether in some sense the community mental health system could not be made into a major response to the service needs of families.

What Is Community Mental Health?

The term community mental health is relatively vague, and, in some sense, it is an ideology rather than a coherent movement, but it is important because it is an ideology tied to a federal funding stream since the early 1960s. As described by Steven P. Segal, community mental health is an effort to focus on an individual's relationship to the social and physical environment.[20] Combining public health and social work approaches, it moves the care of the mentally disordered from the large remote mental hospital and the private psychiatric office to the patient's neighborhood. Its dominant intervention modes are community-based and it aspires to prevention by urging a focus on societal and community problems, and by instruction, guidance, and early intervention where problems exist.

A community mental health center was conceived in the early 1960s as a community "function," not as an edifice: it was to be a cooperative, integrated arrangement of community agencies and facilities that together would carry out five functions ("basic") or ten functions ("comprehensive").

Two more were added in 1975, and the current list calls for inpatient services for the mentally ill, outpatient services for the mentally ill, partial hospitalization (day hospitals, night hospitals, and so on), emergency service, consultation and education, diagnostic services, rehabilitation, precare and aftercare services, training for personnel, research and evaluation, community-based living arrangements, and case-screening facilities. (Parallel and related legislation in the late 1960s and early 1970s created planning and funding supports to develop similar or integrated services for alcoholism and drug addiction.)[21]

The community mental health center movement traces its origins to the failure and horrors of the large mental hospitals ("asylums") and the discovery that open hospitals that were small and decentralized and allowed patients to interact with the normal world were more effective. The theoreticians of mental illness increasingly noted how little of it was organically caused, and they argued, variously, that mental illness is defined by community context, is caused by problems in community living, and/or is "useful" to the community in defining normalcy and establishing social control. Innovative approaches became viable when new drugs made it possible to return many more of the mentally ill to community living safely, while ensuring that most would remain under control.

Public funding and leadership by both the federal establishment and a volunteer citizen movement have spread the ideology and resulted in large-scale service expansion. Significant federal funding has influenced state and local programs and philosophy since the mid-1960s. Psychiatry, social work, nursing, and psychology, funded on a large scale for personnel training, have been in the lead. Members of citizens' movements and politicians have been strong advocates. Normal political and community processes have ensured that community mental health centers are now largely buildings, not community functions. They are identifiable places, describable programs.

The delivery systems do stress community-based care, whether outpatient and day treatment, rehabilitation programs, or a variety of educational efforts as well as consultation to related community institutions. Mental hospital populations have declined, partially in response to these efforts and in part because the aged now often have access to and funding for nursing homes and so-called "adult homes" under various social insurance and assistance programs, and so no longer need to crowd, even if not mentally ill, into the geriatric wards of state hospitals.

Community mental health programs now have contacts at a given moment with almost a million people, some for intensive service, some very briefly. Most operate as outpatient clinics and day hospitals, staffed by psychiatrists, psychologists, and social workers, with some nurses and paraprofessionals. Directors may be social workers, psychologists, or psychiatrists. Treatment must be medically "controlled," whether it involves physical interventions (drugs) or psychotherapy and education, but the control at times is symbolic only. Outpatient care and hospitalization, if only emergency or day treatment, are supplemented by many personal social services and community activities, approximating settlement houses in some places, family service agencies in others.

What Is Achieved?

At best, the community mental health movement has drawn upon substantial federal funds, supplemented by state and local governmental resources and some voluntary money, to improve the delivery of a variety of services to the mentally disordered and the emotionally disturbed. Efforts to address societal issues (part of a community mental health ideology) have faced unclear boundaries; poverty, inadequate housing, and racial tension are hardly subjects reserved for psychiatrists, psychologists, and social workers. Efforts to focus on total community service systems, through so-called preventive educational and consultative efforts or the outposting of staff for intake emergencies, also have had uncertain success. Police, fire departments, and schools can learn from mental health professionals about dealing with disasters and crises and can benefit from insights into human development, but they are equal, not secondary, systems with their own missions, technologies, and expertise. The mental health system cannot be in the driver's seat.

However, a variety of important ideas about the delivery of services to people in need has been elaborated and developed by mental health programs. They have been implemented to different degrees in different places because they all involve social service institutions and providers under several jurisdictions—not necessarily medically oriented and with their own values and interests: continuity of care from one to another agency, a search for meshing of simultaneous and sequential services; case accountability, so cases are not lost in the system; case integration or case management, an administrative assignment to ensure accountability and continuity; parsimonious interventions, that is, doing only what is needed so that personal strengths and normal social supports may play their roles; community service, rather than hospitalizing or removing from the home if unnecessary or for longer than necessary; advocacy and brokerage, helping people in need draw upon rights, benefits, and other service systems essential to their daily living needs; and consultation, helping teachers, police, doctors, and others to do their work and to lessen breakdown and the need for clinical service. This last notion could involve education, consultation, help in emergencies, and so on. Occasionally it takes the form of contributions to housing designs, coping with intergroup relations, writing legislation relating to such social problems as teenage pregnancy, delinquency, drug control, and the like—a move away from treatment to prevention and an investment whose payoff is generally difficult to clarify.

Many of these approaches are shared with advocacy, case integration, and delivery reform efforts in the personal social services, as already noted. The influence is in both directions, although vocabularies tend to vary somewhat. Of special importance in this regard are continuity of care, case integration, case accountability, advocacy, and brokerage service.

Despite literally hundreds of local evaluation studies and many books and journals devoted to the problem of community mental health evaluation, it is difficult to go from a general discussion of influences on thinking about service delivery or the overall reporting of service numbers to any firm assessment. The data prove to be soft. With the wide range of problems and conditions attacked, the literally hundreds of therapeutic strategies, and the decentralized nature of the delivery system, such conclusions are almost inevitable. (One cannot measure impact without specifying targets and interventions with more precision and identifying comparison with control groups.)

Two things are known. First, large numbers of clients, perhaps a majority, do not continue in community mental health centers beyond the initial contact. Second, in 1980, following a request from a Senate subcommittee, the National Center for Health Care Technology began a systematic assessment of three major therapeutic mental health technologies. Even though the community mental health center is not in this assessment, its accomplishments may be examined more closely as a cost-conscious Congress asks whether the Medicare and Medicaid funds buy effective services.

The Connection with Family Services?

Community mental health has its theoretical basis in public health thinking: If possible, stress primary prevention (cut the incidence of breakdown); as an alternative, ensure secondary prevention (early detection and intervention before problems are fixed); but also carry out treatment and rehabilitation, so that suffering is minimized, functional capacity restored, and problems not "transmitted" to one's children and family members.

The general orientation makes it appropriate for community mental health personnel to be concerned with or at least interested in a range of activities covering much of modern family and community life: prenatal care; infant care; sex education; marital problems; child behavior and emotional problems; substance abuse; the quality of community life and citizen participation in agency and community governances; access of people to jobs, income assistance, health services, housing; emergency hospitalization of the mentally ill; outpatient treatment of the mentally ill; rehabilitation service for the mentally ill; community programs for the aged.[22]

Since the 1960s community mental health centers have variously emphasized community organization and anti-poverty activities, community education related to normalcy and disturbance, consultative treatment of the neurotic, unhappy, and mildly disturbed, and treatment of the mentally ill. Congressional pressure, the development of other systems, and a large interest recently in deinstitutionalizing the mentally ill (and others in institutions) has shifted the balance toward integration of community mental health centers with state hospitals and an emphasis on emergency service, outpatient and aftercare services, living arrangements, rehabilitation, advocacy, and referral for the severely disturbed.

In a 1978 overview using 1975 data, the President's Commission on Mental Health reported that of 6.5 million "episodes" of psychiatric care, about 29 percent (1.28 million) were handled in community mental health centers. Elsewhere, an estimate is offered of 1.627 million "episodes" seen in such centers. In another calculation based on analysis of almost one million admissions in 1976 (see above), 6.7 percent of all cases were diagnosed as "social maladjustment" and 13.0 percent as "no mental disorder," 13.9 percent as transient situational disturbances and behavior disorders of childhood and adolescence, and 21.0 percent as "other nonpsychotic." In short, some 54.6 percent of the one million 1976 cases did not involve mental illness in the usual meaning of the term and another 14.8 percent were drug addiction and alcohol abuse cases. It is within this case group of over 500,000 cases that the potentially family-related services (exact totals unspecified) are found within community mental health.[23]

On the basis of our survey, the following statements appear justified. The picture is so diverse and data so inconsistent and incomplete that large numbers of exceptions will be identified.

First, just as public assistance offices that assign eligibility investigations and personal social service delivery to the same social workers find that their major energies must and do go to eligibility certification, community mental health centers seldom successfully do much with prevention if they are seriously concentrated on care and treatment of the severely disturbed. On the other hand, centers that emphasize serving the neurotic and the mildly disturbed as well as "prevention" meet community anger and hospital attack for not supporting a community system in its "primary" deinstitutionalization and "care of the mentally ill" missions.

Second, as community mental health centers do more to meet their assigned missions for the severely mentally ill, they will have even fewer resources for the mildly ill and "normal" individuals and families needing service and help.

Moreover, whereas the early case finding, counselling, and educational activity, along with outpatient treatment of neuroses and mild disorders, attracted a middle-class and working-class constituency, the newer stress on the very disturbed and on deinstitutionalization and normalization has shifted the balance to the welfare poor and the most deprived.

Some families, however, will continue to receive help as a group, and some family members will continue to find help with intra-familial problems and daily problems in living in community mental health centers. This is consistent with the mission of secondary prevention, early case finding, and education.

Finally, as community mental health centers become more successful in developing continuity of care and case integration services, people will move more readily between and among psychiatric, children's, family, and generalized helping services as needed.

Thus far we have talked about services actually based in community mental health centers. Some of these centers in fact are public programs, others only publicly funded. There is another point to be noted: "Mental health" employed as a free-standing term is a loose one, variously applied to helping and treatment programs in which direct work and prevention are carried out by psychiatrists, pediatricians, social workers, psychologists, and educators. Therefore, the family helping programs described in other chapters in this volume (family service agencies and pastoral counselling, for example) may within those systems also be called "mental health" services, whether or not they are functional components of community networks recognized formally as mental health centers. This latter use of the term "mental health" is a reflection both of funding stream requirements (a mental health program directed by a doctor, even if based in a family service agency, may be eligible for Medicaid funds) and of the prestige accorded to services in some way associated in the public mind with psychiatric and psychological knowledge and technology.

Concluding Note

Currently and in the immediate future, many of the American families receiving help and service from public personal social service departments are likely to present severe problems and disorders and to be among the poorest and most deprived citizens. Some of those receiving help from community mental health centers are likely to give evidence of severe pathology and personal disorganization. These facts, as history has proven, will serve to stigmatize some of the services, keeping some people away and affecting the response of those who must come.

But in some communities the take-up is already more general and the image far more attractive. Elsewhere—separated from public assistance programs—these personal social services accept graduated fees from the more affluent as they deem appropriate and continue a trend toward universalism. Community mental health already has a broader tradition.

With universalism and an additional acceptance of the validity of service for the mildly disturbed these services will increasingly meet the types of needs we have placed in the spotlight. Whether they carry the euphemism of "prevention" or the more legitimate connotation of responding to the normal living needs of average citizens, public personal social service programs and community mental health center activities can and should be expected in the near future to offer more in the way of information, advice, education, socialization, and developmental services for families of different types and at various stages in the life cycle.

Even more could be achieved if these systems were joined together to create a broad-gauged, universal, neighborhood-based personal social services delivery system: a new entity clearly not public welfare or a psychiatric clinic. Such a program could make a major contribution to family life in American communities. This could occur, however, only if community mental health centers could separate their large personal social service components from their current responsibilities as part of a medically controlled network for service to the psychiatrically ill, the mentally disordered. Another precondition would be the dominance of a generalist social service practice, family-oriented, where now categorical "problem-oriented" services characterize most personal social service delivery. We state these as desirable directions and possibilities but do not consider them likely: professional and turf concerns, traditional boundaries, and public attitudes, all point elsewhere, at least at present.

Nonetheless, public social services in community mental health centers and public social service or human resource programs do and will meet some of the needs we are highlighting here and could become even more important. To add further to the picture, we now turn to the voluntary non-profit family agency and to family life and parent education, under both public and voluntary auspices.

4 The Family Service Agency

Mention a "family service agency" as a source of help for families, and you are likely to get an immediate and knowing response. Talk to several people, however, and you may find that behind the response are different and even inconsistent images:

"Those agencies are just for people who want to *talk* about their problems. Family service agencies don't give any *real* help."

"That's where poor families go for help. They're not for people like *us*."

"They don't give help to ordinary families. They're just for people with *serious* problems."

Who is right? Or are they all wrong? What exactly is a family service agency?

There is no clear, universally accepted definition of a family service agency. Indeed, the variations among agencies describing themselves as directed toward "family service" are probably larger now than ever before. Any systematic look at such agencies around the country would lead to at least three conclusions: There is no one "typical" or "model" family service agency; what are called "family service agencies" have grown phenomenally in size, budget, and clientele over the past decade—yet the totality of such agencies is not sufficient to touch more than a small minority of all people seeking personal help or service.

And, finally, this expansion in the family service field has not been parallelled by any coherent or consistent view of which families are to be helped, how, by whom, and with what expected results. As a consequence, the family service field is undergoing something of an identity crisis.

In this chapter, we take a close look at these agencies. More specifically we are going to examine: What do family service agencies look like and how did they get to be the way they are? Who comes for help to these agencies and why? Who gets help and how is it given? Why do people come to a family service agency rather than go someplace else for help? What seems to be happening to the private family service agencies now, and what are some of the trends and issues to watch for during the next decade?

112

What Are Family Service Agencies?

Family service agencies differ in size, auspice (sectarian, non-sectarian), operating budgets, programs and services, clientele (poor, working-class, middle-class; racially and ethnically mixed or segregated), problems addressed, and interventions employed. About the only sure thing that can be said about a voluntary family service agency is that it is a non-profit organization, administered under private, non-governmental auspices with a voluntary board, and providing some kind of help for families and family members. At the very minimum such agencies offer advice and counselling regarding family-related problems, marital or parent-child in particular.

Given the looseness of this definition, there is no way to know exactly how many family service agencies there are in the United States today. The most readily identifiable are the member and provisional agencies of the Family Service Association of America, the national association of family service agencies (269 in the United States and 9 in Canada). FSAA membership, however, is limited to voluntary agencies having a certain minimum size as well as certain other characteristics. Moreover, membership in FSAA requires payment of what may be a very significant fee, one that some agencies do not think worthwhile on a cost-benefit basis and that others simply find hard to afford. Thus, a large number of agencies that think of themselves as family service agencies are not FSAA members.

In writing about these agencies in the mid-1970s, one expert estimated that there were about a thousand family service agencies in the United States (half sectarian), of which about three hundred were members of FSAA in 1974 (almost all non-sectarian).[1] In addition to the FSAA agencies, he estimated that there were about four hundred family service agencies under the auspices of Catholic Charities and about a hundred under Jewish auspices. Some years later, in 1979, another expert listed 95 family agencies affiliated with the Association of Jewish Family and Children's Services, including 34 who are members of FSAA, and 545 diocesan agencies and branch offices of the National Conference of Catholic Charities (how many of these are separate family service agencies is not known).[2] The earlier estimate of a thousand such agencies nationally may well understate the number.

Family service agencies range in size from one located on the ground floor of what used to be a private home in an old section of a small town, staffed by one full-time and one half-time social worker, a half-time receptionist-clerk-typist and several volunteers, to a large metropolitan agency with over a dozen branch offices, several residences, more than forty off-site locations where programs are operated, and several hundred staff. Operating expenditures range as widely, from a low of under $50,000 to a high of over $20 million. The source of these funds, however, has changed substantially over the past twenty years, suggesting part of what has led to the change and growth in family service agencies generally, especially in the last decade. In 1959, 94 percent of the FSAA member agencies received more than half their total income from United Way or sectarian federations, falling to 70 percent in 1974. By 1978, the proportion supported primarily by voluntary agency funds had declined to 55 percent. The pattern for the average FSAA agency was about 50 percent of income from private sources and 30 percent from government. The large metropolitan agencies, however, are more likely to look to government for two-thirds or more of their funding.

The program range is equally diverse. FSAA expects its member agencies to have, at a minimum, family counselling, family life education, and family advocacy services, although agencies are not required to have separate and special staff to provide each service.[3] (These services will be described in some detail later in this chapter.) Many agencies provide only these services. Some agencies, instead, provide only counselling, or psychotherapy, to individuals and families, with extensive psychiatric consultation and psychological testing as supportive services. In contrast, other agencies offer a cluster of services. One surburban agency, for example, in addition to its core program, provides adoption services, foster care services, homemaker services, a variety of services for the elderly, Big Brothers–Big Sisters, residences for children and for youth, information and referral services, and training for graduate social workers. Still another provides, in addition to its core services, debt counselling, divorce mediation, sex therapy and counselling, special services for the aged, drug counselling, day care, camping, a special counselling program for blacks and Hispanics, information and referral services, as well as support for training and research activities of several kinds and technical assistance to local self-help groups.

In comparing their service users with the general population, an FSAA survey in 1970 reported that agency clients tend to be younger (with a few fifty-five years and older) metropolitan residents who are slightly higher in education, more often unemployed and/or receiving public assistance, and generally lower in income. The clients are often women, frequently the heads of single-parent families, and they tend to have more children than the average. They are more likely to be black and less likely to be Hispanic, Asian, or Native American.[4] Regardless of whether they come for help for themselves alone or because of some other member of their families, the clients of FSAA agencies are overwhelmingly family members. Few single, unattached individuals come to a family service agency seeking help. Marital problems and parent-child problems continue to dominate the requests for counselling, with problems in individual functioning only a poor third. Other types of requests are likely to be channelled to the non-counselling components of a large agency, or may be referred elsewhere by the more traditional agencies.

Given the range of help sought, it is understandable that the technology of help includes everything from the most intensive psychotherapy to political action. Needless to say, every type of therapy has at least some advocates. Individual, group, and family therapy are standard interventions, as are information, referral, advocacy, brokerage, and a variety of other types of specific, helping services.

Descendants of the Association for the Improvement of the Conditions of the Poor of the mid-nineteenth century and the Charity Organization societies of the late nineteenth century, the family services agencies relinquished their primary role of providing financial assistance to poor families and reforming them in the process only after passage of the Social Security Act of 1935. Relieved of the responsibility of providing money to the poor, these voluntary agencies concentrated instead on problems related to family disorganization and breakdown.

During the 1940s and 1950s Freudian psychoanalytic theory dominated their practice. The Freudian influence became so pervasive, according to one analyst, that "much of the family service casework became almost exclusively a verbal therapeutic process focusing on intra-psychic factors and interpersonal relationship aspects of individuals."[5] Inevitably, the 1960s saw a reaction. With the "rediscovery of poverty" came a growing recognition that the family service agencies had moved very far from their original mission: to serve the poor and disorganized families. These agencies were increasingly described as "disengaging" from the poor, as providing help in a form that was irrelevant to the needs of the poor, and indeed as not addressing the problems of poverty at all.

In response to these criticisms, some agencies began to modify their programs in a variety of ways to make them more accessible to the poor and more responsive to their needs. In 1969, FSAA explicitly urged its member agencies to develop a specialized advocacy role in serving clients. A little earlier, in 1967, an amendment to the Social Security Act had been passed permitting public welfare departments to purchase social services as needed from private voluntary agencies. Thus, at a time when family service agencies were seeking to modify their image and their programs, a new source of funds became available from the public sector, providing both wherewithal and direction. At the same time, Medicaid and Medicare became available as still another source of public monies, as did third-party payment from private insurance companies, albeit of much less significance than the public funds.

The mid-1970s gave still another boost to these agencies. With the passage of Title XX, the first general social service funds were appropriated by the federal government. Given the growing trend toward purchasing services from the private sector, these monies, as well as a variety of categorical funds from such programs as the Child Abuse and Neglect Prevention Act, the Runaway Youth Act, and the Older Americans Act, offered still more in the way of financial resources to creative and entrepreneurial administrators seeking to expand and change the operation of their agencies.

Thus, over the last decade, family service agencies have been transformed from small, somewhat precious, private charitable organizations supported largely by private philanthropy to increasingly large, diverse, multi-program agencies funded largely by public monies. Influenced to a significant extent by the availability of these funds and the constraints imposed by the legislation authorizing funding, the agencies have adapted in a variety of ways. Some have continued in the traditional pattern of providing a low-cost counselling service for family members and individuals with family-related problems. But most have moved in very different directions. Three new models now seem to be emerging as particularly significant.

Mental Health Clinics

Many agencies have responded to the availability of third-party reimbursements, primarily through Medicaid funding, by expanding the provision of psychotherapy offered by trained social workers under the supervision of a psychiatrist. With psychiatrists on staff, private fee-paying patients and Medicaid patients are treated with intensive, long-term psychotherapy, on an individual, group, or family basis. Thus, many family agencies have redefined themselves in all or in part as mental health clinics, often resembling so-called community mental health centers even more than other family service agencies.

Multi-Program Agencies

In agencies following the multi-program model, the family counselling service is often a much less important part of the agency program than before. Instead, existing public categorical funding has been utilized to support a diverse group of programs: for parents at risk of abusing their children; for teenagers at risk of pregnancy or already mothers; for the aged, the bereaved, the drug abuser, and so forth. Mixed in with these services may be still another service. Responding to changes within the family in the 1970s rather than changes in the community or society, FSAA urged its member agencies to develop a special "family life education" program, to be delivered at the agency itself or, more often, at some less stigmatized place, such as the local school, the library, or a church or synagogue.

Agencies That Combine Both Patterns

Expanding their entrepreneurial efforts still farther, agencies may include residences and institutions of different types, as well as the whole cluster of therapeutic and supportive services described above.

What all this means for families and for the kinds of help they get remains to be seen.[6]

Who Gets Help and How?

Almost all requests for help that family service agencies receive are made by the individuals seeking help or by a relative or friend. Calls from staff of other agencies initiating the requests are relatively infrequent. Agencies may refer people for help, and school, courts, and sometimes physicians and ministers do so too, but the actual request is usually made by the person needing or wanting help. Most requests are self-referrals, or referrals through friends, relatives, or neighbors, or referrals coming through use of the telephone book—the "yellow pages" or a community service directory.

Despite the growing numbers of husbands and fathers seen at the initial interview or during the course of "treatment," the overwhelmingly dominant pattern in requests for help continues to be those by women. Husbands or cohabitants may accompany the women, and some of these men may participate actively in the help-seeking process, but it is primarily the women who take the initiative in seeking help for themselves, for their children, for their families. The help that they want may relate to a failing marriage, a problem with a child, a sense of inadequacy in coping with the world or daily life, the problem of caring for an aging parent. There is some evidence that women and couples may be coming more often about problems with adolescents than previously, and that very young couples may be beginning to come for help with family formation problems: "Should we marry? Should we stay together? Should we have children?" Whether this becomes more than a trickle remains to be seen.

In most agencies, the requests for help come largely by telephone. "Ninety-five percent of our intake is through the telephone," said the director and intake worker at one agency. Administrators at several other agencies specified different amounts, but most ranged between 85 and 90 percent. A repeated comment was the relative unimportance of walk-in clients. Only neighborhood-based and neighborhood-focused agencies, especially those in inner-city neighborhoods, find a significant number of requests coming from individuals who drop in to the agency and ask directly for help.

Marital problems are always viewed as appropriate reasons for requesting, and obtaining, help. Few such requests are referred elsewhere. Although most are initiated by women, many lead to first or subsequent interviews with husbands as well as wives, and some may involve one or more interviews with the whole family.

The disproportionately high number of single mothers seeking help is part of a long-standing trend. A more recent development is the growth in the number of working women among those requesting help, described by most administrators as merely a reflection of the tremendous increase in the percentage of women in the labor force generally among the age group most likely to be family service agency clients.

Requests for help may be screened by telephone operators, receptionists, special intake workers, or regular professional staff who rotate the responsibilities of intake by the day or week. Most agencies have a standard series of questions that they ask regarding the nature of the problem for which the caller seeks help, the type of help requested, and, sometimes, previous efforts at obtaining help with the particular problem. If the caller has a history of previous institutionalization for a psychiatric disorder, or has been taking medication, she or he may be referred to another agency. Some agencies ask for the caller's residence, especially when the agency serves a limited geographic area. In most instances, unless it is a specific request for individual counselling, agency staff will suggest that the caller come in, with spouse and/or children depending on the nature of the problem and of the request.

Those who seek help at these agencies have their questions too. As one intake worker at a suburban agency suggested, "During the ten years I have been doing this kind of work I have learned to anticipate certain kinds of questions and to know what is behind them, and what the caller really is asking. Sometimes, I volunteer information that goes beyond the direct question. Often I can tell from the caller's response that I was right."

Among the questions that people are likely to ask when they telephone requesting an appointment for counselling—and the responses they are given—are:

"What is a 'family service agency' and exactly what is it that you do?" "We are a non-profit social service agency providing help for families in this county. We serve individuals with personal problems in their marriage or with their children, or other kinds of family problems." One agency staff member said that she usually adds, "We give help to all different kinds of people—people from different kinds of backgrounds, different races, dif-

ferent religions, and different income levels." At another agency, the intake worker said, "I usually tell people about several different kinds of programs we have, some funded by the county and others by United Way. In this way callers know we are a 'legitimate' agency because the county supports us." In contrast, at a third agency the initial response is supplemented by this comment: "We are an agency that specializes in this kind of help and that is all we do here."

"What kind of help do you provide?" "We provide counselling on an individual, group or family basis." Depending on the agency and what services may be available, the response may end here or be elaborated further to include, as relevant, "and other kinds of help such as . . . [child care services, homemakers, educational courses, residences, and so forth]."

"Who gives that kind of help? What kinds of people do you have working at your agency?" "All our staff are trained psychiatric social workers, college graduates who have returned for post-graduate training and received master's degrees in social work. They are all trained and experienced counsellors." Some agencies describe their staff as "trained and experienced therapists." Some callers ask if there are psychologists available. Sometimes there are. Often the response is that clinical psychologists and social workers have very similar training and experience and do the same kinds of work. Others ask if there are psychiatrists available. Some agencies do have psychiatrists as part-time staff or consultants and say so. Some callers will come only to an agency that has a psychiatrist on its staff. Others view the presence of a psychiatrist as suggesting more severe problems and prefer the term "counselling" to "therapy."

"What do you charge for this service?" Most family service agencies have income-related, graduated fees ranging from nothing to forty or fifty dollars per interview or "session." Family service agencies that define themselves as "mental health clinics" in order to become eligible for Medicaid and other third-party payments are able to meet the full expenses of providing the service. Other agencies are not and find themselves increasingly having to support their counselling services out of their most "expensive" dollars—United Way or other private philanthropy. Average fees may be seven or eight dollars a session, given the high proportion of free clients and the small proportion paying significant fees. The average fee among those who pay is about ten to fifteen dollars an interview. The costs for providing the service are significantly higher than the income from fees; the services thus tend to be heavily subsidized by the agency, often as much as 50 percent or more.

"When can I get an appointment?" Although all agencies are open during the standard 9:00 A.M.–5:00 P.M. workday, five days a week, most

are open, in addition, between two and four evenings a week. Staff often come in early, and hold interviews at 8:00 A.M., too. The pressure for evening hours has grown enormously over the past decade, especially with the growth in the numbers of women working. Daytime appointments tend to be given to housewives requesting individual counselling, or to women requesting help for a child. Evening appointments are saved for couples, families in which both parents will come, and working women. One unusual family agency is designed like a modern settlement house. Open seven days a week, with resident staff available twenty-four hours a day, this agency is a remarkable example of a neighborhood-oriented family service agency, but is not a "typical" agency in any way.

Despite the limitations on schedules, most requests for help can be met fairly quickly. Several agencies pride themselves on being able to make an appointment within twenty-four hours of the request. Most agencies can make appointments within a week if the caller is prepared to come during the day, at least for an initial interview. Requests for evening appointments are more difficult to satisfy and may involve delays of several weeks. Agency administrators are conscious of this as a growing problem, especially as the proportion of young adult women in paid employment, married as well as single, continues to increase. Thus far there does not seem to be any way of resolving the problem, since staff often do not wish to work evenings or weekends. This is where the demand is, however, and pressure is growing for staff to adapt.

Most of those who seek help at a family service agency receive at least some sort of assistance. Whether or not the help is satisfactory from the consumer's point of view is a separate question, as is the question of whether or not it is effective, whatever that may mean.

At the very least, those requesting help for a family-related problem—an unsatisfactory marriage, a conflictual relationship with a child, a behavioral problem of a child or spouse, a change in family structure or roles—will be given help. Such "help" involves talking with an expert about the condition or situation, and gaining some understanding of what the problem is, why it is occurring now, which aspects of it can be modified, and how. Some agencies will also help those whose problems are defined as more personal, problems located within themselves: those who are depressed despite the absence of any special event in their lives to which they can attribute their sense of loss, deprivation, malaise; those who find themselves dissatisfied with their way of functioning; those immobilized by anxiety or irrational fears.

Other family agencies view such problems as symptomatic of mental illness, or of a need for very long-term, intensive therapy. They will recommend to those seeking such help that they look elsewhere.

Some of these agencies will extend the kinds of help offered well beyond "counselling" of all types and will offer also a variety of specific services that families may need and want as they try to cope with the range and multiplicity of ordinary, routine problems that occur in daily life over a lifetime.

Some problems occur that cannot be solved by counselling, however wise it may be. The mother of a three-year-old child who has been offered a well-paying job needs to make child care arrangements and would prefer an all-day nursery school near where she lives. A woman asks for help for her eighty-four-year-old mother, whose worsening arthritis has made it impossible for her to bathe and dress herself, although she can still manage to live alone if a homemaker could come and provide some personal care services. A woman comes in to complain that her fourteen-year-old son has been suspended from school and she cannot find out why. An elderly couple complain that they have no heat in their apartment on a day when the temperature is in the teens. A single mother comes by to say the landlord is threatening to evict her because she has not paid the rent since her husband left home six weeks before.

Obviously, these are "family-related problems" even though the type of help needed may be of a different sort from counselling. In some family service agencies, staff help with these as well as other types of problems. Other agencies may have special staff and/or a special program or service to provide expertise in handling just such problems.

In one family service agency, one such program began as an information and referral service. After about a year, it became apparent that more than information and referral were needed. People were coming in for help with crisis situations that often required some immediate action and expertise that these clients did not possess and could not readily obtain. Other people needed help with identifying or obtaining benefits, rights, and entitlements that played a critical role in their lives. In response, the agency added case advocacy services and a crisis intervention service to its program. Those needing or warranting counselling can also be referred, of course, to that service, but counselling is not the only kind of help available.

But what about those who do request counselling? What kind of help do they receive and how is it given?

Marital Counselling

Marital counselling makes up almost half the cases handled in family service agencies. The following examples, though not necessarily typical, give some idea of the way requests are handled and counselling provided.

A woman, giving her name as Mrs. D, called to request an appointment for marital counselling. She had picked the agency from the telephone book. Mr. Z, one of the professional staff assigned to intake for that day, took the call.

Mr. Z: "What seems to be the trouble?"

Mrs. D: "We've been married for almost two years and we just don't seem to be communicating with each other. We need some kind of help."

Mr. Z: "Have you discussed this with your husband?"

Mrs. D: "Oh, yes."

Mr. Z: "Is he interested in marital counselling too?"

Mrs. D: "Yes, he is. I've been terribly unhappy and he knows that's not good for us. We'll both come for counselling."

After ascertaining where the Ds live, and explaining the agency's policy about fees, Mr. Z set up an appointment for him to see the Ds at 5:00 P.M. the following Monday.

This agency does not have any waiting list and has a policy of responding to requests for service with an almost immediate appointment, if the caller is flexible about time. Evening appointments are harder to arrange, since the agency is only open three evenings a week. These agency hours are very limited therefore, while the demand for evening hours is substantial. Staff are adaptable, however, even when they are not working that evening, and will stay an extra hour or come in an hour early, if necessary, to accommodate clients. In this case, the fact that Mr. D works from 8:00 A.M. to 4:00 P.M. two days a week and 10:00 A.M. to 6:00 P.M. the other three means that he can be at the agency by 5:00 P.M. on Monday. This permits an early scheduling of the first interview. Waiting lists for evening appointments are not unusual in many agencies; at the very least there are delays in scheduling. Even more complicated is a problem of scheduling appointments for those who work rotating shifts. Trying to help policemen and firemen can be difficult. In one agency, a worker told of the problems in scheduling appointments for a policeman and his wife, a nurse, who also worked varied shifts. As the agency administrator commented, for clients with this kind of work pattern "scheduling is either a monstrosity or proceeds on an ad hoc basis."

The Ds—a young couple in their early twenties—arrived a few minutes early for their first appointment. Mr. D, an assistant manager in a local supermarket, was carefully dressed in a suit, shirt, and tie. His wife was dressed much more casually, in jeans and a sweater. Mr. D began the interview:

"We have very different styles of communicating. It's because our family backgrounds are so different. In my family, no matter what the issue is, or how much we may disagree, or how anyone feels, there is no fighting and no shouting. When there's an argument, sure someone wins and someone loses, but it's all done quietly. You may be unhappy about the outcome, but no one would ever know it.

"In Elena's family, it's a whole other thing. Everyone yells about everything. They all argue constantly and everyone has a point of view about everything. There is no privacy in her family. Everybody has something to say about everyone else, and what they do, and how they live, and everything ends up in an argument, with screaming and yelling. And then it's all finished! When it's over they act as if nothing happened! I can't be that way. If I were to blow up like that with Elena, it would mean everything was finished."

Mrs. D joined the discussion to confirm Mr. D's description, but not his analysis. As her voice rose, Mr. D moved back in his seat.

Mr. Z noted that the Ds cannot resolve their differences because every time they argue Mrs. D yells and Mr. D withdraws. The more Mr. D withdraws, the more frustrated his wife becomes, and so she shouts louder, and he withdraws further, becoming angrier and angrier in the process and more and more afraid of exploding at her.

In trying to explore what there was in the relationship to build on, Mr. Z asked the Ds how they met and what made them decide to get married. They explained that they had met three years earlier when both were attending a local community college. Mr. D had first noticed her because she was very outgoing—talked a lot in class and was always surrounded by other students outside of class. "She was very popular. I never thought she'd pay any attention to me." On the contrary, Mrs. D had noticed him because he seemed to be "the quiet, silent type," she said, "always serious and very intense. He looked like someone you could rely on."

They went out together for three months and then, after a party where they both had too much to drink, they had intercourse. After that night they saw each other exclusively, having sexual relations whenever and wherever it was convenient, often at some friend's apartment that was available for a few hours. When they had known one another seven months, Mrs. D became pregnant. She told Mr. D and told him she wanted an abortion. Mr. D, who is Catholic, was disturbed at the idea of an abortion. He told his parents about the situation, and they were prepared to adopt the baby.

After much discussion back and forth, by this time with both sets of parents involved, the Ds decided to get married. The wedding, a ceremony in church and a reception afterward at Mrs. D's parents' home, was already tense. Mr. D described his parents as "German, Catholic, rigid, and authoritarian." His wife's family is Greek. "A fatal combination" was how he described the mixing of the two cultures.

Mr. D said the decision to marry had been a very hard one, and was made under pressure from both sets of parents. It meant his giving up college and he had resented it, although now, he said, "the baby made it all worthwhile. He's very smart and active."

Mr. Z intervened at that point, commenting, "It sounds as if the baby is more important to you than your wife."

Mr. D did not respond.

"Well," said Mr. Z, "what do you want to do now?"

Both responded, "We want to learn how to communicate better." "We want to stay together," Mr. D said. Mrs. D continued, "We want to be able to talk to each other, but without so much pain."

Mr. Z concluded this first interview by explaining that extensive experience in helping people with problems like theirs suggested that couples could improve communication with one another in eight sessions if they really wanted to and were willing to work hard at it. He discussed fees with them and, based on their income, they agreed on a fee of seven dollars per session.

Before the Ds left, Mr. Z gave them some "homework" for the next week. He explained that he tries to assign a task for couples to work on between sessions, to keep them related to the "work" in each session. He recommended to the Ds that they put aside twenty minutes each morning, before Mr. D leaves for work, to talk. Mr. D complained that this would not be spontaneous. Mr. Z agreed, but pointed out, "Since you have not been able to talk to each other spontaneously, you need to learn how. This is a way for you to begin to practice." Mrs. D added, "And it's better than trying to talk at night, because you know what happens, as soon as we talk we fight and if it's at night it interferes with sex."

Mr. Z began the second interview by asking about the previous week. This time Mrs. D took the lead.

"He wouldn't get up in the morning until the last minute and then he said he had no time to talk because he would be late for work. So Thursday we had a knock-down fight, then Friday morning he got up early and we did talk."

"What did you talk about?"

"We talked about the night before and sex. I wouldn't sleep with him when he wanted to."

The Ds talked more about their different attitudes toward sex. Mrs. D accused her husband of "demanding" sex as if it is his right and wanting it "for himself only." Her husband in turn said he resents her withholding sex when she is angry with him. She claimed they have sexual relations only when he initiates them; he rebuffs all of her overtures.

The Ds had developed a very rigid routine regarding sex: specified days of the week, hours, place, and manner. Mr. Z suggested that now, in contrast to setting up a schedule for talking, they should eliminate all routine regarding sex.

The Ds returned to the subject of talking to one another and Mr. D agreed that after a few days it was a little easier to talk. Mrs. D viewed this as a great accomplishment.

Mrs. D then talked about the baby and how much more important the baby was to her husband than she was. From the discussion that followed, Mr. Z noted that one basic problem was that the Ds had been married under pressure. Each had doubts that the other would have wanted to marry if there had not been the pressure of pregnancy.

Mrs. D suddenly began to cry, "And even now, I'm sure if it were not for the baby he would leave."

She admitted she had never said this before, nor had any of these fears been discussed so openly before then. The session ended with each reassuring the other of their love and concern.

The third interview occurred after a hiatus of two weeks. The Ds had gone away for ten days to Arizona to visit Mr. D's parents. Mrs. D had dreaded the trip although her in-laws had paid for it and were longing to see their only grandchild. She had admitted earlier that she always feels under attack by her husband's parents and felt that he always becomes closer to them and more removed from her in their presence.

Mrs. D began the interview by complaining about the visit. Mr. Z asked if it was as bad as she expected. She paused and said thoughtfully, "No, I guess not really."

Mr. Z asked if she had told her husband this and she said no and then immediately began to complain about his not talking to her.

Mr. D responded in a rush of words, "Why should I talk to you? All you ever do is complain and criticize. You never tell me anything positive."

Throughout all of this, Mrs. D watched her husband intently, as she always did in these sessions. As always, regardless of the subject of discussion, Mr. D's face was impassive.

Mr. Z commented that Mr. D must be very angry if his wife never praises anything he does. Mr. D denied any anger. His wife contradicted him, saying, "Of course you're angry. Look at you. Stoneface. You're always like that and you're always angry." Still Mr. D denied such feelings.

Mr. Z pointed out that they both hid their feelings—from themselves and from each other. Perhaps if they told each other in words how they felt, neither would have to guess and often, as a consequence, guess wrong.

The fourth interview began with Mrs. D talking about how much better everything had been until the previous day. Then they had had another "blockbuster of a fight."

Mr. Z accepted this but suggested a different perspective: "Fighting gives us something to look at when you come here. That's how you can learn what is really going on."

Among other problems, each of the Ds was stubborn and opinionated. And both continued to idealize their own families and to bring reports of parental or sibling comments into every argument. Mr. Z urged them to try to identify alternative patterns in resolving disagreements.

The fifth interview began with Mr. D saying that they had had several good talks. "Except for the baby, we have very little in common. I like sports and Elena doesn't. Elena likes to visit her family and I'm not comfortable there, nor is she with mine. We have no friends in common any more. Elena wants to go back to school and I don't see how she can manage it, with the baby and all."

Mrs. D responded that if they really wanted to they could manage to work things out, not just in relation to school for her, but in relation to their marriage, indeed their lives.

Mrs. D commented reflectively, "I want to, but I'm not sure I'm able to. We may find one day we really do have nothing in common no matter how hard we try. Maybe we will end up divorcing."

This was the first time either had mentioned divorce. Mrs. D rejected the idea, repeating, "We can work it out if we want to."

The sixth interview was held several weeks later. The baby had been ill and Mrs. D had not wanted to leave him, and then she had become ill with the flu herself. Mr. D began the interview by saying how much better their relationship was. They were talking to each other more and fighting less. He had told his parents about the trouble they had been having and his parents had urged that they try to work it out together. His mother had called his wife and offered to help in any way possible. Mrs. D was appreciative of her in-laws' support and her husband's reassurance. She again repeated her desire to return to school. Mr. D agreed that, if she wanted to, it was important for her to do so. She could begin by attending two nights a week and he would stay with the baby.

By the seventh session, held two weeks later, Mrs. D had returned to college and the adjustment as well as the work itself had placed a new strain on their marriage. She had high expectations for herself and was already worried about how she would manage. Mr. D commented on her lack of interest in him since school began. She interpreted this as criticism and as insensitivity to her problems in coping with a new and demanding situation.

Mrs. D began to talk about a new subject, how men had always disappointed her, how her father had drifted out of her life after her parents had been divorced and how her husband would probably disappoint her too. She talked a little more and then her husband interrupted to reassure her again that he loved her and that he would stay with her.

Mr. Z cautioned the Ds to be sensitive to Mrs. D's expectation that all men would fail her. He said she might behave in such a way as to provoke this response, and that if she found this happening she might want to obtain individual psychotherapy at that time.

Mr. Z concluded the interview by reminding the Ds that the next session would be their eighth and last. He reassured them that if they felt the need for one more session he would arrange time for it, and that if at some later time a specific problem occurred and they wished to come back and talk again, that could be arranged also.

The eighth session focused more on Mrs. D's expectations regarding college and subsequent work and on the possibility of another child. Mr. D wanted one soon, but Mrs. D insisted that she finish school first. They talked more about managing home and child care routines and how Mr. D felt about having to do more since his wife had returned to school. Mr. D mentioned that perhaps the next year he too might return to college, and maybe they could coordinate their schedules. Mr. Z encouraged him to explore this. At the end of the interview the Ds expressed satisfaction with the counselling experience. They had achieved their goal: they were communicating better; they were talking to each other; they were fighting less. For now the strain was less and their marriage more satisfying to both.

Mr. Z's closing summary, however, noted an uncertain prognosis for the marriage. Mrs. D was clearly building a whole new world for herself through school. Unless Mr. D could find some avenue to personal growth for himself, preferably in a parallel development by returning to school, they would increasingly grow apart. On the other hand, if Mr. D found his own opportunity for development and if it could be a shared experience, at least in part, then their marriage might indeed last.

As we mentioned earlier, although the Ds could certainly not be described as a "typical" case, marital cases do make up about half the cases handled in family service agencies. Husbands do not always participate as fully as Mr. D, but they are far more likely to be involved than previously. Staff in agency after agency commented on the large number of requests for help that begin like Mrs. D's, with an announcement of some trouble in the marriage. When pressed for an explanation of the "trouble," the response is described repeatedly as "lack of communication."

One counsellor explained that, when you talk to these women, it becomes clear that the problem is not really a lack of communication. When you probe a little you find a situation in which the women complain that their husbands do not talk to them and the husbands respond by saying, "You want me to talk to you but I don't want to talk." In effect the husbands are communicating very clearly that they do not want to talk. The problem is not one of the quantity of communication but rather the wives' dissatisfaction with the substance of that communication. The wives want their husbands to change; the husbands either want their wives to change or at the very least leave them alone and not nag them. Often women like these really come for help because they have a sense of unsatisfying and unsatisfactory lives. They attribute their dissatisfaction to trouble in their marriages, which in turn they blame on husbands, who in one or another way fail to meet their wives' needs.

The case of an older couple, Mr. and Mrs. E, who had been married for sixteen years, provides another illustration. Mrs. E, an elementary school teacher, was forty-two; her husband, a foreman at the aircraft factory nearby, was forty-eight. They had one twelve-year-old son, Timmy. Mrs. E had been in psychotherapy for two years following the birth of her son. She believed it had been very helpful to her, but the treatment had never addressed the problems in her marriage and most of what was bothering her now was her marriage. When requesting the initial appointment, she said that her husband was not willing to come for counselling but that she wanted to come nevertheless.

Mrs. E was seen alone by the counsellor, Mrs. Y, four times. Her major complaint was how unhappy she was and how unresponsive her husband was. She talked about her own therapy and how helpful it had been. Apparently its major success had been to enable her to increase her activities outside the family. She had stopped work when she became pregnant and by the time her son was a year old she had become depressed with an increasing sense of isolation and loneliness. She began first to meet other women friends and subsequently became involved in organizational activities of different types, finally returning to work when her son was four.

In the last few years she had become increasingly dissatisfied with her life. Her teaching job no longer stimulated her, yet their financial needs were such that she could not give up working, nor did she want to be at home all day. She described her husband as a "good man," but felt he was neither sympathetic nor sensitive to her needs and that their marriage was "terrible."

By the fourth session Mrs. Y told Mrs. E that there was no way to help her unless her husband came in for an interview. Commenting on the case, the counsellor said, "My experience is that when the *woman* initiates the request for help and blames all the difficulty on her husband, yet continues to come in herself, she probably has a certain amount of leverage within the family. If she really thinks it's hopeless she will move toward a decision to divorce. Otherwise, if she wants to deal with the problem in the marriage, she reaches a point when she decides that her husband should come in—and then he comes. Similarly, in family therapy with such women who are more dominant in the family than they acknowledge, when therapy becomes threatening to the women and they decide the family should stop coming, they stop."

Mr. E was involved by approaching him for participation in a "family session." After being shown the issue as one that involved their son and the family as a whole, the father was willing to come in. As expected, Mr. E was quiet, remote, and withdrawn.

Commenting further, Mrs. Y said, "For the most part in marital cases or family problem cases when a man comes in he needs a great deal of support and approval. It is very difficult for men in these families to acknowledge the need for help and to come here. In order to be helpful in these situations, I take a very active stance in letting the man know that he is important, as are his needs. I try to be explicit and direct in supporting his position and sensitive to some of his problems."

As part of providing support for Mr. E, Mrs. Y noted how Mrs. E chose to seat herself between her husband and Timmy at this first family interview in such a way that Mr. E and his son were separated. They would have had to strain even to see one another. Mrs. Y commented on this directly to the Es without exploring the meaning of the behavior. She did, however, suggest a change in the seating arrangements, placing Mr. E next to his son. Similarly, on several occasions during this interview, Mrs. Y pointed out to Mrs. E how she closed her husband off and did not let him speak while simultaneously complaining about his not talking.

Mrs. Y concentrated extensively on Mrs. E's behavior, pointing out inconsistencies in what she said she wanted and how she acted. Mrs. Y focused very much on how the Es related to one another and how it seemed to affect Timmy, who clearly wanted his father's attention. Mr. E was obviously attached to the boy, but had great difficulty in demonstrating his feelings. Mrs. E interpreted his difficulty in expressing his feelings as disinterest in the boy—and in herself.

The family was seen together in family therapy three times. In one session Mrs. Y focused on the problems created by Mr. E's job. The counsellor said she is increasingly conscious of the impact of work—of jobs—on interpersonal and family relationships. Women will sometimes complain about their husbands that "all he cares about is his job." This may be true, but often it has to do with the fact that this is where much of the man's day is spent and the job also has major impact on whether he comes home relaxed and satisfied or tense and dissatisfied. When both husband and wife work, attention to work and jobs becomes even more important, since inevitably each brings home the spillover from what are often complicated and demanding and sometimes ungratifying experiences. As a fore-man and shop steward at a large factory, Mr. E is the butt of a miscellany of grievances all day long both from the men under him and from his supervisor. Some of the grievances are justified, but many are not, and often there is nothing he can do about them. He must remain controlled all day long under trying circumstances. Mrs. E teaches a class of thirty nine-year-olds who are often unruly and certainly active. She suffers from the absence of adult relationships during the course of the day. When she comes home, she wants companionship.

Mrs. E was seen alone two more times following the family therapy session. Commenting that it was unclear what would happen subsequently, Mrs. Y described the case as a difficult one, because "no single relationship can possibly satisfy the range of Mrs. E's needs." One goal could be to facilitate Mrs. E's return to individual therapy, this time into long-term intensive treatment. However, Mrs. Y thought this unlikely. An alternative goal would be to help Mrs. E to learn to accept her husband as he is, as long as she wants to stay in the marriage, and learn how to meet those of her own needs that are not met within the marriage from other kinds of activities. Thus one positive aspect of the last session was Mrs. E's mention of the possibility of returning to school for training in accounting. Mr. E encouraged her in this step.

Mrs. Y said that she sees many cases like this. The major work of the "treatment" is to provide support for individuals, usually women, while they do the difficult job of looking at their lives, recognizing that what they see is not satisfactory and that in some way they need to accept what is and cannot be changed and to focus on what they can change themselves. "Sometimes when a case is completed, I feel that there has been no satisfactory resolution. Then, a year or two later, I'll get a phone call. The woman will tell me how some months later she got a new job or decided to go back to school, and a whole new perspective emerged in terms of life and daily satisfactions."

Another frequent marital case is the client who needs help dealing with the break-up of a marriage. Such clients do not need to learn to recognize a problem but to learn to cope with it. An example is the case of Jean F, who called another agency in a panic, saying that her husband had just left her and she did not know what to do. She did not even know where to begin, she said, and then asked, "Can I come for counselling?"

Mrs. F was in her middle thirties. She had never thought of facing "this kind of situation" before. Like many women in a similar situation, it was her sister-in-law who finally said to her, "You just can't go on like this crying all the time. You have to do something. Go for help." (Sometimes it is a mother or a friend who urges coming for counselling, but always in situations like this it is somebody close who precipitates the call.)

Mrs. X, the counsellor, explained that many of these women try to get their husbands to come in for marital counselling, at least initially. Usually the men refuse. Often these are men who have moved away from their wives over a period of ten, fifteen, or even twenty years of marriage, yet the wife is "startled" to discover that her husband has been having an affair for several years, or that after becoming increasingly dissatisfied with his marriage he has finally moved out.

Such women often come five or six times to begin to learn how to adjust to what they have already recognized is really going to happen and, perhaps, to test out some new ideas about how to go about establishing new lives for themselves. Mrs. F talked of finding a job in a nearby city even though she still had fairly young children. Women like Jean F come for help to explore how one begins a new life apart from the traditional husband-wife, woman-at-home family. These women are not seeking a radical change but rather an adaptation to a change that has been imposed on them. Usually by the fourth or fifth session they are ready to end their "treatment," and usually they find that it has been quite successful.

A different case is that of Mrs. G, who had finally decided to leave her alcoholic, physically abusive husband after ten years of marriage. The decision had been long in coming, but she knew she was doing "the right thing." "He'll never change," she said to her counsellor, Mr. W. "I used to think he would. He's a decent, hard-working man when he's sober, but a crazy man when he's had a few drinks. And it's happening more often now. The kids are older too, and they see what happens, and Jimmy, our eight-year-old, is frightened and angry when his father hits me. Last week Jimmy tried to get between us and Jim smacked him so hard that he went flying against the wall, fell, and hit his head on the corner of the table. That never happened before. When Jim sobered up he was sick and swore he would quit drinking. But then it happened again yesterday and I decided I was finished. Jim won't try to get help for himself and he can't stop, so I decided I'd better leave while I could still stand, and while the kids were young enough to forget."

Women like Mrs. G come for help in order to get support in implementing their decisions as well as to get practical advice about how to handle the problems following the decision. These women too tend to come five or six times for counselling. Once they have resolved their conflicts and worked out the immediate difficulties they stop. Sometimes, they return a year or two later when they have begun a new relationship with another man in order to test out whether or not this one seems to be a sounder kind of relationship.

Not all marital counselling deals with conventional marriages. Young couples who are living together are now coming for counselling even though they are not legally married. Two cases at one agency resulted in different outcomes: one couple subsequently married; the other decided not to marry.

The first couple, really a family, was made up of three persons: Gordon H, a tall, assertive, aggressive man, thirty-four years old, with long hair pulled back in a pony tail; Linda I, a small, slight, twenty-three-year-old woman; and their eight-month-old son, Bobby. They requested counselling because "we were fighting all the time, so we separated. But neither of us is happy apart and we want to try to work it out together."

In describing the case, Miss V, the counsellor, commented that what suggested a positive prognosis at the outset was that the couple brought their baby, a delightful and responsive little boy. Both parents alternated holding him, watching him when he crawled around on the floor and talking to him. Mr. H was an unusually warm, attentive, and responsive father.

The major problem that emerged in the course of the first session was the fact that they had very different ideas of "the good life" although both of them assumed that personal pleasure was paramount. Neither was interested in deferring gratification. Mr. H had a history of previous alcoholism and drug use and both were using marijuana. Miss I was clearly interesting in making some sort of change from their prior life style. Mr. H worked as a bartender. Miss I felt he should "get out of bars and stop partying" because this was no way to develop any kind of stable life. She was the complainant. She basically wanted more attention from him, more commitment, and a more stable life. His response was that she was nagging him.

Despite their complaints they said they wanted to live together and Miss V focused on this as the goal: learning how to live together.

Having a child clearly was a commitment for Mr. H. But he complained that Miss I criticized him and this made him angry. Later he acknowledged that he was afraid that he would not be able "to make it in the regular world" and could not hold a regular job. Despite her criticism of his life style, Miss I acknowledged some ambivalence; she liked the excitement of his life but feared its consequences over time.

In the course of twenty sessions (this was one of the longer cases seen at the agency), the couple found a place where they could live together. Miss I nagged Mr. H less and began working part time, in the mornings, while he cared for the baby. Mr. H got a regular job, working a 4:00–12:00 shift. They got married. They had clearly developed more structure in their lives and much more of a commitment to one another, and were beginning to build a more mature life.

The other couple was not such a success story. Mr. J telephoned asking for premarital counselling. He was thirty-seven, quiet and withdrawn; his friend, Mrs. K, who was thirty-three, was very dramatic and emotional when she talked. He had never been married before; Mrs. K had a thirteen-year-old daughter from a first marriage. They had lived together for the past three years. Mrs. K complained that Mr. J did did not talk, that they had a communication problem, and that their sex life was unsatisfactory.

Mrs. U, the counsellor, saw Mr. J alone twice and then saw the two together three more times. Mr. J had difficulty expressing his feelings. In the joint interview, it was apparent that, when he tried to, Mrs. K attacked him. The counsellor focused on pointing out her behavior and its consequences.

Mrs. U said that most married couples create their problems together. The technology of marriage and family therapy is to use the way in which couples, or family members, interact in front of the cousellor in order to demonstrate how their interactions create problems for one another. Often the focus is on pointing out how they sabotage what they say they want to achieve.

Family Counselling

Another focus of family service counselling is on the family unit rather than the couple. As we saw in the case of the E family, for example, children may be included in marital counselling sessions, but the focus is on the relationship between the parents. In other cases, it is the children's problems that impel a family to seek counselling. For the counsellor's perspective, however, the problem is often not in the child, but in the family as a system. The L family is an example.

The Ls requested help with their fourteen-year-old son David, who, they said, was "staying out late at night" and was "difficult to handle." The Ls came for counselling because they disagreed on how the boy should be handled. Mr. L was rigid, authoritarian, and moralistic. His wife was passive, long-suffering, and frightened. The goal of counselling was to help them understand how their complaints about their son really were complaints about each other.

Mrs. L accused her husband of being "mean to the boy" and, ultimately, being mean to her. Mr. L's response was that his wife "made too big a thing" out of David and paid far more attention to the boy than she did to him. The reality was that David was not in any serious trouble. He was coping adequately with school, and he had friends. Yet it was clear there was tension in the family.

Mr. T, the counsellor, suggested after two sessions that the Ls come the next time with their three children: David, a girl of twenty-one, and a second girl of eighteen. The family was seen together five times, during which time the counsellor focused on helping Mrs. L to become more direct and more assertive with regard to her own feelings in relating to her husband.

In the family session, initially, David said nothing. The older girls, however, both talked about how feelings were always hidden in the family, yet how their mother was always depressed. The counsellor encouraged Mrs. L to speak up directly in these sessions and pointed out to Mr. L how he avoided hearing her, as well as hearing his son. Although Mr. L found it hard at first, he acknowledged that his relationship with his son improved when he began to take time with him at home, encouraging him to talk about his day. Mrs. L found that she could begin to assert herself more directly, and that Mr. L would respond more appropriately when she did. At the counsellor's suggestion, the Ls began to participate in some recreational activities together as a couple, apart from their children. This too was helpful. No major change occurred after ten sessions, but tension was alleviated for the whole family.

Another case, that of the Ms, illustrates something characteristic of many family treatment cases: The Ms, like the Ls, came for a problem with a child. And, like the Ls, the problem that emerged over time was a marital problem rather than just a parent-child problem.

The Ms were referred by the local Mental Health Information Service. Mrs. M telephoned, saying that they were having trouble with her thirteen-year-old son from her previous marriage. Mrs. M had been divorced ten years before and had married her present husband four years earlier. Mr. M had not been married previously. The couple had two children from this marriage, a girl of three and an eleven-month-old boy.

The whole family came in for the first interview.

The counsellor, Mr. S, began by asking, "What exactly is the trouble?"

Mrs. M responded, "When John comes home from visiting his father, he is withdrawn and surly."

Mr. S turned to the boy, saying, "What do you think the problem is?"

John replied with tears in his eyes, "Pete [Mr. M] criticizes me all the time. Nothing I do is ever right."

Mr. M acknowledged this. "I have a bad temper and I blow up more often than I mean to—or than is good."

It appeared in the course of the interview that Mr. M often lost his temper with his wife too, and that John felt increasingly compelled to defend her against his stepfather. She apparently did nothing to discourage him.

Mr. M complained that John's father is very permissive and "soft." He described himself in moralistic terms, as believing in the importance of "discipline" and "character," clearly projecting the image of an authoritarian and harsh "father."

For John, the contrast between his own father's warm and accepting behavior and his stepfather's rigid and punitive manner was overwhelming. Moreover, this contrast was further exacerbated by Mr. M's immediate questioning of him, whenever he spent time with his own father. Clearly, John felt conflicted about his mother and had become a scapegoat in his new family.

The goal for this family was to reduce the pressure on John by helping Mrs. M to assume greater responsibility for him and to be more assertive in relation to her husband generally. Once Mrs. M began to deal with her husband directly when he attacked her, he began to see that his behavior would no longer be effective. When she began taking more responsibility for John, John felt that he had some support in the family and Mr. M recognized that he could now relate to John as something other than the family disciplinarian. Clearly, it would never be easy for John to move back and forth between the two very different households, but at least the pain was lessened for him, and, perhaps more important, the Ms were able to head off trouble between themselves that would have inevitably emerged over time.

At the end of the case, after nine sessions, the Ms were discussing with John the possibility of changing their current pattern now that he was an adolescent and letting him live with his father the following year while visiting the Ms on alternate weekends.

Thus far we have discussed only counselling for the two-parent family. But a disproportionately high number of family service agency clients are separated or divorced mothers. Many women come for counselling regarding adjustment to separation, divorce, widowhood. A whole other group come some months after the event, because a child is unhappy or behaving badly or seems to have undergone a personality change. Sometimes an apparent adjustment is suddenly disrupted.

Many of these women come as a consequence of school referrals: "Mary has become increasingly unhappy lately. She complains of headaches, doesn't want to be with friends. Has anything happened at home that could account for this?" So reads one note from a teacher concerned about one of her students. Often such problems reflect a child's adaptation to the loss of a parent, especially if a new "friend" comes into the situation. Adapting to different family styles, between weekend visits with one parent and home with the other, can be difficult. Learning to accept the disappearance of a parent can be unbelievably painful for a child who defines such behavior as a personal rejection. Coping with resentment toward a spouse, yet not wanting to project this anger onto a child who is also the "product" of the spouse, can be a hard task.

These cases, however, are the more typical. Others may be of a different sort—in many ways more urgent or difficult and require more active intervention.

Mrs. N, the twenty-four-year-old mother of a seven-year-old boy, Tommy, was referred by the school guidance counsellor. Tommy was given to tantrums, fighting, throwing objects, hitting, and biting other children as well as adults. His teacher had complained repeatedly, and the guidance counsellor noted that Tommy often came to school with severe bruises. Mrs. N came with Tommy to the agency. While talking to the counsellor there, she admitted that she found the boy hard to control and that her own tensions and frustrations made it still more difficult for her, so she coped by beating him. On one occasion she beat him till he became unconscious. Because of her readiness to receive help, the family counsellor tried first to set up support systems at the center and with a grandparent, but these were insufficient. Finally, the agency was able to recruit a foster mother in the neighborhood to care for Tommy so that Mrs. N could visit him every day. At the same time the counsellor arranged for Mrs. N to receive educational and employment counselling and to participate in a parents' group.

Tommy is now attending a special day school, where he can get individualized attention. His behavior is improving and Mrs. N is beginning to feel more adequate and capable of managing her life too. With Tommy living in a supportive, nurturing, yet consistent environment and his mother able to see him while she is supported in meeting some of her own needs, separation and loss for both of them have been minimized. Both need help toward personal growth, which in time will permit reunion.

The Technology of Counselling

All types of counselling are provided in family service agencies. Some agencies provide intensive, long-term, insight-oriented treatment for individuals, similar to that provided by a private practitioner (Chapter 2), albeit at a higher fee. Others use group therapy extensively as the preferred "treatment" for individuals seen first in individually focused counselling. Groups for single mothers, divorced mothers, abusive mothers, and teenage mothers abound, as do groups for the recently separated (men as well as women), the recently bereaved, the recently remarried.[7]

Groups play a significant role in several agencies' family life education programs. Parent groups, groups for new mothers, for the parents of adolescents, and for adults with older parents, women's assertiveness training groups, and many others are all part of the armamentarium provided by these agencies.[8] The focus in these groups, as we will see in our discussion of family life education, is more on "educating" members or participants rather than on "treating" them.

Marriage and family therapy, as already indicated, characterize a large part of what these agencies provide, and as such need no further discussion.[9] Of particular interest is the growing stress in all family service agencies on new approaches to treatment. By and large all these new efforts tend to reflect concern with the high cost of individual counselling, the limited amount of resources available, and the search for less expensive yet effective interventions. Unfortunately, there is little evidence that would indicate which among these various approaches is more—or less— effective, and for whom.[10]

Group therapy is one such obvious response. Another, which cuts across individual, group, and family counselling lines, is the growing stress on short-term, time-limited treatment. Family life education, since it is de- scribed as a kind of "education," almost by definition suggests a time- limited course.

Marriage and family counselling traditionally were open-ended: "until the problem is solved." But this has changed in many agencies, especially during the last decade. In agency after agency administrators speak of the decision to modify open-ended counselling and to focus on what they describe as "brief planned treatment," "short-term treatment," "planned short-term therapy," and so forth. When asked about the precise meaning, administrators describe a counselling program of between six and twelve interviews. Interestingly enough, no one offered a cogent theory as to why they used a particular number of sessions. Indeed, the number seems more arbitrary than anything else, at best "borrowed" from the experience of some other, better-known agency. Different agencies are mentioned as exemplars, yet, when asked, they too give an equally soft rationale.

For some agencies, these time-limited approaches to treatment serve as a reminder to staff to set goals realistically and early and to focus on them throughout the course of treatment. For other agencies these sessions provide a wide screen through which all kinds of requests enter and are met, while the more serious become clearly visible and are then referred for longer, more intensive treatment. Other agencies are relatively casual and flexible, stressing that "brief treatment" is the preferred mode, but permitting staff discretion in deciding when to see clients longer, and how much longer.

Short-term treatment is premised on the appropriate selection of a circumscribed problem and an attainable goal as well as on a clear contract between counsellor and counsellee. One counsellor, explaining how her agency policy was implemented, said, "Around the seventh or eighth session it becomes clear whether the problem we defined has been re-solved or whether there is need for further work. Sometimes, by that time a new problem is identified and the client wants to work on solving that one. The result may be to end treatment at the eighth session [the unit for service at this agency] or to extend it by one or two more interviews. Of course, sometimes the identification of a new problem leads to a whole new contract and another series of eight interviews."

Short-term, time-limited, goal-oriented counselling is clearly the pre-ferred policy in most family service agencies. Not all have been successful in supporting a firm policy with regard to maximum length of treatment. Some agencies get around the rigidity of the policy by specifying diagnostic criteria by which a decision can be reached to see clients longer. Few of these criteria are objective and thus, inevitably, discretion plays a sig-nificant role.

In one agency the focus on "planned, short-term treatment" (up to twelve interviews) was instituted at the end of the 1960s and, in theory, characterizes agency policy for its counselling service in its entirety. The policy is not rigidly enforced, however, and the reality is that the "treat-ment" has been getting increasingly longer over the last few years. The administrator's interpretation is that the longer treatment is a consequence of greater stress on family therapy. According to him, family-related goals take more time to accomplish than individual or marital counselling: "Families come in around child problems. After a while the underlying marital tension emerges. Then you first have to develop a contract for the marital problem." A supervisor in another agency had a different inter-pretation. According to her, length of treatment should vary depending on the presence or absence of certain indicators. Extensive treatment (beyond twelve sessions) is called for if there is a "good relationship" between the counsellor and the client, if there has been some clear progress made in the course of treatment, if the client has limited income and therefore could not afford to pay for long-term private therapy, or if there is no alternative resource in the community for extended low- or no-cost therapy.

Given these relatively loose criteria for permitting more extensive treat-ment, it seems highly likely that counsellors would make their own deci-sions as to whether or not to go beyond the twelve-visit maximum. In a sense there is an open invitation for staff in this agency to extend treatment and no incentive to do otherwise except for personal preference for short-term treatment. Individual counsellors here and elsewhere seem to view anything under twenty sessions as being "short term," further confounding the concept. Moreover, a significant number of "recidivists" return over a period of several years.

The length of "treatment" and the expectations regarding "recidivism" are important issues that are not often discussed in these agencies. Apparently, clients are as likely to be helped by short as by longer treatments. Since resources are scarce and more people can be given help if the help is limited, the rationale for short-term counselling is obvious. On the other hand, solving one problem does not preclude the emergence of a second and subsequent problem. Perhaps successful use of family counselling leads a family to greater willingness to return for more counselling if another problem emerges.

Is this good or bad? Does counselling "make a difference"? Clients say "yes," but how would we know otherwise? Many agencies have attempted to evaluate the effectiveness of their service.[11] The primary measure, however, is either the consumer's assessment or the counsellor's. Neither is objective. Despite this, the requests for counselling at family service agencies or at other sites continue to increase.

Other Kinds of Help

Family service agencies have expanded the kinds of help offered beyond traditional counselling. More and more other services are provided that attract a different kind of clientele.

Financial counselling. A debt or credit counselling service is provided by several family service agencies to help individuals and families with financial management, budgeting, intervention with creditors, and aid and advice at times of financial crisis. A typical case is that of the O family. A young couple in their late twenties, both worked at good jobs. Together their income was $40,000 a year. While they had no children, the Os took vacations, went to restaurants, and lived like any affluent couple. The previous year, however, the Os had decided to have a baby. Now the baby was eight months old, and, although Mrs. O wants to stay home to care for the baby, the Os have not been able to manage on Mr. O's salary of $24,000 a year. Mrs. O made all sorts of purchases on credit cards, and now their debts have piled up overwhelmingly. The Os have been fighting, and Mrs. O has finally acknowledged she must learn to live within Mr. O's salary. So the Os have come for advice about debts and how to budget.

Divorce mediation service. As provided by one agency, divorce mediation is described as a "non-adversarial process helping people dissolve marriages once the decision to divorce is made, and offering individuals the opportunity to negotiate a mutually beneficial separation agreement."[12] This service is provided like other counselling services on a sliding fee basis ranging from ten to forty dollars per hour. The average time to negotiate a separation agreement is about twelve hours, but this is usually accomplished in three or four sessions. Some typical cases are described below.

The Ps are a young couple who have been married six years. Thirty-year-old Mrs. P wants a divorce; her thirty-two-year-old husband does not. They began a trial separation one year ago at the request of Mrs. P. Six months later she insisted that she wanted a divorce. She was not interested in any kind of counselling. The two of them had discussed what the major issues were and had called the agency for divorce mediation help, saying that they had resolved all the issues in the divorce except for the custody of their six-year-old son, who lived with his father but spent weekends with his mother. The case was resolved in the course of one three-hour session in which it was agreed that the couple would have joint custody of their son and continue the living arrangements they had already established.

Another case is that of the Qs, a couple who had been married for nineteen years and had been fighting increasingly over the past six years. Mr. Q had left home three months before, having first told his wife that he wanted a divorce. Mrs. Q, although she did not want a divorce, agreed that the marriage was very unsatisfactory. The couple had two children, one fourteen and the other ten. Given her husband's insistence upon a divorce, Mrs. Q agreed, saying that what she wants is "suitable support and help in starting a new life." The case is still open. There has been one session regarding how suitable support is to be defined. Mrs. Q is also being given an opportunity to go for counselling in the family counselling program.

A third case is that of Sally R, a twenty-three-year-old woman who came in initially for marital counselling. Mrs. R did not want her husband to know she was coming for counselling and refused to have him participate. She complained about a poor sexual relationship and about little communication with her husband. She said her husband closed off her efforts to talk to him by turning the radio up very loud. She talked about how guilty she felt and how inadequate she felt as a wife. She had experimented with two brief affairs with men she had met at work, but had rejected this as a permanent way of life. "After all, I'm only twenty-three years old. There must be something better than this." After four sessions in therapy, Mrs. R had begun to face her desire for divorce. As she began to deal with this, she began to feel much more relieved. She then discussed with her husband her dissatisfactions and her desire for divorce. Her husband came in for two marital sessions with the counsellor. At the end of these sessions the couple agreed that what made the most sense for them was to obtain a divorce. They were referred by the family counsellor for divorce mediation. After one three-hour session with the mediator, the couple resolved their differences. Since Mrs. R worked and had no need for alimony and there were no children, an agreement was readily expedited.

One strategy in this program is to insist that both husband and wife participate jointly in paying for the mediation service. The assumption is that, with an independent mediator and relatively little tension around finances as well as with both sharing in the responsibility for obtaining help, an agreement can be worked out.

Sex counselling. Some agencies provide specialized sex therapy and counselling services. This service is for couples who have problems in their sexual relationships with each other, or for individuals, usually men, requiring help because of their own limitations or their wives' "indifference."

Alcohol and drug counselling. Alcohol and drug counselling programs are being increasingly provided in family service agencies. These may include individual and group therapy for substance abusers, for their families, or both. Often, there are separate, specialized programs for youthful abusers too.

Advocacy Services

FSAA requires that its member agencies include family advocacy as the second component in their core programs in addition to family counselling and family life education.[13] Family advocacy has both "case advocacy" and "social action" implications, so the programs that result are quite varied and often limited. In some instances the advocacy is part of a catch-all department that includes public relations and interpretation. In others, it is combined with all of the "new" services—services other than counselling.

One agency, for example, supplements its family counselling program with an extensive group of family-related services: a parents' group, teen-age nights, a school children's drop-in center, tutorial and homework services, a nursery school program, and an "advocacy clinic." This agency and several others stress the importance of helping people to help themselves and thus focus on facilitating the organization of self-help groups (see Chapter 6). Some agencies may offer technical assistance to launch such groups or provide professional leadership to run them.

The most typical family agency advocacy service is on the level of the case. The members of the social work staff, or case aides, help their clients to obtain access to legal benefits and entitlements, usually by guiding them to the appropriate local public welfare or Social Security office or even making contacts on their behalf. Occasionally there may be legal representation or referral in relation to these programs, public child welfare, or other social service units. Similarly, a family with a housing emergency or a cash crisis may be helped vis-à-vis authorities responsible for helping if such authorities have not been responsive.

Experience with "cases" leads or can lead to class action—initiating or supporting broader local or state (sometimes federal) administrative actions or legislation. Some family agencies are active and effective in this field, especially on the state level, and address themselves to issues that go beyond their own direct-service domains: child care, public assistance, medical services, food stamps, family planning and abortion, appointment of public officials in the social services, public budgets as they affect social services, housing, and so forth. The typical agencies have only modest, if any, advocacy programs of this type, with little or no formal staff assignment. Most depend on the actions of their volunteer committee or board members. A few have staff experts in policy analysis, substantive fields, and lobbying. FSAA as a national organization is also a relatively inactive group in advocacy, concentrating on the White House Conference on Families, creation of a family office in HHS, and a few legislative items. In contrast to the Child Welfare League, for example, it is neither staffed nor oriented for extensive monitoring or lobbying. As much may be said of most other national organizations delivering family services except for Catholic Charities, which has a more active Washington presence.

The commitment to advocacy in principle is strong and widespread among family agency personnel, but lobbying and monitoring are costly and difficult to finance. Moreover, board and staff members concerned with helping families find it easier to agree upon an agency service repertoire or on advocacy relating to ensuring benefits or services for a particular case to which the public bureaucracy has not been sensitive than to arrive at consensus about and to shape legislative and administrative reforms that affect views of government and its responsibilities. Nor are those who are expert in direct services or family life education necessarily legislative or policy experts as well.

Why a Family Service Agency?

The variety of services provided by family agencies do more than just expand the nature and range of help available to those needing assistance. They also provide a multiplicity of "doorways" so that individuals and families seeking aid can define their problems and their needs in different ways. Not all "help" is counselling, but many family agencies continue to define it as their central task. Not all view counselling as the primary form of help, but clearly many do. Information and advice have long been defined as essential services, as have brokerage and advocacy. Now it appears that so are support services (encouragement, enhancement, facilitation) provided through counselling and the gaining of insight into problems or behavior through talking to someone who is wiser or more experienced. None of this precludes the value of more concrete support services other than counselling, or all of these kinds of help when provided informally through relatives or friends rather than through formal institutions. Perhaps what emerges as most significant is that none of these problems are unique, nor is much of the kind of help that is provided. It is only that societies are more complex, as are our lives. Thus, the need for help may be more readily identified and more acceptable. For some, family service agencies offer help in a useful way. For others, help is not offered, or not available, or not useful. Some of these seekers go elsewhere.

From talking to administrators, staff, and clients, as well as from reviewing case records, we get a fairly clear picture of who comes to these voluntary family service agencies, and what kinds of requests they bring. Chapter 3 underscored the absence of a publicly operated family service as part of the public personal social services. Certainly, families do not approach these public agencies expecting to find such services provided there, although they might go expecting to be referred to an appropriate resource. What is unclear, thus far, is why some people come to these private family service agencies while others go elsewhere. Why do some seek out informal help or self-help groups or read a book while others explore a community mental health center, a private practitioner, a marriage enrichment program, a pastoral counselling service?

Only a consumer survey would clarify how much is accounted for by deliberate choice and how much by happenstance. Each service has its own view of why some consumers prefer the help they offer while others go to another service. Family service professionals are no exception. Here are the reasons some professionals give.

Why Not a Private Therapist?

Obviously, as we have indicated, not all requests for help are for counselling. Moreover, even when the need for help includes the need for counselling, many requests are multi-dimensional and a variety of other services is needed too. Where a multiplicity of services is needed or wanted, a private practitioner is inadequate, unless he or she is part of a group practice that provides services other than just counselling and therapy. For the most part individuals and families requiring multiple and diverse forms of help at the same time require the services of a large organization rather than an individual practitioner. Indeed, only economies of scale can make such diversity possible. Thus only a large organization can provide them.

Counselling, on the other hand, can be provided by an individual in private practice, or by an individual based in one of several different kinds of agencies. What do family service professionals view as the distinction between what they provide and what may be obtained from a private therapist, and what kinds of people with what kinds of problems go to which?

A supervisor at one family service agency who also has a private practice, as many others do in a similar position, described the service provided by her agency as "a time-limited, problem-focused, inexpensive form of therapy." She says that the major difference in treatment between what is provided by the staff at a family service agency and what a private practitioner provides is the length of the treatment and the degree of insight expected of individuals coming for help. "The treatment I offer the individuals I see privately is designed to enable them to obtain insight into their functioning and the nature of their problems. The premise is that the problem is located within them, not outside of them. These are intrapsychic problems that are troubling them. Thus, much time must be spent on learning about themselves and as a consequence, the treatment is long term and expensive." Other agency staff and several therapists in private practice agree with this position. But some agency executives dispute such a characterization.

Why Not a Community Mental Health Center?

The distinction between family service agencies and community mental health centers is much less precise. Indeed, some family service agencies view themselves as mental health clinics and are funded as such. Moreover, community mental health services do serve a relatively similar population. The dominant age group is between twenty-five and forty-four. Like the family service agencies, the community mental health centers serve a slightly better-educated group than the average American (largely a reflection of the age of the population coming for services). Finally, these centers are increasingly serving groups that have been described as "the worried well" rather than the severely disturbed, once again the same group served at family agencies.[14]

Family service professionals suggest the following as reasons for selecting one or another of these helping resources:

People come to family service agencies because they feel "healthy" or "healthier." If they feel very disturbed they go to a community mental health clinic. While waiting to see her counsellor at a family agency, one woman volunteered, "I came here for help because I have a problem with my life, not because I think I'm going crazy! If that were the case, I would go to a psychiatrist. If I could afford to see one privately, OK. Otherwise, I'd go to a mental health clinic." Staff at family agencies agreed, repeatedly stressing that they saw a much healthier population than did the local clinics.

In those family agencies that define themselves as "family services" and not "mental health clinics," the distinction regarding who is referred to a clinic may be clearer. One counsellor illustrated this by explaining, "When a woman calls and asks for help around a specific problem—'I want to go get a job but I'm afraid to'; 'My husband left me, and I don't know what to do'; 'My mother lives with us and it's getting to be impossible; I just can't manage'; 'I want to leave my husband but I feel so guilty'—I make an appointment for her to come in and discuss counselling at our agency. If the request for help is diffuse, and the description of depression and anxiety 'free floating,' I refer her to a psychotherapist or to a mental health clinic." She proceeded to describe a typical call: "A woman called this morning saying, 'I'm upset and depressed. My husband is great; my kids are wonderful; but something's wrong. I don't know what it is. I'm sure it's my own fault, but I don't know what to do or how to do it. I want some help.' This woman I referred elsewhere."

For agencies such as this one, there are other distinctions too that permit a quick decision. A previous history of hospitalization for psychiatric problems or regular use of medication usually leads to referrals to a clinic.

Several administrators and counsellors were even more specific: Community mental health centers primarily treat individuals, even though they may see other family members, around problems that they define as within themselves. Family service agency clients, on the other hand, come overwhelmingly for problems that they locate in their family situations. The counsellors view these problems as systemic and focus their treatment accordingly.

Community mental health clinics look for pathology; family service agencies seek out "strengths." As one counsellor said, "The people who come to see us are functioning. If they don't get help from us they may have more or unnecessary pain, but they're not going to fall apart. We give them a sounding board, expert or informed advice, an opportunity to explore alternatives, a new or a different perspective. And it often helps. Maybe not forever, but until another hard problem comes along."

Although community mental health centers experienced a 50 percent decline in the percentage of patients diagnosed as schizophrenic between 1970 and 1975, they still see more severely disturbed individuals than do family service agencies. They also provide medication if necessary, something the family service agency does not do unless it has also been licensed as a mental health clinic.

The reality is, however, that many of those treated at a community mental health center also could be treated at family service agencies. And a large group of family agencies have medical consultants or "directors" and are licensed as mental health clinics, and thus are increasingly likely to serve an even higher proportion of similar requests for help and similar individuals seeking help.

Family Life Education

"Family life education" (which we will employ as the broader term encompassing education for parenthood) is the third program element regarded by FSAA as an essential offering for all family agencies. Depending on definitions, it is also a major family-related activity in secondary schools and colleges, community centers and settlements, churches and synagogues, youth organizations, adult education programs; and it receives major attention on radio and TV, in the daily press, and in the publishing business.

While we place our discussion of family life education in a chapter devoted to the family service agency, other settings thus are involved as well. We have made some mention of the topic in the "market" chapter and, particularly, in the chapter on church services, which follows. Here we will focus, first, on those activities carried on by family service agencies. Then we will attempt to characterize the broader field.

Family Life Education in Family Service Agencies

A representative national committee made up of big and middle-sized city agency directors urged FSAA to make family life education a coequal program element and the recommendation was adopted in 1974.[15] Clearly placed in a "preventive and developmental" context, the service is targeted at people who are self-directing and enter voluntarily even though they may or may not be experiencing pain or conflict.

Less threatening or demanding than therapy, more time limited, far less intense in its relationships, family life education focuses on the development of knowledge, understanding, and behavioral skills in various proportions and does not deal with the defense structures of the personality. Unlike counselling or therapy, the program requires no diagnostic doorway and is offered to the general population (apart from some targeted outreach to specific problem groups or deprived minority populations). While continuous at the extremes with therapy or social advocacy, most of the family life education groups are essentially educational in mode and intent, and are premised on conveying knowledge and experience in such fashion as to contribute, variously, to role competency, social functioning, improved self-esteem. There is belief that knowledge and understanding, made available in a supportive context, can have such impact. Such results require trained leaders, usually university-educated, from one of a number of fields, careful educational planning, and the availability of books, pamphlets, handouts, film strips, or plays that can be performed and discussed—in short, a variety of other materials. The enterprise requires sensitivity to cultural, regional, ethnic, and religious differences.[16] The focus of most programs is summed up in the following:

> Family life education helps group members to understand and anticipate the normal patterns and stresses of individual family and community living in order to prevent and reduce situational crises, to improve and expand the range of coping capacities, and to stimulate self-actualization and growth.[17]

Efforts are being made to support such programs with manuals and related materials addressed to the social work group leaders and other mental health professionals in family agencies. In recent years FSAA has published four manuals as part of a series of "Workshop Models for Family Life Education": *Couples Communication and Negotiation Skills; Separation and Divorce; Parent-Child Communication;* and *Career Planning for Women.*[18] The session subtopics offer helpful elaboration. The manuals deal as well with techniques, handouts, and administration. Two of the topic listings will serve our purposes. *Career Planning for Women* has an eleven-session model: "Job Finding—You Need the Right Strategy"; "Getting to Know Yourself" and "Getting to Know about Jobs"; "Interest Inventory" and "Exploring Employment Resources"; "Self-directed Job Search" and "More Ways to Find Out about Job Openings"; "Members' Career Profiles"; "Job Applications"; "Getting Ready for a Job Interview"; "Schooling"; "How to Combine Work with Family Responsibilities Successfully"; "Setting Ongoing Career Goals"; and "Follow-up: Where Am I Now in My Career Campaign?"

Similarly, the six-session model for *Parent-Child Communication* is close to the field's traditional mainstream: "Behavior Is a Statement of Feeling"; "Sensitive Listening and Responding"; "Sensitive Expressing"; "The ABC Method of Problem Solving"; "Using the ABC Method of Problem Solving"; "Discussion of Individual Concerns and Questions."

People who join Choosing Parenthood groups in a Rhode Island family service agency program are offered a "menu" of the following topics from which to choose a six-session program. Each group seems to choose differently:

1. Lifestyles of the childfree.
2. The two-career family.
3. Shared parenting.
4. Dealing with a person's family: in deciding when to have children; in deciding how many children to have; after deciding *not* to have children.
5. Pronatalism.
6. The single person as parent.
7. Maternal instinct theories.
8. Pregnancy: physically, psychologically.
9. Unmarried couples as parents.
10. Adoption.
11. Sterilization.
12. Cost of having and raising a child.
13. Mobility and children.
14. The "best" age for pregnancy; the "best" age for raising a child.
15. Relationship changes after the decision: to have children; not to have children.
16. Genetic considerations.
17. Feelings about children.
18. Rivalries between: the man and the children; the woman and the children.
19. Parenthood for interracial couples.
20. Available support systems.
21. One-child families.
22. Society's reaction to childfree people.[19]

Depending on setting and the conceptual-theoretical orientations of staff, programs focus variously on child development, problems faced by children, parents, or families, life cycle issues, relationship or role or parenting skills, family management, and so forth. The programs range from impersonal public lectures to intensive small group interactions. They are conducted by psychiatrists, psychologists, pediatricians, social workers, nurses, high school and elementary school personnel, guidance counsellors, family life sociologists, the diversity of counsellors and therapists described in the several chapters of this volume, neighborhood "indigenous" personnel, organizational volunteers. They are more or less structured and use material, tests, evaluations, feedback, audiovisual materials, and so forth. They may be long term or quite brief, have a closed continuing membership or be open and changing in participation. They may be free (supported by taxes or charity) or quite expensive for the participants.

Despite the strong case frequently made for offering family life education for all prospective or current parents and to average, normal people generally, some of what goes on under this rubric is in fact remedial and compensatory. There is a history beginning early in the century of middle-class use of parent education to guide and "upgrade" the child rearing of immigrants and the "lower classes."

As we have illustrated already, other programs are sometimes used in conjunction with or to complement counselling and therapy. The adult education or group education format may be employed for group therapeutic programs, with all concerned recognizing what is involved. Again, this is not the major thrust of family life education in the United States.

Indeed, as currently organized, most family life education serves typical, average families, not defined as being in particular trouble. If anything, there is a clear tendency to concentrate on the middle and upper classes, not on the poor and disadvantaged. What, then, does the broader field look like?

The Broader Field

It is not necessary to recite once again all the social changes that limit the learning through personal experience of young people who will become spouses and parents. And it is the limitations of personal experience and thus of usable knowledge that apparently motivates some of the large numbers of willing participants in family life educational programs. A few of the relevant themes merit mention, however, even repetition. Growing up in families smaller than the historical family, even the "usual" family of modern times, young people see less of parent-child interaction and observe far less of the details of parenting at various life cycle stages than was true in four-child or six-child families. Since children grow up in households from which mothers go to work outside the home, whether part time or full time, either continuously or with some interruptions, there may be some loss of exposure to knowledge and role models for childbearing and child-rearing activities. (These, in any case, seem to be reasonable inferences based on available knowledge in a surprisingly undocumented area.) Moreover, social change places all contemporaries in a world in which roles of men and women, of young children and adolescents, are changing in many ways whether or not both parents are in the workforce. It is a world of mobility, communication, and technical change that nobody has fully experienced before; therefore it is not surprising that members of the several different adult cohorts, especially those about to have children and the parents of young children, are particularly curious about the experience and thinking of others. They are prepared to share knowledge and perceptions and even, jointly, to shape norms. In addition, as more people live longer, particularly in the post-retirement years, there are still other roles and relationships to be worked out, from the side of adult children and from the side of their post-retirement parents.

Finally, and also significant, there is the current widespread interest in lessons from the behavioral and social sciences. Our society believes that science can improve upon tradition. Science magazines are constantly expanding their circulations. The readers of millions of books of popular sociology and psychology want to know what the lessons are for their personal lives. As we have already noted, just as people are constantly interested in articles about diet and exercise, they are prepared to read in magazines, newspapers, and books about intimacy, parenting, and child-bearing. They also follow TV programs on such subjects. Therefore, it is hardly a surprise that large numbers of adults and adolescents are prepared to enroll in family life education courses and programs—whether carried out by family service agencies, in community mental health centers, in settlement houses, as elements in youth organizational programs, or offered as part of adult education series in local schools and colleges. (Church-based or derived programs are discussed in the next chapter.)

These and other considerations make most "consumers" quite comfortable about their use of these family-support services. Dale Hoffman, a magazine reporter, explained her interest in this way:

> Three years ago, my husband and I brought a five-day-old infant home from the hospital. Despite our planned parenthood and compulsive reading of anything with "baby" in its title, we soon discovered we were unprepared for parenting. We are, we've learned, typical. So typical that there are now dozens of parenting courses, workshops, and discussion groups designed for people like us—men who want to be participatory fathers, and women who have worked at careers and now want to work at mothering.
>
> Our own mothers didn't have workshops or groups. But many of them did have extended families—which meant role models, a mutual-support system, and continuity of child-rearing methods. Most of them relied on pediatrician-gurus for advice and hand holding (no one I know goes to a pediatrician for anything but colds and shots). And few of our mothers expected child rearing to be meaningful and fulfilling, an expectation that is a legacy of the women's movement.[20]

In her own explorations, Hoffman found it useful to classify parenting groups as emphasizing "mutual support" or "communication." Many of the services she identified, however, seemed to "defy classification," ranging from large public lectures to instructional group discussions and "exercises" featuring "stars" like Dr. Lee Salk and many types of professionals. The services almost all involve fees, but range in auspice from the commercial to the non-profit.

In the most comprehensive available overview of a large part of this domain, David Harman and Orville Brim accurately describe parent education as "a new kind of support."[21] They offer some helpful distinctions. If the overall rubric is parent education, it is useful to recognize a difference between preparation for childbearing, or education for future parents, on the one hand, and education to improve child rearing, or education for parents, on the other. While not all of adult education, they note, is parent education, most parent education clearly is a form of adult education, and the educational and organizational experiences of adult education apply. Our own view is that parent education, in turn, is a subcomponent of the larger field of family life education, which also encompasses family-planning education, a focus on family relationships and roles beyond child rearing, education in relation to budgeting, family economics, and household management, and family-oriented health and nutrition education. While overlap with some fields, particularly health education, is common and inevitable, the programs we are interested in here see this kind of content as relevant and consider it, also, as a vehicle for consideration of parenting in the narrower sense.

Since they are delineating a domain, Harman and Brim quite legitimately include within their purview three categories of programs: anonymous mass modes (books, booklets, pamphlets, newspapers, magazines, radio, TV, films, filmstrips and slides, public lectures); group modes (parents meeting under leadership in more or less formal ways); individual modes (education in the context of counselling and therapy). For our purposes, and with family support services as the organizing point of departure, we have elected to review the mass modes, except for public lectures, briefly under the marketplace and shall say more about this type of educational activity in the church chapter. The individual mode is of course recognized as a component of counselling and requires professional analysis in that context. The unique contribution of family life education to the program of family agencies, educational institutions, youth organizations, churches, centers, and settlements is in public lectures open to all and in several group modes, on which we shall focus here. Harman and Brim quote from an early article by Aline Auerbach:

> We are focusing specifically on the experiences of parents meeting under skilled professional leadership in small discussion groups. . . . The attention of members is not focused directly on the group process or the role they play in it. While there is reason to believe that if they learn to function more effectively in a group, they may function more effectively in other human relations, the primary purpose in coming is to become better parents, not better group members.[22]

As the field has developed and expanded, there are great variations in the size, duration, formality, process, curriculum, and leadership of the groups. The educational mode is stressed, but there is an experiential component and an emotion-tapping process featured in some of the programs. The range will be noted, again, in the discussion of sectarian and secular marriage enrichment and related programs in the next chapter. For the most part, however, the programs assume participation by competent and normal people who are motivated to improve their role performance and are capable of cognitive learning. This assumption does not preclude outreach efforts, creation of motivation, and careful attention to the socioemotional context in which learning is enhanced. These efforts are built on a tradition of upper- and middle-class socialization of new immigrants, of re-education of deviant groups, and of professionals sharing their expertise with laymen.

Some adult education theoreticians and researchers have attempted to contribute to the knowledge base for family life education so that the essential choices may have an objective basis, but one would judge from the Harman-Brim review already cited that the endeavor in this sense is primitive. Concerned largely with effecting changes in parental role performance and with upgrading child care practice in the home, the parent education subfield has yet to resolve many issues relating to techniques, motivation, content, leadership, and values, and to distinguish its impacts from general cultural developments. As much may be said about the broader concerns with supporting other aspects of family life in the face of change and crisis. Serious attention needs to be directed at the reasons that many programs—some allege, the majority—terminate because of waning interest among participants. Nonetheless, from all indications, continuation and growth are to be expected. Despite the inherent difficulties of standardization, evaluation, and measurement (and the limited efforts to do even what would appear possible), carefully elaborated by Harman and Brim,[23] it is clear that people want and use help in their family role behavior and that they turn increasingly to family life education. It seems reasonable to expect more and better measurement of consumer response, more rigorous studies of short-run outcomes as related to techniques, more longitudinal assessments, and continued preoccupation with relating techniques, content, methods, and auspice to goal and client characteristics or what has been helpfully called "situation specificity—making the program fit the participants."[24]

5 Churches Help Families

In both formal and informal surveys, people identify priests, ministers, and rabbis as major sources of personal advice and help. In one major study, more people (39.6 percent of those interviewed) said that they would turn to clergy with a problem needing professional help than to any other profession. The "dean" of pastoral counselling notes that by long tradition pastors are expected both to preach the gospel and to heal the sick. The latter function implies counselling.[1] Increasingly, this help has been systematized in ways that make it a relevant component in the picture we are assembling in this volume.

Among the church-related or church-derived programs or service systems that families turn to are family life education, encouragement for self-help activity, structured experiences under such labels as "marriage encounter" or "family enrichment," formal counselling or treatment for individuals, groups, and families, and less formal programs of pastoral counselling.[2] Some of these programs clearly are bastions of defense of traditional family values. Others, depending on denomination and geographic location, represent an effort to understand and support living groupings, whatever their formal status. The extent to which such programs are joined together or separated also varies with their location in one or another Protestant denomination, the Catholic Church, or a Jewish synagogue program, as does their scope and scale. Moreover, while many of these activities enjoyed much or all of their initial growth out of church-based initiatives, a considerable component of the activity now crosses denominational and religious lines or lacks formal religious affiliation. The formal counselling, in fact, seems in some places to be as much a church borrowing and adaptation of the therapeutic initiatives that have developed in secular psychiatric, psychological, and social work programs as it is an evolution out of the counselling responsibilities of the pastor.

Thus, this chapter covers a diversity of activities: some of them are actually programmatically unified in some places and for some denomina-

We are indebted to Susan Neibacher, who conducted most of the interviews with pastoral counsellors reported in this chapter.

tions, while others do not define themselves as interconnected or even church-related at all. Nonetheless, the device of placing all these elements in relation to one another does serve to define some issues. Also, it may clarify where many millions of Americans turn for help, how they define their needs, and what the total service repertoire contains.

Church and Family

The Scope of Family Ministry

The experienced director of a counselling service in a large Protestant church on the east coast comments on her function as follows: "The task of psychotherapy is to help people find a strong and authentic sense of self that comes out of their own awareness of their own values, their own needs, and their own feelings—as opposed to a sense of self that is based on meeting external requirements, living up to what other people expect of you. A person attempts through psychotherapy to find an authentic sense of self which is strong enough to cope with a lot of things, because it involves self-esteem. The task of faith that goes along with that is to help people find a sense of meaning and purpose in life that helps them connect to other human beings and to something larger than that self—friendship, community, and responsibility in the world; connection with other people and God. Pastoral counsellors are more aware of not being value-free and of a concern with the meaning of life." Here, then, is the case and the possible contradiction: self-expression within a religiously based value system. This is seldom a problem for private practitioners, but can be important in officially sponsored programs.

One type of client involved in intensive treatment with a pastoral counsellor remarked: "I've had therapists who say they don't want to hear about God. Or they consider the stuff sick and say that's not what we should be talking about." Like this client, there are many people who, in their struggle with emotional problems, are trying to develop an interpretation of the religious beliefs they have learned that can be congruent to their overall needs. Pastoral counselling seeks to respond to this need. As a church-related professional mental health service recently interpreted itself: "Being fully pastors and fully psychotherapists is the art for pastoral counsellors. . . . Our work is of God, and it also measures up to the [standards of] other professional therapists."

On the other hand, there are those who come to the church-connected service without special interest in its religious aspect at all. They come simply because it is a convenient, not-too-expensive counselling service that they know about.

The east coast counselling service mentioned above is staffed by personnel called "therapists" who have a background in both ministry and therapy. Another Protestant church of a different denomination with access to a church counselling center next door considers the minister to be a pastoral counsellor whose role is distinct from the more formal role played by psychiatrists, psychologists, social workers, or ministers with specialized and advanced training in counselling and psychotherapy. A minister who does not consider himself a specialist remarked: "They come to us as ministers because we are the first line of the helping professions. We don't have a title. We are not psychiatrists or psychologists. So if there is an emotional problem, they don't have to confront it right away in such language. You don't have to admit you are sick or have a neurosis. There is also another reason for coming to the minister: he is in the first line of people known outside of one's own family and friendships. Besides, formal help is expensive and time-consuming. We are available and people expect the help in return for their tithe."

Thus, one pattern to be found resembles the structured adult clinic or family service agency. The second builds on the pastoral tradition in which priests, ministers, and rabbis have always visited and served prisoners, hospitalized parishioners, victims of accident and disaster, and almshouse residents, or served as military chaplains.

But the range of church-related family helping services is far wider than traditional ad hoc counselling and more formal clinic and social service counselling programs. In 1978, after an intensive planning period, a joint task force of the National Conference of Catholic Bishops and the United States Catholic Conference published a plan of pastoral action for what the churches call "family ministry." This term describes the total family educational and support program in some churches but does not encompass counselling and formal treatment in others. The Catholic plan was discussed and local units, on the diocesan level, were encouraged to devote 1980 to the planning of family-oriented activity in several categories: a ministry for pre-marrieds and singles involving preparation for family life, including sexual education; a ministry for married couples, emphasizing the development and enrichment of the marriage relationship; a ministry for expectant parents, young parents, and parents of adolescents to assist them in understanding their roles in a time of social change; a ministry to stress the "social mission" of the family by creating "supportive associations" to inspire family spirituality through home prayer formations, family nights, and religious and cultural events; a ministry for "hurting" families, to include specialized counselling, reconciliation, a variety of services responsive to poverty, aging, alcoholism, drug abuse, homosexuality, divorce, separation, handicap, and so forth; and a ministry for leadership couples, to give support and renewal to those who are in the forefront of this work and must continue to learn skills and have their own needs met.[3]

One could substitute several similar lists from major Protestant denominations as well.

Educational and social action activities in the field are illustrated by the program of the National Council of Churches, Commission on Family Ministries and Human Sexuality, the focal point for cooperative efforts in the area of family and/or sexuality for thirty-two Protestant and Orthodox bodies with a combined constituency of forty million. The Commission's present involvement includes work in family violence, remarriage of divorced persons, homosexuality and families, parents as sex educators of pre-adolescent children, and abortion.

Along with the Commission's work, the NCC's Office of Family Ministries and Human Sexuality assists other projects and deals with public policy issues that touch families. Recent examples of these include an extensive research project on death, grieving, and funeral planning; a consultation on religious affirmation of sexuality in the later years; testimonies on tax reform, guaranteed income, and amendment of the civil rights legislation to disallow discrimination based on sexual orientation or practices; and the publishing of a study book on human life and the new genetics.

There usually are three elements in the concept of family ministry: a strong educational component that joins family life to religious commitment; a mutual-aid, participatory experience variously interpreted as including educational and socioemotional components; and a therapeutic-counselling-service program that may be quite formal and professionalized or, as we have seen, a component of the pastor's daily church routine. While the Catholic program here outlined asks for diocesan planning to encompass all of this, a national perspective that includes all groups suggests diverse organizational, associational, and professional patterns for the division of labor.

In category 2 of the Catholic plan, "the development and enrichment of the marriage relationship," the local church carries out marriage and family enrichment programs and is the base and recruitment point for a series of so-called "movements," of which "marriage encounter" is the most visible and (as we shall see) touches the most people. By now, this movement has secular and religious branches, denominational and ecumenical operational patterns. One of its leaders explains: "The core of Marriage Encounter, . . . the initial experience, is a weekend in which ten to twenty-five married couples are given an opportunity to examine their lives together free from everyday distractions. They are urged to explore their relationship—their individual weaknesses and strong points, their hidden hurts, dreams, disappointments, their joys and frustrations—openly and lovingly in a face-to-face encounter with the one person they have chosen to live with for the rest of their lives." The weekend is presented by a team of two or three previously "encountered" couples and a minister, usually a priest. It runs from early Friday evening to late Sunday afternoon.[4] There are also secular encounters, without minister or priest. Sometimes the groups are smaller; one couple may lead. And the unit of attention may be the entire family, a couple and their children, not, as is more typical, the couple alone.

Thus we note a series of church and synagogue approaches that clearly concern themselves with people who define their participation in different ways: hurting and needing help; wanting to enrich their personal and family lives in an interpersonal or self-realization sense; ready to help others directly or through mutual aid; seeking information, explanation, or guidance as tools for living. Clarification of the place of all this in an overview of where Americans seek and find help, and in relation to the roles of churches in this country, requires a somewhat more systematic look at church and family, at pastoral counselling in its more traditional and its professional-therapist forms, at educational and other family enrichment efforts, and at the family-centered "movements," especially "marriage encounter."

How Various Churches Regard the Family and Organize Themselves to Deal with It

The United Methodist Church, based in Nashville, Tennessee, has taken the lead in shaping a concept of "family ministry." Dr. Leon Smith, its director of Education for Marriage and Family Life, has pioneered in developing methods for marriage enrichment programs and family life education. He has been chairman of the National Council of Churches Family Ministry Staff Conference (an organization for denominational secretaries in family ministries). Like many of the others in such work he has supplemented his education for the ministry with in-service training in a marriage counselling program and is active in professional associations made up of personnel serving families.

Smith's theme is that "church and family belong together." He says:

> Family ministry is not a segmented compartment of church work. It is conceived rather as an *integral* part of the total ministry of the church to persons as family members.
>
> Family ministry is not an occasional "program" but a continuing, ongoing ministry of the whole church to all its families. This is a much broader concept than the church "putting on" particular programs for families. It envisions *families assuming responsibility* for the Christian nurture of their own members, for their participation in the life of the church.[5]

The family is important, he adds, *"in itself* to its own members," to provide food, shelter, clothing, basic physical needs, but "especially to each other as persons" to meet personal and affectional needs of all family members across the life span. The family is also important to society as the primary unit in the social structure, as producing and caring for children and helping them mature, as providing for the needs of adults, and feeding into their culture values that undergird creativity and stability. And the family is important to God as a basic structure of human relationships, "providing community for individuality, . . . as a channel for God's unconditional love, . . . as an opportunity for the kingdom of God to come to earth within families and society."[6] Thus, in this view, the local church coordinator of family ministries has a job that "affirms families": the focus is on families or persons as family members, on families as units, on forces affecting families, "on the potentialities of families in the church and in society."[7]

While vocabularies vary, specifically with exposure to sociological and psychological work in the family field, there is a commonality across many denominations and religions in justifying a family focus. Their affirmation that the "family is important" adds a religious dimension to the usual sociological, psychological, and psychiatric observations.[8]

Recent Catholic statements place emphasis both on the help to the family and on the protection of the family as an institution by the Church and as a vehicle for strengthening and building the Church:

> Thus at a time when many in our society are predicting the demise of family life and sacramental marriage, a new found hope is appearing in the pastoral life of the church.
> The pastoral concern of the bishops for the family is more than evident. The family is seen as the first place of evangelization, as the first school of life, as one of the major forces in the expansion of the Gospel and the implanting of the mission of the Church.[9]

A sophisticated, sociological perspective on the complexity of designing a pastoral approach to issues "in regard to love, marriage and the family" is offered by Dr. John L. Thomas in an analysis prepared for the United States Catholic Conference. In the overall context of the majority culture, he writes, it cannot be assumed "that the faithful fully understand the total Christian context of relevant beliefs within which acceptable solutions must be formulated." As members of a religious minority, albeit a large minority, they must deal with their major decisions and practices in what they must regard as "a morally pathological social system." The attainment of one's own distinctive family values becomes extraordinarily difficult because of the "normalcy of the pathological, institutionalized in the system by the dominant majority."[10] One might extrapolate this analysis as well to all except the most dominant of Protestant denominations in formulating a rationale for introducing into personal and family counselling, and family life education as well, personnel whose identification and training permit them to cope with the moral issues and core values central to personal identity.

Those who do the work often define its mission in both church and individual terms. As one Protestant program puts it: "Many people find their way into the church or 'back' into it through special pastoral ministries making alive or suddenly meaningful its context."

The marriage encounter literature, too, views family as both end and means, varying with branches of the movement and their particular leaderships. Most of the discussions see the enrichment of marriage—and thus of its members—as a prime goal. Some authors focus more on the family as institution. Fr. Gabriel Calvo, who brought the movement to the United States and is its charismatic leader, is very direct and specific: "The purpose of the weekend is not to focus on feelings; it is to focus on God's plan." Some find this disappointing. One couple, more interested in an ecumenical approach, concluded that "the purpose of marriage encounter was the renewal of the Catholic Church."[11] But thousands of others continue participation with no apparent sense of tension between such goals.

Most of the program material in family ministry, generally, and in pastoral counselling, specifically, takes a relatively traditional view of the family as its point of departure and indeed seeks to reinforce and strengthen the family in its most traditional sense. Much of the programming is premised on nuclear units made up of a husband who works and a mother who stays at home with the children. There is attention as well to divorced and separated couples, varying somewhat by denomination.

In response to family structural changes, and to give support to groups facing stigma, discrimination, and disadvantage, some of the religious groups and denominations, particularly the more liberal ones, actively affirm the worth of deviant or diverse family forms. There also is increasing evidence of the recognition of female-headed families as a common form (the living arrangement for one child in five in 1980) and of the need to offer support and help where once there was condemnation and only substitute care for the child. Strangely, this is not matched as yet by any substantial deliberate consideration of the life routines and program needs of two-earner and two-career families, except for some attention to day care, despite the statistical importance of this almost dominant mode.

Several of the pastoral counselling programs give special attention to serving homosexuals, particularly in programs conducted as private practice or agency spin-offs by priests and ministers not working in formal church context. In a concern with non-traditional family forms more generally, Dr. G. William Sheek, director of the Family Ministries and Human Sexuality Office, National Council of Churches, has written an elaborate theological rationale for accepting family diversity and regarding the extant "household" rather than the traditional biological or legal unit as the focus of attention:

> Family unit living has always been determined by various conditions of society and therefore familial modes have differed. . . . God has confronted personkind with relationship imperatives about love, but the groupings people live in to express those imperatives are not necessarily nuclear families. . . . If the church embraces qualities of human life over structures, then the church should function to empower persons to claim these qualities. . . .
> We need not feel guilty in supporting a variety of living units. . . . If public policy narrowly restricts the definition of acceptable family units, we will need to oppose that.
> Societies can find strength in strong supportive units which are often by blood, marriage, or adoption, but it can find equally strong support in units which are bonded together by commonalities of various kinds. Where doctrine deems the concept of families as households, we have an educational job.[12]

Sheek is, however, atypical. Most of the family ministries, as contrasted with some private and semi-official pastoral counsellors, focus on mainstream families, often facing largely toward middle America.

The several different tendencies express themselves through both formal and informal division of labor. One clear illustration is offered by an agreement among the National Conference of Catholic Charities, the National Conference of Catholic Bishops, and the United States Catholic Conference. In general, there is recognition of two streams of action: the more formal social service programs of Catholic Charities (family service agencies, child welfare programs, programs for the aged and for adolescents, and so forth); and the preventive and developmental activities of the diocesan Family Life Office.

There are elaborate procedures for ensuring some initiative in all dioceses during the 1980s. Since Catholic Charities or a Family Life Office is not everywhere available, the divisions are not firm. In general, however, Catholic Charities focuses on "hurting" families and its formal agency activities approximate those described in Chapter 4, even though many are too small or too poor to join the Family Service Association of America. In fact, Catholic Charities, along with FSAA, the Child Welfare League of America, and the Association of Jewish Family and Children's Agencies, is currently a member of the standard-setting unit in the field, the Joint Council on Accreditation. Like other social work services, from the early 1970s the Catholic Charities units and the coordinating body, the National Conference of Catholic Charities, have sought to reorient their work to ensure a focus on poverty and minority populations and to increase participation of all interests in policy and program decisions. Direct service is supplemented by policy initiatives and social action. Given the increasingly high levels of public social funding, the local Catholic Charities agencies operate with a level of resources unavailable to the in-house family life ministry activities.

There is no way to specify the scale of all Catholic Charities activities since local service definitions vary, as do statistical procedures. While there is an annual report, the service units tabulated are not standardized. The scale is large, however: more than one hundred agencies; hundreds of "programs"; several hundred thousand people, largely for brief service; some small-scale financial aid for lay charity societies; marriage preparation and related educational activities; programs for the aged, and for families, children, and youth; many for unmarried mothers.

The diocesan family life programs take on the developmental, socialization, and educational activities already cited above: specific programs for pre-marrieds and singles, for married couples, for parents with very young children and with adolescents, for families at various points in the life cycle, for leadership families. While programs for "families who are suffering" are also encouraged, this clearly is the primary Catholic Charities domain where such a program exists. [13]

Protestant denominations are more diverse. One of the most active, the United Methodist Church, has developed an elaborate family ministry program featuring parent-child issues, marriage, and sex education. Elaborate study units (each involving thirteen sessions) are prepared for local Sunday school use, mostly by lay teachers. A quarterly magazine is distributed in the churches as a basis for parent education classes. Materials are prepared for parental use (on the first child and on other stages through elementary school) in a "parental guide" series.

In addition, the United Methodist Church, in its own variation of the marriage enrichment movement, has trained over eight hundred couples for leadership over the last fifteen years, and some ten thousand couples participate in forty-eight-hour weekend marriage enrichment experience sessions each year. There are also mid-week and one-evening-a-week classes. The basic orientation is that the husband-wife relationship is the key family relationship. These eight hundred couples have included people from twenty-eight denominations in fifteen countries (with about 50 percent fallout after a few years). In any case, the Methodists serve as a central training resource. Standards are protected by the "cooperative certification process" of the American Association of Couples for Marriage Enrichment (ACME), founded in 1973.

Some denominations join educational and counselling activities in their programs. Some stress the educational. One of the family ministry leaders in the American Baptist Churches states his view as follows:

> The orientation of much church effort on behalf of families is a counselling orientation. I stand somewhat against this, feeling that counselling is best left to those professionals and agencies thoroughly trained to do it. I see the church, rather, as an educating institution, doing preventive work with families. I believe lay persons are less intimidated by an educational approach to family ministries, and the data I have tell me churches do more in family ministries when lay people are planning the programs.[14]

The Southern Baptist Convention offers another illustration. A broadly conceived program of family life education is strongly supported as one of four church priorities and is implemented in the conglomerate of 35,000 churches with 12 million members. Attention is directed both to typical, traditional families and to family types with special problems and needs: single-parent families, handicapped individuals, the divorced, the widowed, older couples with special problems.

The overall goal of the Baptist educational effort, as stated by Dr. Joseph W. Hinkle, its director, is to "strengthen the family unit" through traditional forms of parent education, supporting a family enrichment program (for example, they trained about one hundred leader couples and reached a thousand couples with the program in 1979), premarital education, and circulation of materials. During 1979, the totality of seminars, case workshops, leadership training sessions, activities with family life education ministers, and so on involved some 32,000 participants in small and large groups. A monthly *Home Life* magazine circulates 800,000 copies. Three parenting magazines are published quarterly, purchased, and distributed by the churches: one dealing with pre-schoolers has a circulation of 140,000; the one devoted to elementary school children and the other for older children circulate 40,000 each. The psychological orientation is eclectic. As part of a series of publications for use in church workshops, there are such titles available as *Money Management, Marriage Enrichment,* and *Sexuality.* A follow-up study is under way on the effects of marriage enrichment retreats after three to five years.

The family ministry program repertoire also is exemplified by the plan, reported earlier in the chapter, developed by the National Conference of Catholic Bishops and the U.S. Catholic Conference (USCC). The dominant concept is that families should be "empowered" rather than made dependent. Whereas schools, hospitals, and other institutions tend to see and deal with people as isolates, the emphasis here is on viewing people as family members. Thus, while the social agencies of Catholic Charities, like all social agencies, tend largely to focus on helping individuals with problems, seeking in some instances to achieve a more coherent family focus, especially in "family therapy," the family life program is throughout premised on work with families per se. As much may be said of several major family life programs among the several Protestant denominations, in contrast with their own denominational, specialized social service agencies.

The USCC has prepared an ambitious and attractive resource guide with the title *Marriage and Family Enrichment*. This guide is intended to inspire local diocesan family life personnel by suggesting specific program resources. The perspective is educational, developmental, and inspirational. The parish is invited both to be hospitable to national "movements" and to adopt and adapt nationally prepared program materials for use in parish family life programs that are conducted by specialists and volunteers. Catholic Charities is sometimes an initiating or cooperating body, but it is more often the source of specialized help to which referrals are made.

The major resource guide topics suggest the range: "Christian Family Action," "Human Sexuality/Family Living," "The Elderly," "Family-Centered Programs," " Marriage Encounter Movements," "Marriage/Family Spirituality," "Marriage Renewal," "Natural Family Planning," "Newly Married," "One-Parent Families," "Parenting," "Separated, Divorced, Remarried," "Singles," "Widowed."[15] Under each heading is a listing of organizations and movements with program ideas and materials that are available for local use, or that could be locally sponsored. Many non-Catholic sources are cited. Some of the offerings are available for a family's adoption in its own home. Some of the resources apply to several headings. A partial listing of citations under "family-centered programs" and "marriage encounter movements" (described in detail in our final section) are especially relevant. "Family-Centered Programs" includes: "Families for Prayer," "Family Nights," "Hi, God," "Christian Family Concert," "Family Learning Films," "Family Retreat," "Love Happens in Families," plus the "marriage encounter" entries and many others. "Marriage Encounter Movements" lists National Marriage Encounter, Worldwide Marriage Encounter, FIRES (Family Intercommunications Relationships Experience Services), Evenings for Couples, and the Family Weekend Experience, among others.

In general, the orientations of the family ministry programs are developmental, not therapeutic. The basic activity is educational. As we shall see, however, lines are not sharply drawn. What is of interest, too, is the sense in which family ministry programs are truly couple- and/or family-unit-oriented, in contrast to pastoral counselling and church-related social services, which are more often focused on the individual as client.

For the Methodists—and they characterize much of the Protestant writing—the core unit is the married couple, but there is a life cycle perspective reflected in the literature, as illustrated by Dr. Smith's heavy reliance on the theoretical writing of Evelyn Duvall.[16] In addition to the educational and enrichment programs already described, there is recognition here, too, of the need for more formal counselling and therapy, whether in church-related or in general community service programs.

Black churches are often family-oriented in their programming and are generally tolerant of less traditional family forms. However, they seldom can afford full-time staff and materials, or to give high priority to explicit family programming. An exception is the effort under the Board of Christian Education of the Church of God in Anderson, Indiana. This church has a fifty-year tradition of family ministries. The director of the program, Dr. Alvin Lewis, has a background in research and university teaching of family life education. The program is geared to all black churches, not to the Church of God alone. Its main vehicle is the "conference," a kind of intensive seminar experience, which is employed with pastors and laymen. The goals include sensitizing pastors to the importance of family life education as strengthening both families and church, enriching church programs by offering programs that they cannot mount alone, and recruiting and training lay leadership to expand the work.

The typical conference meets from 7:00 to 10:00 P.M. on Thursday evening and again on Saturday from 9:00 A.M. to noon. This schedule permits participation by clergy and working families. Typical topics, repeated in many communities by Dr. Lewis and his colleagues, are dating and courtship, financial planning, the single parent, the unwed mother, divorce and remarriage, human sexuality. There often is an emphasis in the conference on marriage enrichment.

Most of the conference leaders are college graduates, many of them pastors, social workers, or professionals in related disciplines. The conferences span the country and have reached about one thousand people over the past thirty months.

Personal help and therapy, whether developed by, referred to, or supported by Protestant and Jewish denominations, follow several patterns, which are not necessarily seen as mutually contradictory or in competition, since different functions or relative advantages may be ascribed to them. First is a church social service program. Catholic Charities has been mentioned. The Lutheran Church has elaborate social

service in a pattern of similar scope and range. Jewish social agencies—
family service and child welfare—relate both to the local Jewish Welfare
Federation and the community-wide social services, but cooperate in the
family life education efforts of the local synagogues and community
centers.[17] Next is the general community service system, public and private, to which the church refers. Third are the pastoral counsellors within
the local church programs, sometimes functioning as specialists, but more
often including counselling as a segment of the minister's role. Finally
there are the private practitioners of psychiatry, psychology, counselling,
and psychotherapy.

Pastoral Counselling, General and Specialized

The classic work in the field of pastoral counselling, authored by Seward
Hiltner, the recognized "dean" of the field, was published in 1949. As we
have already noted, Dr. Hiltner defines the pastor's task as including both
preaching the gospel and healing the sick. The latter role requires a
counselling function. He sees the pastor as a general practitioner, not a
specialist, who combines compassion for people "with a sense of their
responsibility for bringing on their own special predicament." The focus,
however, is on helping the sinner, because it is society that is the greater
sinner in creating conditions that breed crime and prejudice.[18]

Dr. Hiltner describes the counselling methods in terms that will remind
social workers of the secular social casework texts of the 1940s and 1950s:
"the attempts by a pastor to help people to help themselves through the
process of gaining understanding of their inner conflicts, . . . sometimes
referred to as an emotional reeducation, . . . should teach people how to
help themselves with other problems."[19] What makes this activity different
is the view that, in helping people find their own way, the pastor embraces
both the "social adjustment" and "inner release" perspectives and sees the
need to go further. Beyond these views, he also believes in a force in all
human nature that revolts when basic needs are not fulfilled ("objective
ethics"). For this, Christian theology offers an undergirding: the ethical
character conditioning man's life is God-made and supported. Thus, pastoral counselling works in a unique setting, the church, and with a special
view of human nature. The denominations may differ on the details of the
latter, but their position, in turn, is distinguishable from secular views.[20]

As we already have noted, the work of church counselling began with
battlefield, prison, asylum, and hospital service. It is carried on informally
as an aspect of the overall pastoral task. Most church personnel now have
some preparation for this kind of work in their general seminary courses
and some special courses. Others take more specialized programs within

the seminary. Still others enroll in specialized pastoral counsellor or psychotherapeutic training, offered in many forms and in many places, preparing themselves for more complex helping as an aspect of the pastoral role, or for specialized work within the local church, or for even more specialized roles in social service and counselling programs. Some move into free-standing social agencies or to private psychotherapeutic and counselling practice, still identifying themselves as including the religion-related identification (and sometimes content) as helpful or relevant. A similar range of activities is also visible in the several Jewish religious tendencies, especially the Conservative and the Reform.

There are no complete national data, but we have the impression that most pastoral counselling is church-based, that it is part of a role. There are, however, also large numbers of minister-counsellor specialists in church-based and church-related services or agencies. Private counselling and therapeutic practice by people with training in the ministry is growing, especially in a few large cities.[21] The response of higher church authorities varies, and a final pattern clearly has not emerged. The local bishop, for example, determines the range of choice for the priest who becomes a specialist. The diversity, the differences between generalists and specialists, and the search for clarification are illustrated here with some specifics.

A minister for whom counselling is an aspect of his overall daily role, not a specialty, describes a recent experience: "A mother asked for help with her thirty-three-year-old daughter, who was unable to leave her house. She asked me to make a home visit. The daughter will see a minister on a home visit. I regard it as an intake interview, perhaps even working with the mother to get the daughter hospitalized. The mother is the real client." The minister is a seminary graduate, has served as an associate pastor in a suburban church for seven years, and has completed a two-year, one-day-a-week course in pastoral care at a leading institute. He stresses the minister's home visit: "People feel more comfortable; it is their own turf." Again, the problems dealt with here could be found in other settings too. They involve adolescents creating problems at home, not doing home-work, acting out sexually; difficult problems in marriages; separation and divorce; crises in the family. If he tries to help people by going beyond the referral of complex pathology, his efforts remain informal: in the hallway before a service, after a meeting, "a ten-minute contact and not formal arrangements for seeing clients." This is a common, widespread pattern in many religious groups and denominations.

At the very beginning of this chapter we referred to a more formal, specialized counselling service within an east coast Protestant church. Its personnel are called "therapists." Many of the patient-clients come to it because of its church affiliation; others see it merely as competent, convenient, inexpensive.

They are referred, variously, by ministers and other church staff, a local health service, other churches, and mothers' groups at the church. A few of the more sophisticated patient-clients see this as a place that will not challenge their religious convictions, unlike orthodox Freudian settings, which may have negative attitudes toward religion.

The caseload statistics, however, are not very different from those of many clinics and family agencies: 70 percent of the work is with individuals; 25 percent is marriage counselling; 5 percent is family therapy. The workshops that are conducted cover topics that are common to some family life programs in family agencies and in other programs in churches and community centers (although, again, the orientation reflects the setting): separation and divorce, women's issues, struggling with self-esteem, personal faith, stress, mid-life crisis, parenting, nurturing, couples unable to have a child.

The way in which the religious affiliation can become relevant is further illustrated in a self-report after treatment by an unusually articulate forty-five-year-old woman, described by the therapist as terribly overweight, who long felt unattractive and not worthy of love and who indulged in infantile behavior. After a successful period of therapy, the therapist characterized her as follows: "She is a stimulating and vital person, has a quick-witted intelligence, and knows the Bible better than I do. She is a well-known artist and has achieved financial and social recognition." The self-report follows:

"I went to that service because I was disillusioned with traditional therapy. I thought I would get something different from a priest or minister who was a therapist. I guess I was just trying to cover all the bases. I assumed I would get a wise old man. Instead I got you. I never thought it would work. First of all you were a woman—I thought a man would be better. Second, you were tall and thin—all the things my father had wanted me to be. I disliked you for that immediately. For a long time, even after I'd decided you were a good therapist, I never thought of you as a minister. Now I think of you as my therapist and my spiritual guide.

"What worked? It seems very simple to me in some ways. You listened to my entire story. I told you things I had never told anyone before—things I was ashamed of—things I thought were awful and unacceptable. You always told me the truth, and helped me understand why I felt that way. You never humiliated me or made me feel bad when I became demanding or angry. Even when I walked out on you.

"You made me feel that you loved me. Sometimes I wished that I had really had you for a mother. It's silly, isn't it—you're so much younger than I am, I never thought I would think of you as a mother—but I do. I never like to admit you have other clients—even when I've sent them to you. But I can send you other people because I know that I am very special to you.

"I think I see myself much more realistically now. Once you told me that I had never learned to express fear or hurt—only anger. I've accepted myself more as I am. I can admit that I don't want a man anymore. I don't want sex. That's a relief. . . . Even then all I wanted was the approval. . . . I like my way of life now. I like living alone. I like painting without interruption. I like my friends. I feel I have been given a second chance.

"I think I stopped blaming other people for everything—my parents and other people in my life. . . . I think I've learned to accept responsibility for myself. . . .

"It's been very important to me to talk about God with you. I used to feel there was a deep hole in me that only God could fill. I was afraid to be alone—afraid to lose control. I think that's why I couldn't pray very well. I've kept using priests for confession—still covering all the bases. But I've never before felt connected with God. I was always looking for something churches couldn't really provide—the right answer—the sure thing. That's probably why I've never stayed with a church. You helped me to believe that the answer is not out there—it's within me. God is within me all the time—that's what you've taught me. I am the kind of person who can't grasp God in abstraction. I have to understand God from other people—from the way God works in their lives. It's the human story that moves me. That's what's been so important to me about you. I can only experience God's love when I experience it through people."

Two programs within one hundred miles of New York City offer further illustrations of common Protestant and Catholic patterns. The MN Council of Churches is a cooperative venture of Protestant ministries covering two large and populous counties (3 million people). The cooperating denominations are United Presbyterian, United Methodist, United Church of Christ, Lutheran, Episcopal Reformed Church, and American Baptist. Individual cooperating congregations also include the African Methodist Episcopal Churches as well as Congregational and Evangelical Covenant congregations. This total cooperative Protestant mission effort covers work with migrants, a blood bank, emergency services, Bible distribution, a radio program, housing programs for the aged and work programs for youth, and so forth. Within the cooperative pattern, there also is a major cooperative counselling service. Separately incorporated and dependent wholly on sliding scale fees, the service is considered to be completely professional and oriented both to individuals and to families. It is based in two major offices and several satellite locations across the two counties and employs ten counsellors (offering a total of five thousand counselling hours a year).

Although several other mental health professionals participate, most of the staff are Protestant ministers who have completed full-time post-graduate training in psychotherapy and who (in the words of the agency's brochure) seek to combine "the skills of the mental health profession and the perspective of meaningful religious commitment." The credentials of the director suggest a pattern that is now not unusual in the country at large, especially within Protestant programs: an ordained minister (Presbyterian), parish experience, full-time training in an institute for three years, and standing in the American Association of Pastoral Counselors and the American Association for Marriage and Family Therapy.

The services offered cover individual, group, and family counselling, as well as premarital counselling, marriage and divorce counselling, and personal help with a variety of types of individual "inner distress." Cases may involve couple conflict, loss of a family member, terminal illness, sexual difficulty, adolescent-parent tension, and so on. The service also offers pastors supervision and consultation for their own parish counselling work (what we refer to as non-specialized pastoral counselling), as well as frequently conducted clergy workshops.

In the same general geographic area, a large local Catholic church offers its surrounding community the following services, largely through volunteer activity: information and referral; "supportive counselling," largely on a group basis, for widows and single parents, as well as parent education and hospitality to Alcoholics Anonymous and a chapter of the Divorced and Separated Catholics; educational activity; family therapy (only the director is involved in this limited effort); advocacy vis-à-vis the public welfare and the local Catholic Charities agencies; emergency food, fuel, clothing, and rent help; and friendly visiting and transportation help.

The church building is this program's service center. There is twenty-four-hour telephone coverage for emergencies. The core staff of eleven is completely volunteer, carries out the assessment and case management activities, and participates in continuous in-service training, on the foundation of initial training by the local Catholic Charities. Some eighty auxiliary volunteers, most of them from the Society of St. Vincent de Paul, are responsible for much of the concrete service, outreach, friendly visits, and telephone contact work. The agency coordinator, the only professional on the staff, is a nun with full social work graduate training. The total budget in 1979 was $11,000, all raised locally, but this is augmented by much contributed space, service, and equipment.

Where the judgment is that a mental health service or more skilled facility is required, cases are referred out. There are close ties with the relevant local Catholic Charities, which, as already indicated, offers the more traditional, professional family service and child welfare programs.

Preparation for this work is not standardized. All theological seminaries have their own content in the core curriculum and some have specialized offerings. Many pastoral counsellors take degrees in family sociology, social work, or psychology. In large centers in several parts of the country, specialized institutes have also developed. An illustration (hardly typical, since no program at this stage is typical) is offered by New York's Blanton-Peale Graduate Institute of the Institute of Religion and Health. The institute is state-chartered, an amalgam of two programs that date, respectively, to the 1930s and the 1950s, reflecting both the large demand for counselling experienced in the churches and the desire of clergy, psychiatrists, and others to discuss "the relationship of health and behavior and its relevance to issues of faith and the wholeness of men." The program has grown to a point where its main clinic and three pastoral counselling center branches conduct over 750 hours of counselling each week. Some seventy men and women are enrolled in training programs. The Institute now also serves as a national organization with twenty-five affiliated counselling centers and publishes the *Journal of Religion and Health.* It sees itself as having two roots: "the religious wisdom of the Judeo-Christian tradition and the new knowledge of modern psychology."

Blanton-Peale offers two main full-time programs, a Pastoral Psychotherapy Residency and a Marital Therapy Residency.[22] The former is open to graduate ordained clergy with two quarters of training with the Association for Clinical Pastoral Education (ACPE), or similar qualifications, and sufficient experience to give evidence of emotional maturity.[23] It is a three-year program combining class work with extensive supervised clinical experience. Parallel personal therapy is required. Completion of this certification opens the door to relevant professional affiliations and (with modest additional work) a doctorate of ministry program in pastoral counselling at Andover Newton Theological School. (A small number of people are also admitted to this program on a part-time basis.)

The Marital Therapy Program is open to all allied professionals and stresses supervised clinical work. It prepares people for membership in the American Association for Marriage and Family Therapy. This program, too, requires a personal therapy involvement.

The course programs show a general psychoanalytic and developmental psychology orientation, considerable attention to the ego psychologies, a rather eclectic theoretical bent, and concern with both individual and group methods. There is little religious content as such in the formal outline. However, the catalogue states:

Residents are helped to integrate their own religious heritage and experience with psychodynamic theories of behavior and the modern modalities of treatment used in the clinic. Opportunities for dialogue take place in multi-disciplinary conferences, regular course work and the several papers and projects which occur during training on the relationship of religious experience to psychological theories of growth, development and pathology. The theology and tradition of each resident is respected as the resident moves on a pilgrimage toward new levels of awareness and an integration of skills and knowledge.

Blanton-Peale also serves the non-specialists. Its one-day-a-week pastoral studies program is designed for staff of local churches, synagogues, and pastoral centers. A certificate is awarded for a two-year program that emphasizes the counselling process and a perspective on one's functioning.

While in the Jewish community most of the non-market counselling and therapy is agency-related and not synagogue-based, almost all these tendencies do also appear in relation to synagogues. For example, Rabbi Z, a Reform rabbi, who is hardly typical, divides his professional time between staffing a small synagogue and servicing a counselling center in a small town along the eastern seaboard, and referring from one to the other. Apart from his rabbinic training, he has devoted eight years of study to preparation, participating in full-time and part-time work in a "marriage and family" (sociology-oriented) program, a pastoral counselling and a group therapy experience, and a doctor of ministry program in a Protestant theological seminary.

His counselling work developed largely out of problems related to Jewish intermarriage, which still represents almost one-third of the load. He has made a speciality of this and holds untraditional views. Referrals come from people formerly served (60 percent), people he met through officiating at marriages (20 percent), and miscellaneous professional and speaking contacts (20 percent). There are no referrals from other rabbis. Half the caseload is non-Jewish.

His service "modalities" include three marriage enrichment groups meeting at the synagogue on Friday evenings once each month (for "solid marriages" and not seen as treatment), individual treatment, couple treatment, group treatment, sometimes a family unit in treatment. Half the caseload consists of individuals with marriage-related or child-related problems. He cites cases such as the following: conflicts that arise when one spouse wants a child while the other does not; apparent sexual problems, often covering basic relationship problems in the marriage; problems between a parent and a child; problems in coping with divorce and separation. The program also includes seminars and workshops focused on parenting and human sexuality. The counselling program pays for itself through user fees.

The rabbi sees himself as "eclectic" in method, but working within a general psychoanalytic framework. His explanation of the marginal advantage of the pastor (condensed and edited) is similar to explanations from various Protestant ministers:

"It is easier for people to go to a rabbi because they do not have to see themselves as sick—as they would with a psychiatrist, less with a psychologist. In this sense the social worker is closest to the rabbi. With a psychiatrist you have to be pretty bad. People find it easier to tell their parents they are seeing a rabbi. They are usually people with some exposure to a church or synagogue. For many it is an entry into therapy.

"It often is difficult to know what comes from being a rabbi. But I identify with that part of a person that is healthy—or what in religious terms one might call the divine part of self."

Generalization would be premature. It would take an elaborate, long-time survey to identify the variety of theories guiding pastoral counselling, the multiplicity of views as to the depth of the counselling or psychotherapy that is appropriate, the schools of thought and the numbers of their adherents and client-patients, the multiplicity and numbers of various types of settings—and we would still lack data about the impact on individuals and families. Clearly this is a field that is developing and not yet consolidated. It could merge with the broader, secular human services field or with private psychiatry, psychology, and psychotherapy. Or it could become even more structured, standardized, and specialized.

The Hiltner volume is close to its pastoral roots in discussing the special resources for pastoral counselling, in addition to humanistic values and general psychological insight: the pastor's religious identification and what it means to specific individuals, prayer, the Bible, religious literature, Christian doctrine, sacraments and rites. By contrast, another early volume is in many ways part of the stream of short-term psychoanalytic psychotherapy, even though it considers itself less directive than the psychoanalytic posture as it interprets psychoanalysis. It urges that the counsellor be seen as "directive, non-directive, or educative," depending on the specific situation. In any case, the pastor's task is to help at many life crises and "to deal with the immediate situation in a manner that at least does no harm, and if possible promotes growth and stability."[24]

Contrast these early formulations with the self-reports of several counsellors whose roots are in the ministry and in religious settings, but who have trained in one of several "institutes" and divide time between formal counselling settings and private practice:

"I have psychoanalytic training but am most comfortable with Arnold Lazarus' multimodal behavioral therapy and social learning theory. I use insight therapy but am eclectic, including hypnosis, gestalt techniques, bio-feedback, medication."

"The most important theoretical framework for me is object relations theory. I've been interested in sociological 'marriage and family' theory and psychodrama. I've also been influenced by meditation, healing, work in bioenergetics."

"My institute training was psychoanalytic (ego and integrative). To this has been added behavior theory, assertiveness training which I actively use, transactional analysis, gestalt, sometimes existential, and psychodrama."

"I am trained analytically but am free to use non-traditional ways of treatment: hypnotherapy, psychodrama, gestalt."

These are atypical interviewees, most of them quite experienced, often working in private practice and identified with a free-standing service concept, even if using a religious identification from pastoral training and experience. More often the traditional psychological training in counselling or the sociological "marriage and family" orientation is predominant, and serves to guide less intensive counselling on the varieties of life problems. The national standard-setting and certification organizations described are seeking to guide the development but cannot, of course, control the practice.

The "Movements"

We have already introduced the "marriage encounter movements" and their various educational and experiential offshoots as constituting a significant component of family ministry. These programs receive church referrals, may be housed within church family life programs, or are reinforced by local church action. A distinction should be made between "marriage enrichment," focusing on couples, and the support systems and education known as "family enrichment." There are both religious and secular variations. Marriage and family enrichment should, in turn, be differentiated from the specific programs that often take the form of a "movement," called "marriage encounter."

The most common marriage encounter pattern involves a structured experience, under the guidance of others who have gone through it, to develop the capacity to communicate, express feelings, achieve joy and satisfaction in joint activity, based in the family-marriage relationship—and the church relationship too, in many instances. The guides and materials are both didactic tools and devices to encourage interaction and self-expression. There is a stress on the program "rhythm" for the weekend, the day, the evening, as the interaction is developed, guided, climaxed, and resolved in line with overall goals.

Thus one concept of a marriage encounter weekend pattern, inspired by the teachings of Fr. Calvo, begins with a presentation and sharing of their experiences by the leadership couple. This "fans the coals." Then, there is a period of personal reflection to be written out and shared. A dialogue—an open, two-way, free-response exchange—follows. At the end a family member reports to the others as moderator. Each phase is stimulated, supported, guided, by structured presentations, exercises, prayer, group meals, and musical, cultural, and spiritual experiences.[25]

In one formulation, the "stages of the weekend are summarized as follows:

The first stage of the weekend: The encounter with self or "Why am I afraid to tell you who I am?"

The second stage of the weekend: The encounter with each other or "Does our marriage indicate symptoms of spiritual divorce?"

The third stage of the weekend: The encounter with God or "Dialogue alone doesn't save."

The fourth stage of the weekend: The encounter with the world or "A sign for all to see."[26]

Many of the programs offer experiences, courses, and seminars, while sometimes trying to change ongoing family living patterns. Some continuity is offered by such movements as National Marriage Encounter, Worldwide Marriage Encounter, the Catholic Family Movement, and CANA. Generally, however, there is no continuity. Some of the leaders in the National Marriage Encounter express the hope that the special weekend patterns may eventually translate into a new form of local community life.

Where couples are unable to get away for a "traditional" forty-four-hour structured marriage encounter weekend, there has been local development of "marriage enrichment" variations in the church. Several models exist, such as the four-session, two-day, one-and-a-half-day, and one-day models, with specific programs, exercises, and processes.[27]

We have cited statistics from two Protestant denominations. Clearly these are large endeavors, but it is difficult to assemble hard data, given overlap, multiple participation (it becomes a way of life for some couples), and the casual nature of some of the contacts. (Even the more formal social services report rather poorly.) Catholic leadership estimates that over the past twenty years some 15 to 17 percent of all Catholic families have been "touched" by the various encounter, enrichment, and charismatic movements.

National Marriage Encounter, an ecumenical movement that, nonetheless, is dominantly and visibly Christian and to a good degree Catholic in its operation and literature defines its purpose as "the renewal of marriage and family life." Early in 1980 it counted 220 affiliate groups in the United States and Canada that were conducting programs continuously.

Many of the programs rely less on religious definitions and identifications. For example, one of the many secular variations of the marriage enrichment weekend is conducted in conjunction with a counselling program for couples at the University of Pennsylvania Medical School. The initiator, Dr. Larry Hof, states: "It in no way replaces therapy for couples who need therapy. But it is helpful and, I think, shortens the therapy required." In any case, this program does interrelate encounter and therapy, an approach quite different from that of the church-related movements. A journalist summarizes Hof's approach as follows:

> When couples who are undergoing counselling at the medical school center agree that they want to salvage their marriage, they can sign up for an enrichment weekend. The program, a model for similar sessions being developed elsewhere, is held at a conference center outside Philadelphia, and its basic aim is to help the couples participating gain greater mutual respect and confidence.
>
> On Friday evening the couples hear an introductory talk and are encouraged to set "personal goals" for the upcoming weekend. The idea is to "share" goals with one's spouse, then with others in the group. The evening ends with what Hof says is a group circle, with the couples entering into "a very light physical-touch experience." For example, they might sit in a wide circle and meditate on the possibilities of a better marriage, as they touch hands. The idea is to provide a sense of intimacy.
>
> Saturday starts with a "marriage lifeline session" in which the couples tell about their marriage and about where they feel they are heading in it. There are more exercises, such as writing down individual marriage objectives and responsibilities as well as a "marital intimacy checklist" to help achieve greater closeness.
>
> The weekend closes with a renewal of a couple's marriage vows. "It can help troubled people who still care," says Thelma Dixon-Murphy, a New York City marriage therapist. "Some couples come back with an emotional 'high'—the question is, can they sustain it?"[28]

While the couple is generally the unit of attention, some of the programs include children as well. The following, from a major book in the field, describes the beginning of a report on a "family enrichment weekend":

> Jack and Mary Ann and their children, Kathy, Bill, and Anne, were huddled cross-legged on the floor. The children were looking intently at their parents. Kathy had just asked her mother and dad how and when they met for the first time.
>
> "You kids remember how we met, don't you?" Jack asked with a "surely you do know, don't you?" look on his face.
>
> The children's faces reflected their total lack of information. Not one of them could recall anything about the unique and exciting events which surrounded Jack and Mary Ann's first introduction to each other and their wartime romance.
>
> In the next few minutes Jack and Mary Ann related their first meeting, a blind date arranged by Mary Ann's roommate with a young serviceman

who was then home on leave from duty. Something of their joy and excitement was communicated as they told the children about their first date and the remaining evenings of Jack's leave that they spent together. Mary Ann's face was radiant with the joy of memories as she shared with the children how deeply she and Jack had felt about each other and how much they had enjoyed being together. Jack filled in the details of their wedding, which took place when he returned from the service several months later.

The Traberts were "playing detective," which is the first activity in the Family Enrichment Weekend. The children were looking for "clues," and Jack and Mary Ann were responding by telling them about their introduction, their courtship, their marriage, and the circumstances surrounding the birth of each of their delightful children.

The occasion was the first Family Enrichment Weekend. The "Wesley Weds" (the church school class which we attend) were sponsoring the weekend at a youth camp twenty miles from Des Moines.

It all began when Jan Boelter, the program chairperson of "Wesley Weds," asked us to lead a weekend experience for class members and their children. "We want something that will help our families—something that will draw us closer together and help us to communicate better," Jan said. "We don't want to just go to a camp and goof around and have recreation; we've done that. We would like to have some growing experiences with our children."[29]

Despite the strong sense of fellowship and an ecumenical spirit in the marriage encounter movement,[30] there are diverse conceptual and methodological currents even in the programs with religious ties. There is general agreement that the origins were in Spain and that National Marriage Encounter came to the United States as a service to couples in 1967. It was organized as a weekend experience. Two direct affiliates, Worldwide Marriage Encounter and FIRES (the organization in which Fr. Gabriel Calvo, the initiator of the movement, now works), are large and popular. The split between National Marriage Encounter and Worldwide is largely the difference between a dominantly Christian ecumenical program (with some Jewish participation) and one that is overwhelmingly Catholic. There is a Jewish Family Encounter too, another offshoot. Many related forms of programming have also emerged in a completely secular vein. About a dozen religious and secular enrichment movements and programs exchange views and cooperate through CAMEO, Council of Marriage Enrichment Organizations.

The core elements appear to be leadership by previously encountered couples; the use of questions, workbooks, cassettes, self-reports, and structured dialogues to elicit materials that participants produce and reflect upon together; a strong degree of social group and peer support, even inspiration; a specific time-phased rhythm that tends to create a climax and sense of accomplishment in the form of enriched mutual understanding and love. The quality of this approach and some of the procedure are further suggested by an excerpt from one of the most "specific" of the "process" reports:

M.E. Materials
Guidelines for Dialogue

W   1. Make your reflection a love letter.

2. Do your written reflections separately but with your partner foremost in mind.

3. Describe feelings in fullest detail to trigger partner's memory.

4. Refer to partner with direct address frequently in the letter, using name or endearing term, but avoiding sentimentality for its own sake.

5. Be honest, but make it attractive; invite your partner to feel it—even though feelings can be shared with gentleness.

E   6. Exchange notebooks lovingly, and without comment; go to your partner's notebook seeking the person, not information.

7. Work at the reading and dialogue proper with as much intensity as the written reflection.

8. Read the reflection twice, once for the feelings and once seeking the person behind the feelings.

D   9. After two readings, identify and share the feelings triggered. Begin conversation with, "What are your feelings now that you have read my letter?"

10. Select the feeling(s) most meaningful to the relationship which would be explored so the relationship may grow.

11. Describe your partner's feelings back to him, suggesting tentatively what you're picking up, giving him/her an opportunity to share more of himself/herself.

12. Search through your partner's feeling until you live it as your own, working along with your partner—word pictures, intensity, duration, a time you felt the same way—manifesting a desire to know the person more.

13. Avoid attacking or judging your partner's feelings or defending your own.

14. If any decision comes in dialogue, it's not a dialogue.

S   15. Select question for next dialogue.[31]

Inevitably there are different interpretations of the conceptual founda-
tions and key dynamics of the processes. The general premise for marriage
and family enrichment programs, as put by Otto, is that

> all persons and all relationships are functioning at a fraction of their
> potential and that, in every couple or family, there is the potential for
> growth in the relationship as well as the possibility of personal growth,
> leading to a more fulfilling togetherness. It is a further hypothesis that
> every union, or family, can be strengthened through the periodic regen-
> eration and renewal offered by marriage and family enrichment
> programs.[32]

Despite the widespread notion that "enrichment" is for normal, successful couples, however, even Otto states that "the need for enrichment and
personal growth is often not recognized by couples, and this can lead to a
subtle and insidious debilitation of the relationship over a period of time."[33]
One report suggests why participants appear to have normal lives yet
respond to the "encounter" opportunity:

> In these "gray" situations, one spouse or the other has turned gray or
> translucent in the eyes of the other. The image of the other spouse has
> become almost invisible against the background of the environment
> within which the couple is living and operating. One of the marriage
> partners has lost sight of the other and usually cannot realize why.
>   The classic case I dealt with involved a couple in their early thirties,
> with two daughters, 11 and 8. The husband was employed in a semi-
> supervisory job with a large manufacturing concern. They were buying a
> very nice middle-class home, had two cars, went to church regularly,
> had a significant sum in savings, and had every appearance of having "the
> world by the tail on a downhill pull."
>   In my interview with the wife, her answers to all the usual questions
> about his drinking habits, his running around with other women, and his
> being financially irresponsible were answered in the negative. All he did
> was work, bring her the pay check, come home in the evenings, play
> with the children, have dinner, watch TV for a while, then get up the
> next morning and start the process all over again. They were both quite
> active in the activities of the church, and had both attained about average
> educational status.
>   After about fifteen minutes of discussing the problem with the client, I
> remarked that about 95% of the women I knew would probably trade
> places with her, sight unseen, if given a chance to. Her response was,
> "That may be so, but I can't take it any longer. I am under a doctor's care,
> am taking tranquilizers regularly, and feel I am going to be ready for the
> head-shrinker if I don't get out of this trap."

Her real problem was that her husband and her marriage were getting lost in the woodwork of her life. . . .

There are many variations and manifestations of the Grayness Syndrome which I have encountered, but the essential element of the problem is always the same. The two have never approached unity. There is none of the drunkenness or violence or infidelity or fiscal irresponsibility which are comparatively so easy to cope with. Marriage Encounter may hold the only hope for coping with the Grayness Syndrome.[34]

Fr. Calvo also rejects the notion that marriage encounter is reserved for couples without problems: "In the beginning weekends were not just for 'good marriages.' This is a false division. . . . It also gives the mistaken notion that some couples have made it. . . . Any sincere couple has to admit that there are many times when they are in trouble."[35] Nonetheless, it certainly is the case that the weekend retreats and related activities are conducted in a context of normalcy, competence, and mutual aid. Efforts are made to screen out the obviously ill and troubled. People whose marriages are in crisis or who ask for counselling are not accepted in most encounter programs. The programs recruit people who define their marriages as going well, but who want even more satisfaction. Self-selected and enthusiastic couples seek to qualify as leaders and to complete ACME certification requirements.

A balanced perspective is contained in Otto's summation:

There is also a widespread recognition by members of the helping professions that a large proportion of marriages and families are "subclinical"—subclinical in the sense that they have problems with which they need help and that they are functioning much below optimum despite the couple's love and dedication to each other and their commitment to continuing the union. The vast majority of these families will not seek help, because the problems are of the low-level debilitating kind, never severe enough to precipitate a major crisis for which help must be sought. Recognition of the presence of this subclinical stratum in turn has convinced many professionals of the necessity for preventive programs such as the enrichment movement, which is essentially preventive in nature.[36]

The literature of the field confirms the conclusion of David Mace that these major so-called marriage encounter activities are not encounter groups in the sense that they do not employ confrontational tactics or deliberately evoke negative emotion. Participant couples are not pressured if they wish to hold back.[37] By now, however, the broader label "marriage enrichment" also covers a diversity of educational and group programs loosely derived from T-group and sensitivity training of earlier decades, the human potential movement, and the various types of encounter. These intensive group experiences may take various forms.

Similarly, while Fr. Calvo denies that the essence of the goal is improved communication, because to him "openness means sharing my relationship with God," there are others, particularly in the derivative or independently developed parallel secular programs, who focus on communication skills per se. The Interpersonal Communication Program (formally known as the Minnesota Couples Communication Program), for example, which reports that it has served some 75,000 couples over ten years and has trained 1,500 instructor teams throughout the United States, Canada, and several other countries, cites twenty-five "impact evaluation studies" as evidence of its effectiveness, measured largely through the development of self-disclosure skills and self-reported marital adjustments and relationship patterns. A recent assessment, however, shows that much of the communication skill has been lost by follow-up time, even though some relationship gains persist.[38] Dr. B. G. Guerney and his collaborators have developed an approach to strengthening the family known as "relationship enhancement." The emphasis is on training in the skills of interpersonal reaction: the approach has been applied to husband-wife, parent-child, and therapist-patient relationships. The techniques fit under the general rubric of "behaviorist" but are in an educational tradition and have some "humanistic" roots.[39]

This explicit focus on communication skill and process, in Relationship Enhancement, Interpersonal Communication, and similar programs, rather than on content per se, clearly is secular and is heavily didactic. Unlike some of the national movements, it does not draw upon or assume religious content. It stresses skill training rather than positive emotional experience alone. We have described such programs in this chapter rather than in Chapter 4 and offer the excerpt below only because both the secular and the sectarian enrichment programs must now be seen as sizable, as covering a wide range of activities, ranging from the experiential emphasis of the encounter to various forms of skill training, and as not always easily distinguishable:

The following excerpt is from a feedback episode in the Minnesota Couples Communication Program—group members are providing feedback to Jim and Carol, one of the participant couples, immediately after a three-minute dialogue between them. In the exercise each couple discusses a real issue for three minutes, and then receives five to ten minutes of feedback from other group members. Feedback focuses on the skills used or missing in their exchange. The exercise occurs towards the end of Session 2, at a point when group members have been introduced to several of the skills and concepts taught in the program. . . .

Participant A: "I heard you make a clear 'intention statement,' Jim, when you told Carol that you would like some time for just yourself when you get home from work."

Participant B: "Yeah, he did, and I heard Carol . . ."

Instructor: (interrupting) "Will you speak directly to Carol?"

Participant B: "Okay, Carol, I heard you make a clear 'intention statement' when you told Jim that you want some adult companionship after spending all day with the kids."

Participant C: "I heard some 'checking out' from both; for example, Jim, when you asked Carol whether she thought you were trying to avoid her when you bury your nose in the newspaper, and, Carol, when you asked Jim how he felt about your wanting more of his company in the evening."

Instructor: "Did you note the absence of any skills that you would have liked to hear Carol and Jim use in their dialogue?"

Participant C: "I can't recall either of you saying how you *felt*—no 'feeling statements.' Carol, I was especially aware of this when you were talking about being alone all day with the kids and then Jim comes home and starts reading the paper. I was thinking you might be feeling deprived, or hurt, or angry, or . . ." [another participant, interrupting] ". . . All of the above."

The focus is on skills, on process rather than content. This is an education program in which partners practice using effective communication skills in dialogue around meaningful issues and receive immediate feedback from other participants on skills demonstrated and skills missing from their dialogue. (If one of the group members begins to offer solutions, or begins to speculate about why a couple is having a particular problem, the instructor will interrrupt and encourage the participant to limit his feedback to identifying skills used or skills lacking in the dialogue.)

In addition to skill practice in the group session, structure is provided for transfer of learning to situations outside the group through practice assignments to be carried out at home between group sessions.[40]

The range of program forms is also suggested with reference to the Family Clusters program, an educationally oriented effort that is unified largely through the training activities of Dr. Margaret M. Sawin of Rochester, New York, a doctor of education whose activities go back to 1972. The model is specifically differentiated from therapy; its educational activities generate a small-group support structure. It has some "community organ-

ization" aspects, serving to help new residents to find their way in suburban areas and facilitating cooperative child care and grocery purchases.[41]
We quote from an explanatory brochure:

> Family Enrichment is the process of enriching or bettering the
> strengths and attributes which provide growth for family members and
> the family as a complete unit. It is an educational process for well-
> functioning families to make family life even more mutually satisfy-
> ing. . . .
>   A Family Cluster is a leader-led group of four or five complete family
> units who contract to meet together periodically over an extended
> period of time for shared educational experiences related to their hopes,
> concerns, joys, problems, dreams, questions of living in relationship
> with the family. A Cluster provides mutual support, provides training in
> skills which facilitate their living within families, and allows for celebra-
> tion of their life and beliefs together.

The methods are a direct outgrowth of the "training laboratory" models
of the National Training Labs. There are three types of foci for each
laboratory: for family groups, including children and youth; for persons in
training; for experienced leaders.

> Its variables include a *weeklong residential* setting with families who are
> organized into clusters. It also includes a number of skillshops for
> learning skills and theory related to the Family Cluster Model (i.e.,
> human interaction skills, design/planning skills, family systems under-
> standings, group dynamics and leadership, and other related skills).
> Trainees will lead cluster sessions and will receive supervision by skilled
> staff persons. The Laboratory Training School builds total community of
> everyone present: family members, persons-in-training, and staff.[42]

The activities are church-sponsored, covering a range of Protestant
denominations and some Catholic parishes. They are strongly represented
in Unitarian fellowships and churches.

All training events are ecumenical in nature and open to persons of
various faiths and denominations. They are also open to persons affiliated
with "secular" agencies or organizations interested in preventative
education with multi-family groups. Training events have a theological
base which is existentially-oriented rather than doctrinaire-oriented.[43]

Herbert Otto sums up a 1973–1974 study (one of the few surveys
available) based on information from thirty professional workers in this
field. While the numerical estimates must be seen as guesses, the variabil-

ity of theory and practice is tapped: the techniques of this "movement" as a whole, as seen by these experts, involve group discussion, structured experiences, two-person experiences, and non-verbal experiences. There are sensitivity sessions, encounter sessions, occasional use of films, and many kinds of structured "exercises" to increase sensitivity and to facilitate discussion; it is mostly a cognitive approach to the development of insight.

The weekend is the most popular time for the programs to operate, but some combine classes with weekend retreats. Only about 15 percent do not involve residential or overnight facilities. Groups vary from four or five couples to ten or fifteen. Classes tend to fifteen couples. Classes meet in churches or private homes; fees vary substantially and some only meet costs if they are church-related. There is a fair amount of use of evaluation forms, feedback, questionnaires.

Given these reports, the label "movement" must be considered as loosely applied. It is an eclectic development and one that may not be a movement at all since "at one end of the continuum would be the Roman Catholic Marriage Encounter Program, where there is maximum structure with group interaction restricted to feedback; at the other end of the continuum would be the programs utilizing mostly or entirely sensitivity or encounter sessions." At the latter extreme, the sensitivity or the encounter overwhelms the cognitive material, and it is not clear what is in and what is not in. There are also some "leaderless" marriage and family enrichment and encounter groups and "family clusters," which may in turn be self-help and cooperative enterprises (see Chapter 6) or also weekend group experiences.[44]

Otto's informants in fact report on a diversity of family enrichment weekends, family camps, an enrichment program called a Care Lab, "Family Home Evenings," Christian marriage retreats, ecumenical marriage encounter, Gestalt and transactional variations. A variety of detailed programs are presented from several "enrichment" labs with emphasis on exercises and techniques, including detailed schedules for days and weekends, and a bibliography of books, cassettes, and exercises that can be purchased. The various authors in the field continue to have different explanations of what is going on. Thus, Douglas A. Anderson, who writes about the family growth groups (family clusters), regards this as a mode of family education. Similarly, a description of family camping cites it as an opportunity for parents to model their marriage as they would like children to see it (as opposed merely to parenting behavior). In short, some of the marriage and family enrichment reports and papers stress training in relationships or simply freedom created in an encounter-type setting to communicate, whereas many others are educational, offer modelling, and suggest norms and values in the very way in which they structure the operation and offer exercises. Otto himself is quite critical of traditional family education since it teaches individuals, not families as groups, does not see families as growing and changing systems, and does not involve all family members. He believes that the family enrichment movement corrects this.[45]

In contrast to the big-city-centeredness of some of the more specialized pastoral counselling elaborations, and the appeal to the middle-class parishioner-clients of the more intensive therapeutic services, one gains the impression of a largely, but not exclusively, lower-middle-class and skilled working-class, middle-American appeal of these encounter programs. Its obviously large appeal suggests the potency of a church base, of church sponsorship, or—in the secular variations as well—of these relatively structured and non-threatening pathways to education, training, and larger community interrelations.

A variety of researchers has called attention to research weaknesses of most (but not all) efforts to validate marriage enrichment formally, but they argue, too, that one cannot dismiss the overwhelming weight of testimony that the initial marriage enrichment weekend experience "creates an interpersonal atmosphere of acceptance and trust which is conducive to increased mutual self-disclosure and awareness of marital strengths. Many couples report an increase in positive feelings toward their partner and their relationship as a result of participation in such a program."[46] It is argued that the strong motivation to work on one's relationships and to accept change that results from the experience should then be utilized to facilitate participation in longer-term skill-oriented (relationship enhancement) programs. One such sequential model moves from "intensive retreat," to special "spaced relationship skill training," and then to an "ongoing support group."[47] This is one of several proposals that marriage enrichment become part of the full professional repertoire of family support services, whether secular or religious, and be integrated with other components for individual use—whether in therapeutic or "preventive" contexts.

Is There a Church-Related Helping System?

Whether one refers to the church educational activities, the "movements," or the range of helping services under the general rubric of pastoral counselling, the programs described in this chapter touch large numbers of people. They are a significant element in the picture of who helps families; no policy or programming discussion realistically can or should ignore them, yet they are often "unknown" or considered irrevelant by the human services community.

Evidence as to effects and effectiveness is inevitably spotty and some of what occurs in unregulated free-standing counselling, on the face of it, can hardly seem responsible or competent in the eyes of observers. Nonetheless, self-directing citizens participate in large numbers and come back. Consumers spend their money for fees. Religious leaders are enthusiastic about results. Some narrow research studies are available and do report effectiveness. For the present, little more should be expected by way of assessment of so diverse a group of activities offered to so many types of people, with many different individual and institutional goals. In the long run, systematic evaluation will need to focus narrowly, program by program, group by group, to describe impact precisely, whether to improve methods or to argue for or against support. For the present, programming and policy questions clearly are in need of open discussion.

It could be argued that some of what we have described here is not a "family" service, in the same sense that traditional child welfare does not always focus on family units. Nonetheless, if we consider the three "clusters" of activity, we note that each is somewhat family-related: Some of the pastoral counselling intervenes with the family unit or the couple as a unit, although much of it focuses on the individual or individuals together in a group. (As much was said in our discussion of family service agencies.) Much of the family ministry activity that is educational in form is family- and couple-oriented. Indeed, family ministry is typically a family program. Much of marriage encounter and the marriage and family enrichment is a family or a couple program. Again, this is more characteristically a family activity than are practically all modes of counselling.

Not all of these programs we have described are religious in method, orientation, or derivation. Indeed, there is substantial evidence that church and synagogue personnel have responded to secular educational, service, self-help, and treatment developments and have adapted them to their own contexts. On the other hand, there also is a clear trend to build new forms of service into the pastoral role, to use the pastoral role for case finding and linkage with other helping services, and to give some counselling and group programs special character that derives from religious content. In some programs (some of the family cluster and marriage encounter activities, for example), there is clear and deliberate use of a theological base. Depending on the auspice, it may be generalized and ecumenical or oriented to a particular church or doctrine. On the other hand, at the end of the pastoral counselling continuum, which reaches into the private practice of psychotherapy, the religious connection is only occasional and case-specific, as it might well be in any type of setting with a sensitive practitioner.

As we have seen, what starts as pastoral counselling sometimes becomes a free-standing agency or an independent practitioner without church relatedness. One of our informants made what to us seems to be a relevant comment: "I guess you could be a religious man at large; but a pastoral counsellor really is part of an agency, a community."

Is there, then, a separate church-related service system? The answer appears to be yes and no. A Catholic diocesan program, integrated with a local Catholic Charities effort, offers a case-finding network based in the parish, educational programs that are family-focused, close support of and hospitality to the social enrichment and encounter movements, and specific ties to religious programming. Several Protestant denominations offer well-structured family ministries as well, featuring elaborate family educational offerings, strong participation in marriage encounter and family enrichment programming, active pastoral counselling integrated with the ongoing work of the minister, and close linkage (depending on the denomination) with either secular or religious personal social services and counselling programs. This much said, it also is true that many of the secular and religious educational "movements" and counselling offerings are free-standing, operate on a community and not a church-related basis, and do not closely link with others. Thus we have service "systems" under this overall rubric, evidence that other service "systems" could be created, but also considerable evidence of fragmentation, unrelatedness, diverse standards, and sometimes even a semblance of irresponsibility and anarchy.

But is the question really fair? Does not a concern for "system" make this kind of service to families too formal, thus sacrificing the values of church-relatedness? Yes, in the sense that all bureaucratization is different from primary group experience. If a church program truly is conceptualized and organized as system, however, it would appear able to offer users, as needed, some of the advantages of either primary group or formal organization. We have reviewed the range of possibilities. There are, first, the self-led informal family educational efforts and "enrichment" programs. Then, the "movements," led by couples who have "made an encounter" one weekend. Also, the informal help by the priest, minister, or rabbi in the context of his religious role, an occasional, incidental, not structured, intervention. Then, the somewhat more organized courses, seminars, and treatment and helping groups. Finally, professionally offered and controlled individual service and treatment.

When each of these elements is understood and used in its appropriate way, such a continuum has distinct advantages: people want and use help and service at various points on three continuums—from the didactic-educational to the intensively experiential therapeutic, from the self-help to the professional, from the secular to the deeply religious. A pluralistic helping society will value each of these and offer it a secure base for development.

6 Families Help Each Other and Themselves

There is no "typical" self-help group or "typical" self-help group meeting. In fact, many self-help groups have no regular member meetings. Many of the groups are oriented to the needs of the severely troubled or outcast; some are focused on social action. Any given self-help organization does not necessarily address itself to the questions or the families on which we are here focused. Where there are groups whose activities can be described as "helping families"—or families helping themselves—and where such groups have member-participation sessions, the meetings may not be accessible to outsiders.

In a classroom of the local university, tables were pushed to the side and chairs were set up in a circle for the 7:00 P.M. self-help group meeting. Eight members arrived, women and men in their thirties to fifties—a retired plumber, a Hispanic bookkeeper, a black librarian, a media consultant, and several housewives. These people had been brought together by a very important factor: each of them had an aging, ailing parent.

Blanche, a stout woman in her fifties, acted as the group facilitator this evening. "I'd like to welcome you to our monthly meeting. I'll begin as usual by reading the guidelines we've developed for our group discussion. First, everything said here is confidential. Members can feel free to say anything they wish. Share as much or as little as you want. Second, speak in the first person. Talk about your own experience. Third, ask questions for clarification of what is being said but avoid asking 'leading questions' that require analytical responses. Okay, I know we're anxious to talk about what we've been going through these past few weeks. Who would like to begin?"

Marv, a dark, curly-haired man in his fifties, divorced and recently unemployed, leaned forward. "You know that I moved into my eighty-three-year-old mother's home after she became too ill to stay alone. I really don't mind being there doing things for her. There's a certain comfort and security I feel in this role. She took care of me and now it's my turn to take

The major part of this chapter was prepared by Brenda G. McGowan. We have rewritten it to meet the needs of the volume as a whole.

care of her. The problem is she resents it when I leave the house for more than an hour. She cries. I feel like I'm abandoning her and I feel guilty as hell. I don't know what to do. I've got to get out—see my friends, take care of personal business. Also, I'm gonna go nuts if I don't."

"God, I know how you feel. Have you thought of bringing in a homecare attendant to take care of her when you can't be there?" someone suggested. "That way she'll feel that you do care about her and you'll be able to get away and live your own life a little."

"Yes, I thought of that, but I really don't think she would allow a stranger in her house and I can't afford something like that," responded Marv.

Fred, who lives in a neighborhood not too far from Marv, offered, "There's a homecare agency that I've contacted and they send me very reliable people. And they'll be able to tell you about financial aid available for this type of service."

"Which reminds me," said Blanche. "It might be a good idea to have someone from the Department for the Aging come in and talk to us about benefits and services for the elderly."

Marie, a thin, nervous woman, said to the group, "You know, I'm just beginning to realize why I'm here. I thought at first I came for my mother but now I realize I came for myself. I was beginning to develop all kinds of psychosomatic illnesses—chest pains, tiredness. Since I've been coming and talking out my fears and guilt and learned that everyone else in this room has similar doubts and anxieties, I don't feel so crazy. For instance, I heard someone in the group say how angry and resentful she felt after being awakened for the third time in the middle of the night to help her mother to the bathroom. I realized that I'm not the only one who reacts selfishly sometimes and that it's perfectly normal. It's okay to be angry with my mother sometimes but love her too."

Another member remarked on how important it was for members to take care of their own health, physical and mental. She encouraged Marv to get out once in a while and not to punish himself for it. "If you were to get sick or develop emotional problems, then you really wouldn't be of any help to your mom."

At 9:00 P.M. Blanche thanked everyone for coming and sharing. She reminded members to talk about the group to friends and neighbors and invite interested persons to the next meeting. "Meanwhile, we all have each other's phone numbers, and can feel free to call one another if we need to talk."*

Although there has been steady growth in the range and number of self-help groups in this country since World War II, the vast explosion has

*This example was provided by Carol Eisman, Associate Director, New York City Self-Help Clearinghouse.

occurred since the mid-1960s. A directory of self-help groups compiled in 1961–1962 listed 265 different groups;[1] an estimate made in the mid-1970s assumed as many as one-half million groups;[2] and in the late 1970s the *Hastings Center Report* suggested that "about 5 million people in the United States now belong to self-help groups of various kinds. Every major disease, organ, condition, and complaint has a group. Their names provide an encyclopedia of modern physical, mental, and social ills."[3]

Unfortunately, there is no way at present to catalogue the self-help groups currently in operation. New ones are started daily; others frequently merge, shift focus, or cease operation; and many of the smaller ones have no formal organizational base. However, a brief look at the dates of relevant publications reveal that the self-help phenomenon has only recently begun to attract extensive professional attention.[4] Therefore, as more effort is made to study this phenomenon, attempts will undoubtedly be made to obtain more precise data regarding its scope. A National Self-Help Clearinghouse was established in New York City late in the 1970s, and a national research institute on self-help was launched at the same time by the Center for Urban Affairs at Northwestern University. These developments not only offer the possibility of obtaining systematic data on self-help groups, but they also mark the institutionalization of the self-help movement.

Despite the information gaps, there appears to be agreement that during the past decade the self-help movement has emerged as a significant, if unanticipated, component of the changing social scene. Frequent and extravagant claims are made in both the professional literature and the popular press regarding the scope, durability, and efficacy of the movement. Questions clearly should be raised here as to what role self-help groups play in the provision of family services: Who uses these groups? What needs do they meet? Why are they expanding so rapidly? What relationship do they have to services provided under more traditional professional agencies?

Why Self-Help?

The self-help or mutual aid tradition has roots in man's earliest history. Evolution involved not only the survival of the fittest in the Darwinian sense but also an ongoing parallel process of mutual support and social assistance among people struggling to survive in a hostile environment.[5] By the time of the Middle Ages, the practice of mutual aid was widespread in Europe. This aid was extended, however, only to members of particular in-groups; outsiders had to struggle on their own. Consequently, to ensure that each local parish would provide for all its poor, the Elizabethan Poor Laws were enacted, initiating a policy that has led to almost continuous expansion and bureaucratization of formal service provision for people in need. Dissatisfaction with the very restrictive provision of the Poor Laws, in conjunction with adverse social conditions created by the Industrial Revolution, led to the spontaneous development of mutual aid associations among groups of industrial workers. The most noteworthy of these were the Friendly Societies established in England during the nineteenth century and the consumer cooperatives established at the same time in a number of European countries.

Although early residents of the American colonies carried on the European tradition of mutual aid, the vast expanses of land available to individual families and the absence of strong social controls soon promoted an ethic of rugged individualism that undercut the early communal tradition. Nonetheless, the Industrial Revolution in this country also led to the development of consumer cooperatives and mutual aid associations among workers. Mutual aid was important, too, in frontier settlements. Although many of these efforts did not survive the disruption caused by the Civil War, the establishment and growth of the trade union movement during the late nineteenth and early twentieth centuries carried on the tradition. And this same period witnessed the widespread development of religious and ethnic organizations that encouraged mutual assistance among various immigrant groups.

It is interesting to note that the earliest mutual aid involved "average" people in shared circumstances. The more problem-focused self-help groups that have proliferated so rapidly in recent years were unknown during this early period. Alcoholics Anonymous (AA), for example, the first and perhaps the best known of these latter groups, was not established until 1935.[6] One explanation for this relatively late development is that, as long as most people were preoccupied with problems of survival, they had little time or energy for individual psychological needs or behavioral problems. Alfred Katz hypothesizes a common theme:

> Historically, then, the essence of mutual aid has been the need for and creation of group coping mechanisms that ensure man's survival in the face of environmental threats and deprivations.
> People with like needs and goals persistently seek each other out, no matter what the historical circumstances. The problems people face and the approaches they take to solve them may differ, but there is a constant element in people's need to give and take help from one another.[7]

Why the recent upsurge, then? Many theories have been advanced as to why the self-help concept has come into prominence. For one thing, despite our tradition of rugged individualism, the movement is consonant with such other American traditions as populism, pragmatism, pluralism, and the Protestant ethic. In addition, a number of more immediate antecedents can be identified—so many, in fact, that it has been suggested that the movement's growth is overdetermined.[8]

Almost all commentators on the self-help phenomenon relate the rise of this movement to the conditions of modern society, pointing out that the formation of self-help groups is a natural response to the alienation and powerlessness people experience in the face of urbanization, industrialization, and dehumanizing social institutions.[9] Implicit in this explanation is the assumption that there is a universal human need for supportive primary group ties and that during every period of history man has found different ways of affiliating with others in order to satisfy this need. Sol Tax, for example, comments:

> Normal human individuals require social support: and self-help groups established for any purpose may be presumed to provide significant support. In a society like ours so many "social functions" have been preempted by impersonal institutions that traditional primary and small groups have tended to wither away. . . . The movement toward increasing development of *ad hoc* self-help groups is therefore understandable, whether or not these might serve the need better or worse than might the strengthening of traditional primary groups.[10]

The interesting question then becomes, "What is it about our current society that makes it appropriate for such fundamental bonding to begin to occur around adults faced with common afflictions or patterns of deviance?"[11] One explanation is that, in European countries where a comprehensive approach to institutionalized social welfare programs is accepted, multi-focus self-help efforts often enjoy active government support and are able to concentrate on devising ways in which programs can best be implemented because there is little conflict regarding social goals. In contrast, the United States, where the ethic is reluctant and provision episodic in many fields, groups must often concentrate on changing public policy and attitudes in order to establish the validity of their goals and programs. Hence they are forced to adopt a single-issue or single-problem focus in order to have political impact.[12]

The growth of bureaucracy and professionalism has also stimulated the recent development of self-help groups. The convergence of bureaucratic and professional influence in modern human service agencies has created a monolithic force in response to which self-help organizations may represent an effort "to substitute the autonomy and solidarity of members . . . for bureaucratization and professionalization."[13] Similarly, as Matthew

Dumont points out, "the conjunction of this growing reliance by government on professionals and the increasing complexity of professionalism
leads to a concentration, authority, and unaccountability of power that
would stagger the imagination of the authors of the Constitution." Dumont
goes on to suggest that two of the major developments of the 1960s,
advocacy and consumer control, arose in response to this "professionalization of power" and that the self-help movement is a natural culmination of
these developments.[14]

To say that professionalism is a major factor contributing to the development of self-help groups, however, does not address the issue, suggested
by Morton Lieberman and Leonard Borman, of why the response to this
concentration of power tends to be the establishment of formal groups
organized around a single issue or problem. By specializing in this way,
self-help groups would seem to be adopting one of the primary elements
underlying the bureaucratic and professional forces they are attempting to
oppose. As suggested earlier, it may be necessary for such groups to
specialize in order to acquire sufficient power in the public policy arena;
but the very fact that many of these groups endeavor to exert some type of
public influence lends credence to an alternative explanation for the rise of
self-help groups offered by commentators who focus on unmet needs
and/or inadequate service provisions.

One commentator suggests that the self-help trend "reflects the serious
cutting back in political and professional resources to meet people's needs.
But at the same time it is a response to the newly widening gap between
America's social promise and its social practice."[15] Others who take similar
positions highlight the tensions created by inadequate resources, ineffec-
tive service strategies, and consumer desire for a more egalitarian relationship with service providers.[16] In a related vein, Frank Baker offers the
following hypothesis regarding the rise of self-help groups:

> Natural support systems come into existence or disappear in a cyclical
> sequence in counterpoint to developments in the professional caregiving
> network of a particular community. When a problem becomes acute
> among a significant element of a population without being given ade-
> quate attention and recognition by formal caregiving systems, natural
> support systems arise to meet the need. As these natural support sys-
> tems spontaneously evolve, they tend to move towards a formal struc-
> ture and the leaders of the movement become increasingly
> professionalized.[17]

Since the self-help movement is clearly not a unitary phenomenon, all
these explanations may be valid under certain circumstances. As different
groups arise to meet different needs, so they are likely to derive from

different sources. In an attempt at an overview, Katz and Eugene Bender have suggested that the minimal conditions identified as essential to the development of all social movements also seem to characterize the establishment of a wide range of self-help groups:

> There must be some source of dissatisfaction arising from a person's day-to-day living pattern. These discontents are shared with others and not merely internalized as private agendas to be reckoned with at some future, unspecified date. The dissatisfaction contains an element of *deprivation*, otherwise collective action is unlikely to occur. The individual perceives that some *possessed quality* (status, power, material goods, social acceptance) has been taken away or withheld when it is his due.[18]

These conditions, however, would seem to be applicable only to the formal, single-issue groups on which Katz has focused his research efforts. As we will see, there are many different views on what constitutes a self-help or mutual aid group, and further research is needed to determine what factors give rise to natural support groups organized on a more informal basis, many of which have a multi-issue focus. This is important, because it is these groups, not those of the type described by Katz, that are most likely to provide broad-based family services.

What Is a Self-Help Group?

The literature on self-help or mutual aid groups, although relatively limited compared to that on other types of family services, is very broad, somewhat uneven, and occasionally contradictory. In an article entitled "Mutual Help Organizations: Interpretations in the Literature," Marie Killilea has written a superb analysis of the categorizations of mutual help organizations found in 220 different sources. She identifies twenty different interpretations of self-help groups ranging from secular, religious, social-movement, and agent-of-social-control definitions to alternative caregiving system, professional adjunct, and intentional community.[19]

In relation to family services, there would seem to be four interpretations of self-help that need to be considered. First is the "do-it-yourself" concept manifested most dramatically in the recent rash of self-help books on almost every facet of modern life. One need only visit any local book-store to realize that we are fast becoming obsessed with the idea of doing it ourselves, whether in the area of auto mechanics, health care, interior decorating, or parenting. As we note in Chapter 2, these self-improvement manuals and courses are often the first resources used by people, some of whom may need intensive family services. As Michael Rossman has suggested, the very fact that some of these books exist indicates a breakdown or change in some of our major social and cultural institutions. Although the books address private needs, they raise public issues in that these "arise in individual lives precisely at the places where our collective structures of meaning and cooperation are breaking down, perhaps to be reformed." Rossman goes on to point out that it should be possible to learn about sexual functioning, parenting, the skills of daily living, driving, and so forth through families and friends; but people simply do not talk very much about anything that really matters to them. It is easier to go to a book, workshop, or organized workshop on whatever issue is of immediate concern. Yet such forms of "self-help" reinforce the idea that one must rely on experts to solve every human need, thereby undercutting the potential for mutual aid that exists in natural social groupings.[20] In this regard, it is useful to consider Rossman's distinction between *self*-help and forms of help that are truly *mutual*.

A second view of self-help uses the term very loosely to refer to a wide range of efforts that are part of the whole move toward consumer participation and control of human service organizations. For example, although Anthony Vattano does not offer a definition of self-help, he includes as part of the self-help movement, which he sees directed toward enhancing the power of service consumers, community organizing efforts with distinct social action goals—such as those of Saul Alinsky and Mobilization for Youth—as well as encounter-sensitivity groups led by non-professionals.[21] In a similar vein, Alan Gartner and Frank Reissman emphasize the convergence of what they call the service society and the consumer participation ideal, suggesting a vast expansion of the existing service network with the consumer as the primary producer of services.[22] Any significant development in this direction could have an impact on traditional forms of family service, and could provide whole new modes of family service. At present, however, it would seem that this concept of self-help essentially refers to a service development strategy (no matter whether this is viewed as a therapeutic device, a group process, or a community organizing technique) rather than to a distinct service domain. But if the term self-help is defined so broadly that it includes elements of every service sector and different modalities, it becomes impossible to specify what is distinctive about this type of service. Consequently, this concept of self-help does not seem very useful, at least for our purposes.

A third view of self-help or mutual aid has been developed most fully by Gerald Caplan and his colleagues at the Harvard Laboratory of Community Psychiatry in their work on natural support systems. Caplan defines support systems as "attachments among individuals or between individuals and groups that serve to improve adaptive competence in dealing with short-term crises and life transitions as well as long-term challenges, stresses and privations."[23] He suggests that kith and kin groups, informal community caregivers, voluntary associations, and mutual help organizations, as well as individual professionals and formal service organizations, can all be elements in support systems. He also notes:

> Both enduring and short-term supports are likely to consist of three elements: (a) the significant others help the individual mobilize his psychological resources and master his emotional burdens; (b) they share his tasks; and (c) they provide him with extra supplies of money, materials, tools, skills, and cognitive guidance to improve his handling of a situation.[24]

In *Support Systems and Mutual Help*, their most recent publication on this topic, the Harvard group employs a rather broad and flexible concept of mutual help, omitting any precise definition. Unlike the authors discussed above, however, they place a strong emphasis on mutuality and reciprocity in their discussion of various mutual aid efforts, thus suggesting at least one distinguishing characteristic. Moreover, the concept of mutual help they employ is closely related to the issue of family services in that one of the major thrusts in the field today is the effort to identify ways in which professionals can enhance informal support networks or organize new ones in order to help people with normal life crises and transitions. As will be discussed later, this approach is illustrated by the social network intervention approach of Ross Speck and Carolyn Attaneave, the Day Care Neighbor Service described by Alice Collins and Diana Pancoast, and the Widow to Widow Program organized by Phyllis Silverman.[25]

The last and perhaps most common interpretation of self-help or mutual aid groups is described most fully by Katz and Bender:

> Self-help groups are voluntary, small group structures for mutual aid and the accomplishment of a special purpose. They are usually formed by peers who have come together for mutual assistance in satisfying a common need, overcoming a common handicap or life-disrupting problem, and bringing about desired social and/or personal change. The initiators and members of such groups perceive that their needs are not, or cannot be, met by or through existing social institutions. Self-help groups emphasize face-to-face social interactions and the assumption of personal responsibility by members. They often provide material assistance, as well as emotional support; they are frequently "cause"-oriented, and promulgate an ideology or values through which members may obtain an enhanced sense of personal identity.[26]

A number of other authors employ similar definitions. Some have operationalized the concepts suggested in Katz and Bender's definition more precisely in order to carry out empirical studies, but they highlight similar distinguishing characteristics.[27]

Although groups of this type serve relatively few families experiencing "normal" family crises and transitions, they form a distinctive service domain and have been the subjects of study and analysis. It is possible to examine their potential role within the range of family services.

A number of classifications of self-help groups have been proposed. Edward Sagarin, for example, uses the approach to the management of deviance as the critical variable, distinguishing between those groups that attempt to reform their members, such as AA, and those that attempt to reform social norms, such as gay liberation organizations.[28] Another approach to classification distinguishes between groups that focus primarily inwardly on the needs of their members and those that focus outwardly on effecting some reform in the larger society, such as some of the women's rights organizations.[29] Katz and Bender propose a fivefold typology: groups primarily focused on self-fulfillment or personal growth; groups primarily focused on social advocacy; groups primarily focused on creating alternative living patterns; "outcast haven" or "rock bottom groups," such as Synanon; and mixed types, which have the characteristics of more than one of the other groups.[30]

In an empirical study of sixty self-help groups in a medium-sized northeastern city in 1973, Richard Steinman and Donald Traunstein identified four types of groups: the "anonymous" model, such as AA and Parents Anonymous; the "underground" model, such as street schools and some militant minority groups; the "big timers," such as the National Association for Retarded Children; and the "masqueraders," those groups that are commonly described as self-help groups but did not meet the minimum criteria for inclusion in their study, such as the requirement that a majority of the board members or their children benefit directly from the group's program.[31] In preparation for a study of self-help groups funded by the National Institute of Mental Health, Leon Levy developed a fourfold typology based on purpose and group composition: groups that have as their primary goal some form of conduct reorganization or behavioral control; groups whose members share a common status or predicament involving some degree of stress, such as Parents Without Partners; groups composed of members who are discriminated against or labelled deviant; and groups that have as their primary goal personal growth, self-actualization, and enhanced effectiveness in living.[32]

At present there is no single, generally accepted typology of self-help groups. Thomas Powell, however, has identified three major dimensions that should be considered in relation to any group: the group's posture regarding integration with the dominant society and collaboration with professionals; the nature of the problem addressed by the group and the way in which this is defined; and the nature of the group's program and activities.[33] These dimensions seem to capture many of the variables employed in the typologies described above and should probably be considered in any effort to develop a typology with more universal applicability.

Service Delivery: Doing It Oneself

Why do people join mutual support groups, however defined? What needs do they meet? How? Do they serve functions different from those served by professional service systems? Before we address these questions, it is important to discuss briefly the structural elements in self-help groups.

Structures and Dynamics of Self-Help Groups

Since self-help is not a unitary phenomenon, there is wide variability in the way self-help groups are organized. As a general rule, however, most groups tend to be small (usually fewer than twenty members) and, if they are affiliated with a national organization, usually enjoy a good deal of local autonomy.[34] Many display few of the bureaucratic characteristics of traditional human service organizations. For example, almost three-quarters of the self-help groups in one medium-sized city had annual budgets under $5,000 and over one-half used amateur means of fund-raising such as bake sales and dues. Although the vast majority had an elected board, only about two-thirds had an incorporation certificate, less than one-half had secured tax-exempt status, and only about two-fifths issued an annual report.[35]

There is extensive contact between new and veteran members in most self-help groups, and members enjoy equal status. Since the professional role tends to be minimized, leadership is achieved rather than ascribed. Although the early leaders often display charismatic qualities, leadership roles usually shift over time and are open to any member. The more highly developed and strict the ideology of the group, the more structured the group tends to be.[36]

Katz has identified five stages in the development of self-help groups: its origin; an informal organizational stage; the emergence of leadership; the beginning of formal organization; and the beginnings of professionalism. Some groups, however, resist moving into the third stage and even more avoid the fourth and fifth, thereby challenging Michel's Iron Law of Oligarchy. Those that do move into these later stages, like the National

Association for Retarded Citizens, may eventually become so professionalized that they are indistinguishable from more conventional, voluntary
organizations.[37]

Many theories have been advanced to explain why and how self-help
groups work, what factors motivate people to join such groups, and what
benefits are conveyed by membership. One factor is what Dumont terms
the "dynamics of peer influence," whereby self-help groups are able to
maximize the well-known phenomenon of peer group influences on attitudes and behavior.[38] Another is the phenomenon of "going public," where
individuals tend to move through a spectrum of behavior from private
concern to open declaration about a personal attribute to broader political
action: "People seem to help themselves as they become collectively
involved in broader social and political issues which concern them
particularly."[39] In differentiating between self-help and other modes of
service provision, two factors may be critical: that self-help groups stress
ongoing emotional support and advocacy for members, two types of service
given relatively little attention in the public service sector; and that self-
help groups tend to "normalize" needs while professionals tend to "prob-
lemize" client situations.[40]

There are also other, multi-factored, explanations for the way self-help
works. Frank Riessman, for example, gives strong emphasis to his "helper
therapy" principle, but he also stresses the importance of four other
factors: consumer intensity (the degree to which the consumer is involved
in the production of services); the aprofessional dimension (ways in which
self-help groups counterbalance some of the predominant characteristics of
professionalism such as elitism, monopoly, mystification, and lack of
accountability); indigenous service providers, who are closely involved and
identified with service consumers because they come from the same
community or client group; and the implicit demand that individuals do
something for themselves because they need not feel powerless, especially
in a group. Thus, the underlying theme in Riessman's analysis is that
self-help groups work because they are empowering.[41]

Based on his observations of self-help groups that have a significant
psychological component, either in explanations for or consequences of the
problem addressed, Leon Levy takes a very different approach. He has
postulated eleven processes that may explain the helping process in such
groups:

Processes with a behavioral focus . . . :

1. Both direct and vicarious social reinforcement for the development
   of ego-synotic behaviors and the elimination of problematic behaviors . . .

2. Training, indoctrination, and support in the use of various kinds of self-control behavior . . .

3. Modeling of methods of coping with stresses and changing behavior . . .

4. Providing members with an agenda of (and rationale for) actions they can engage in to change their social environment . . .

Processes with a cognitive focus . . . :

1. Providing members with a rationale for their problems or distress, and for the group's way of dealing with it, thereby removing their mystification over their experiences and increasing their expectancy for change and help . . .

2. Provision of normative and instrumental information and advice . . .

3. Expansion of the range of alternative perceptions of members' problems and circumstances and of actions which they might take to cope with their problems . . .

4. Enhancement of members' discriminative abilities regarding the stimulus and event contingencies in their lives . . .

5. Support for changes in attitudes toward one's self, one's own behavior, and society . . .

6. Reduction or elimination of a sense of isolation or uniqueness regarding members' problems and experiences through the operation of social comparison and consensual validation . . .

7. The development of an alternative or substitute culture and social structure within which members can develop new definitions of their personal identities and new norms upon which they can base their self-esteem.[42]

As Levy has suggested, these processes may well characterize a whole range of professional and non-professional helping strategies, not just self-help groups. Nor are all these processes likely to be present in any one group. However, the list seems to capture the critical psychological components of self-help.

Probably the best summary statement is Marie Killelea's list of seven critical elements in self-help:

1. Common experiences of members
2. Mutual help and support
3. The helper principle
4. Differential association

5. Collective willpower and belief
6. Importance of information
7. Constructive action toward shared goals.[43]

Thus, self-help groups are characterized by the intense personal involvement of members with others who share common experiences and needs in
an ongoing process of mutual support, help, and advocacy. Members relate
on an equal-status basis, defining their problems and needs in normal,
non-stigmatized ways, and strong emphasis is placed on cognitive and
behavioral, rather than emotional, change. Strength is found in the power
of the group, and reinforcement for desired attitudes and behaviors is
sought through association with others who share similar experiences and
views. There is a strong emphasis on activity as a means of developing a
sense of competency and personal responsibility and learning new behaviors. Members are expected to help other members and to contribute
to the work of the group as a whole, both to help themselves and to share in
the attainment of common goals.

The Professional's Role in the Self-Help Movement

In a later section we shall examine these dynamics in relation to the
provision of traditional family services, but first it is important to look
briefly at the role of the professional in the self-help movement. There is
wide variation in the degree to which mutual aid organizations make use of
professional services. Some oppose any professional involvement in their
activities. Others have clearly defined roles for professionals. Each local
chapter of Parents Anonymous, for example, is required to have a professional sponsor. Most permit and encourage some professional involvement
but insist that the membership retain control of the organization, at least in
the early stages. It is questionable whether groups that become fully
bureaucratized and professionalized should still be defined as self-help
organizations.

Since staff members of traditional family service agencies may work with
self-help groups, it is important to point out that a number of roles have
been identified for professionals in relation to mutual help efforts.[44] Baker,
who has explored this issue most fully, suggests five possible roles. First,
professionals can encourage mutual aid efforts among their client populations. Second, they can actually help to organize new self-help groups.
Third, they can provide consultation and/or technical assistance to existing
groups. Fourth, they can refer individual clients who might benefit from
membership in self-help groups. Finally, they can learn from successful
efforts and pattern some of their own behavior on the helping strategies
used in mutual help organizations.[45]

Certainly self-help efforts raise policy issues for the professional community. Ralph Tyler suggests that professionals should attempt to encourage mutual help organization by publicity, technical assistance, and so forth but should abjure any efforts to order and regulate the self-help phenomenon, lest they change it by controlling it.[46] Katz suggests that, since self-help groups have emerged as an important social development, providing many benefits to their members and influencing the structure of social support systems, it is essential that professionals develop ways of cooperating more effectively with them. He warns, however, against the risk of over-romanticizing the potential contribution of the self-help movement or of capturing it through attempts to influence and even dominate groups that are struggling to establish themselves in the community.[47] Victor and Ruth Sidel present a more skeptical perspective. Although they acknowledge that self-help groups are serving essential functions in modern society by providing needed services, enhancing members' sense of competency and self-worth, and creating new links among people, they warn that these groups tend to respond to symptoms rather than to underlying social problems and may at times exacerbate these problems. For example, without a shared set of social goals, self-help groups may contribute to the maldistribution of power and resources among different groups and to the fragmentation of communities. Moreover, the ideology of many groups supports a blaming-the-victim mentality and encourages further division between consumers and professionals. Hence, they imply, although the self-help movement should be supported, professionals and policy makers should be wary of encouraging all self-help efforts uncritically, without concern for a framework of broader social goals.[48]

Self-Help and Family Services

Despite the recent, rapid development of the self-help movement, few self-help organizations are concerned with families experiencing normal developmental crises. At first this seems surprising given the many tensions of modern family life. But the model of the "pure" self-help group is not especially appropriate for many types of family problems. There are several reasons for this. First, self-help groups tend to form around people who share a common problem or condition that has tremendous personal salience, distinguishes them from other people, and often carries a stigma. Obviously, by definition, normal family problems do not share these characteristics. Second, most self-help groups demand intense personal involvement over an extended time period. Again, almost by definition, normal family crises are unlikely to stimulate such involvement because they are time-limited: a family experiencing the stress created by a mother's return to work might benefit from associating with other families experiencing similar stress, but once they have made the necessary adjustments, they are unlikely to continue this affiliation or to want to devote much attention to an organization focused solely on this problem. Finally, and perhaps most important, families experiencing any one of the common stresses of family life such as childbirth, children leaving home, retirement, or moving can usually obtain the information and support they need from members of their natural support networks. The very fact that these are normal family problems means that one or more of their relatives, friends, neighbors, or co-workers are likely to have had similar experiences and can probably provide the necessary assistance.

This is not to suggest that traditional types of self-help cannot make major contributions to family life. It is probably not an exaggeration to say that Alcoholics Anonymous may have done more for families in this country than all the family counsellors and therapists combined. What it does suggest, however, is that self-help groups are more likely to serve as a major resource for families experiencing exceptional problems than for those seeking assistance with normal developmental crises. Organizations like AA, the National Association for Retarded Citizens, Parents Anonymous, Parents of Gays, Reach to Recovery (for women who have had mastectomies), and Al-Anon are all likely to provide essential services to special groups of families, but they are not suitable for larger population groups experiencing "normal" transitional problems.

Two national self-help organizations, the La Leche League and Parents Without Partners (PWP), present an apparent contradiction to this statement. (Make Today Count, an organization serving families with a terminally ill member, probably belongs in this category, but given its early stage of development, full characterization is difficult.) It is important to note, however, that both of these organizations were established at a time when the needs they address were not defined as normal. The La Leche League was organized in 1956 by a group of nursing mothers in the Chicago area who found it difficult to obtain the information they needed about breast feeding from family members or physicians.[49] Similarly, Parents Without Partners was established in 1957, when single-parent families were far less common than they are today. In recent years, in fact, some have criticized the name Parents *Without* Partners because it conveys a deficit status. Although many people obviously obtain benefits from membership in both groups, most could now probably find other informal supports if the resource were not available.

The La Leche League is an international self-help organization that focuses on the experience of mothering, thereby helping members cope with the transition to motherhood. The organization has been described as follows:

La Leche League now numbers more than 1,000 groups, and is a highly organized, centrally controlled operation. The usual La Leche group consists of from 1–30 mothers who learn of the organization through doctors, nurses, friends, and newspaper announcements. . . . A series of four meetings with a structured agenda is repeated several times during the year. The topics covered are: (1) the advantages of nursing; (2) overcoming difficulties in nursing; (3) baby arrives and joins the family (including a discussion of labor and children); (4) nutrition and weaning (including understanding of toddlers and sibling rivalry). Some groups add meetings to include fathers.

The formal part of each meeting is directed by a leader who presents information in didactic fashion. This is followed by informal conversation around specific problems and solutions. Literature . . . is available, and each member receives a regular newsletter. Telephone consultation with leaders and other members is encouraged, and a regional hotline is maintained.

New group leaders are chosen carefully, following their observation within the group and their relationships with their own children. Personal training workshops are then provided by the national organization.[50]

The La Leche League provides help to its members in developing an accepting personal approach, in preparing for the birth of the child, in handling problems in the hospital, in understanding the period of exhaustion following the baby's birth, in preparing to face the shock of the sudden, full-time task of motherhood, in physically preparing for nursing, in understanding the baby's physical problems and the mother's own socioemotional problems and behavior, and in dealing with generalized feelings of guilt and anxiety.[51] Since these problems represent the full range of difficulties women may experience in the transition to motherhood, the group can be said to be providing a clear family service. Given the high degree of structure and centralized authority in the organization, however, it is difficult to know whether it should still be classified as a self-help group.

PWP is an international organization of approximately thirty thousand single parents who belong to over two hundred local chapters. The membership, which is primarily middle-class, tends to have a strong psychological orientation. The group emphasizes its educational function. Ethel Gould, a professional advisor to the president of PWP, described the organization as follows:

Members' purposes are basically educational; and with some professional help they conduct a program in which lectures, discussions, publications, and recreational activities aid the single parent with many problems and dilemmas that must be faced in his home.

They have family activities, in which men and women participate with their children. State and local seminars, workshops, and conferences are held as well as an international annual conference, in which top professionals in allied fields participate. . . .

The organization is by nature one of transitory membership. It is a flowing stream wherein the frightened and troubled new member enters, grows, and moves on to leave room for the next one. Members leave the organization through marriage, or because they have gained enough direction and purpose that they no longer feel the need for the PWP, Inc., program.[52]

PWP also serves social and psychological functions: "Its goals would seem to be its members' short-term survival from the traumas of family breakup and widowhood and support in helping them get back into the competitive social/sexual rat race of dating and remarriage."[53] One major study concludes, however, that PWP's main function may be to provide new resources and relationships to help reduce potential sources of distress inherent in being a single parent: "the absence of a sustaining community; the absence of similarly placed friends; the absence of support for a sense of worth; and the absence of emotional attachment."[54]

The structure of PWP is very different from that of the La Leche League. PWP places strong emphasis on individual responsibility and participation and all members are expected to assume some type of leadership role. Although there is a national office and each chapter is expected to adhere to certain program guidelines, there is a good deal more decentralization of authority. It is clearly a member-controlled organization.

Perhaps the most interesting question that can be posed in relation to the classification of PWP as a self-help organization for families experiencing normal developmental crises is whether PWP views itself as helping with "normal" problems. As we suggested earlier, the very name of the organization implies acceptance of a stigmatized status for single parents. And Katz and Bender have commented:

PWP, in general, poses no criticism of the society or its values, but implicitly, does castigate individuals who have not "made it," according to prevailing standards. It is thus a short step for PWP members to internalize these "failures" at the marriage game, to emerge with a poor view of themselves, as mirrored in society's stigmatization of "single" parents, and to seek to change that condition as soon as possible.[55]

So far we have been discussing the role of traditional, formally organized self-help groups in the provision of family services. As we noted earlier, however, there are several other concepts of self-help, all of which have relevance to the provision of family services. Certainly, the "do-it-yourself" phenomenon is having a major impact on the design of family service programs in that potential consumers of service are now much better educated about child development, parenting tasks, and so forth and have much more knowledge about the range of services that could be made available to them. Consequently, many clients are beginning to shop around for the service program they feel is best suited to their needs, making heavy use of service modalities such as Parent Effectiveness Training that give them greater cognitive mastery of their life situations, and demanding more direct input and control of service programs.

Similarly, the growth of small, grassroots mutual support and social action groups is having a major influence on the family service field. The phenomenon is best illustrated by the vast number of consciousness-raising groups spawned by the women's movement, all of which help their members to deal with the typical problems associated with marriage, parenting, work, and sexuality that might also be brought to family service agencies. Although women's groups are perhaps the best known and most widely utilized component of this grassroots movement, other groups such as neighborhood and block associations, gay rights groups, parent groups, and consumer cooperatives also affect the family service field by providing alternative sources of support to their members and stimulating traditional service providers to develop special programs targeted on specific population groups. The recent interest in programs for battered women is a clear illustration of the latter trend.

The concept of mutual aid that seems likely to have the most significant impact on the provision of traditional family services is that developed most fully by Caplan and his colleagues at the Harvard Laboratory of Community Psychiatry and focused primarily on the role of natural support networks. Caplan already has been quoted in Chapter 1 as suggesting that the family itself is a major support system for individuals in need, carrying out a wide range of supportive functions. Based on this analysis, Caplan suggests that social policy should be geared toward promoting the "intactness, integration and mutuality of extended families," and he goes on to specify a wide range of ways in which service agencies could begin to implement such a policy.[56]

As professionals have begun to recognize the tremendous potential for healing and growth inherent in people's natural support networks, they have started to initiate service programs designed to enhance the functioning of existing networks, create new networks, or attach isolated individuals to existing networks.[57] In order to convey a sense of the types of activity that are taking place in this area, a few of the efforts will be described briefly.

Family Network Intervention

Ross Speck and Carolyn Attaneave, who have developed the network therapy approach most fully, base their work on the "retribalization" phenomenon found in many cultures by which entire tribes are brought together in crisis situations in order to initiate the healing process and discover appropriate solutions. The social network is defined as the total relational field of an individual; it includes family, friends, neighbors, and so forth, and may have from fifteen to a hundred or more members. In Family Network Intervention, the entire network of an individual (usually forty or more people) is invited to participate in a series of sessions designed to set in motion "the forces of healing within the living social fabric of people whose distress has led society, and themselves, to label their behavior pathological." The sessions are led by a team of approximately four "network intervenors," who attempt to use the power of the assembled group to redefine the problem, identify potential solutions, and set a change process in motion. The network intervenors do not attempt to define or reach a final solution, but rather concentrate on mobilizing the healing potential of the natural support network.[58]

Family Clusters

The Family Cluster program was started by the Unitarian Church as a means of bringing together people isolated from their families in order to create artificial extended families. A family cluster is composed of people of different ages and marital statuses who agree to meet regularly in order to develop meaningful personal relationships that are enjoyable and provide a mutual support base. Family clusters often celebrate holidays together, help each other out in emergencies, provide opportunities for cross-age socialization, and generally function as extended family units.[59] Its relationship to the marriage enrichment movement is discussed in Chapter 5.

Day Care Neighbor Services

The Day Care Neighbor Services program was started by Alice Collins and Eunice L. Watson as part of the Family Day Care System in Portland, Oregon, directed by Arthur Emlen. In this project, the professional staff attempted to identify "natural neighbors"—people who by virtue of their role or personality are likely to serve a central, helping function within their natural social networks—who might serve a natural helping role for families in need of day care service. They then developed a careful method of consultation with these natural neighbors in order to enhance their capacity to connect family day care users and providers and to provide assistance when problems arose in the user-provider relationship. On the basis of this experience and their analysis of other natural helping networks, Collins and Diane Pancoast have developed a fairly sophisticated strategy of intervention for professionals who wish to work with natural neighbors.[60]

Women In Self Help (WISH)

Created by three professionals in the Baltimore area in 1974, Women In Self Help is a telephone service to help women in traditional nuclear families with everyday problems and needs. The service was started on the premise that many women in a modern mobile society feel isolated because they do not have the opportunities for communicating informally with other women that were available to residents of closely knit communities. The telephone service is staffed by volunteers who are encouraged to use a peer counselling approach. Although the program was organized by professionals and the volunteers all receive training, the emphasis is on the commonality of experience between caller and listener. Hence it is viewed as a self-help organization, and effort is made to highlight the voluntary, peer-group nature of the program.[61]

Widow to Widow Program

Widow to Widow is one of the best known of the preventive intervention programs initiated by the Harvard Laboratory of Community Psychiatry. Started by Phyllis Silverman in the mid-1960s, the program was designed to provide support to newly bereaved women in the hope of preventing some of the mental health problems associated with loss. The program was staffed by non-professional aides who had been widowed. The aides provided help to recent widows in learning to make decisions independently, learning to be alone, and learning to make new friends and develop new support systems. Evaluation of the project suggested that the fact that the caregivers were also widows was critical in establishing initial trust and allowing the recipients to express their feelings and test out the appropriateness of their reactions. Also, over time it was discovered that many of the service recipients were able to move into caregiving roles, helping new widows in their own neighborhoods and thereby perhaps helping themselves.

It should be noted that, as the funding for this program was running out, a telephone hotline called the Widowed Service Line was established in an effort to reach a wider group of recently widowed people. The program was administered by three aides from the original program, but staffed entirely by widows and widowers who volunteered their time.[62]

As these brief program descriptions suggest, there are many ways in which professionals can and do engage in and stimulate the mutual aid process in order to help families experiencing developmental crises. Not only do service strategies of this type make economical use of limited professional resources, but they also provide a means of reaching families who might never utilize more traditional services, and they seem to be relatively effective. None of these efforts, however, can be classified as pure self-help efforts in the traditional sense because they all seem to have required some professional involvement, at least in the initial stages. Also, they tend to be small, locally organized efforts and do not attempt to establish national associations similar to those of the major self-help groups. Certainly this does not alter their potential usefulness in the family service arena, but it does raise questions about traditional service classification schemes.

The New Support Network

There would seem to be six types of self-help or mutual aid efforts that contribute to the provision of family services: self-help groups for family members with special problems or needs (Alcoholics Anonymous, Parents Anonymous, Fortune Society); self-help groups for relatives of people with special problems or needs (Al-Anon, Al Teen); self-help groups for parents of children with special problems or needs (National Association for Retarded Citizens, National Cystic Fibrosis Foundation, United Bronx Parents); self-help groups for families with special problems or needs (Council on Adoptable Children, Foster Parents Association); self-help groups for families experiencing special transitional crises (La Leche League, Make Today Count, Parents Without Partners); and professionally mobilized natural helping networks for families experiencing normal needs or transitional crises (Widow to Widow, Day Care Neighbor Service, WISH, Family Network Intervention, Family Clusters). Grassroots organizations such as women's groups formed without any professional assistance may also help their members to cope with many family problems, but since this is a secondary benefit, not their primary purpose, they are not included in this typology.

The traditional self-help group would seem to be a major resource for individuals and families experiencing any sort of special problem or need; but since this model requires intensive, continuous member participation, it is unlikely to be as viable a resource for families experiencing developmental crises or needs. On the other hand, mutual help organizations and natural support networks in which professionals provide the initial organizing impetus and guarantee some continuity over time can serve as an important resource for families in need of transitional supports. Although the latter model of service is still in a very early stage of development, it seems likely that this will become an increasingly important mode of family service provision. For example, the Indiana State Mental Health Commission sponsors a statewide program of mutual support groups to help people deal with situational crises such as the birth of a handicapped child, illness, death, and marital separation.[63]

There are two somewhat contradictory themes underlying much of the current interest in self-help and mutual aid. First is the growing recognition that many people with special needs who might formerly have been referred to professional organizations might be better served through self-help groups. The other is the realization among professionals that because of changes in family life and geographic mobility, many people do not have ready access to the natural support networks that have traditionally helped families cope with normal problems in living. Thus we have the two simultaneous trends: increasing consumer utilization of self-help groups in preference to professional services, and increasing professional involvement in encouraging natural support systems that were historically independent of the organized service sector. Because these developments are so new, it is difficult to know what, if any, conflicts they may create. It is clear, however, that the role of the professional in natural support systems is changing, and further research will be needed to determine which roles can be carried out most effectively by professionals and which by consumers and how responsibilities can best be allocated between professionals and members of natural helping networks.

There are a number of other issues that require further study, especially in relation to the role of mutual aid in the provision of family services. For example, we need to learn more about structural elements in self-help groups and the way these organizations evolve over time, the actual helping processes that occur in mutual help organizations, and the patterns of relationship and influence among self-help groups, professionals, and formal caregiving institutions.[64] We also need to explore the differences between groups that demand ideological conformity and those that encourage individual freedom and acceptance of differences, as well as the processes of goal displacement and the contrasts between groups that focus inward on the needs of members and those that emphasize social change.[65] We need to identify who is not served as well as who is served by self-help efforts and to begin to develop some more precise evaluation criteria,[66] and to examine which people are helped with which problems, the relative effectiveness of self-help groups in serving different socioeconomic classes, and the effectiveness of current organizational formats and ways in which the de-alienating function of self-help groups is carried out.[67]

Perhaps the most critical issue is to be able to recognize what the appropriate public policy stance should be in relation to mutual help organizations. Should the public sector attempt to support the growth of the self-help movement? Can all groups be supported uncritically? What is the risk of cooptation—capture of the groups as they become dependent upon institutional recognition and support? Should the relationships between self-help groups and existing service structures be formalized? Should planning efforts initiated to develop more rational systems of service delivery make provision for mutual help organizations, or should these groups be allowed to flourish or flounder independently? Additional research is needed before it will be possible to answer these questions with any degree of certainty. It is possible, however, to make some tentative judgments and recommendations based on the present overview.

First, it must be emphasized that the self-help movement is having an increasingly important influence on the entire social service field. Perhaps the most dramatic illustration of this impact is the fact that, of the eight major areas of concern identified by the President's Commission on Mental Health in 1978, the first was the development of personal and community supports for people with mental health needs.[68] It would appear that neither the millions of citizens now participating in various types of self-help groups nor public policy makers now advocating an expansion of mutual support networks are willing to wait for a thorough professional assessment of different aspects of this movement. The issue posed is, given the knowledge now available, how can the self-help phenomenon best be utilized in the provision of family services?

It seems likely that the primary reason for the increasing popularity of self-help groups is that they provide a high level of consumer satisfaction. It is also possible, however, that people are turning to self-help groups because these are the only resource available for responding to some needs or problems. Therefore, their existence does not per se mean that they are a full response and that professional practitioners and agencies should take no initiatives.

Where appropriate, self-help groups clearly provide a cost-effective means of reaching large numbers of unserved people. Minimal professional involvement in various types of mutual support groups can have a large multiplier effect in that the specialized knowledge and skills of professionals need be used only for tasks requiring their expertise while other people can carry out the many non-expert tasks involved in the provision of services.[69] For example, many lay people are capable of teaching basic parenting skills; individualized teaching does not have to be carried out by child development experts. Similarly, a friend or volunteer helper can often provide as helpful a listening ear as a professional to a person going through the crisis of divorce or the death of a spouse, and the lay person is more likely to be available at night, on the weekend, or on holidays, when the person in crisis may be most in need of help.

Another major advantage to the use of self-help groups is that they provide much greater diversity than traditional family service programs in terms of the types of problems they address and the range of their potential participants. Because they tend to be relatively specialized, such groups can develop expertise in helping people with particular types of problems. Since family service professionals usually are expected to be able to help people with a wide range of problems, they are less likely to be familiar with all the resources available in a particular problem area or with all the types of concerns people with that problem are likely to experience. A member of a single parents group, for example, may know much more about child care, unemployment, social service, and housing resources for a recently divorced mother of pre-school children than will a family service worker, who must also know about resources for the frail elderly, adolescent drug users, battered wives, families with a terminally ill member, and so forth.

The other advantage inherent in the diversity of the self-help movement is that it provides a means of reaching people who might never approach traditional family service agencies. Because of the inevitable social distance between professionals and the poorer, less-educated segments of the population, many of the latter are distrustful of professional service providers and reluctant to expose their needs or concerns. Similarly, because of the cultural diversity in this country, professionals frequently do not understand some of the family patterns and traditions of minority groups and do not know how to provide services that bridge these cultural differences. In these situations, members of self-help groups from similar socioeconomic backgrounds may be able to reach out and support each other in ways that are foreign to traditional service providers.

As we saw in an earlier section, by involving their members in the provision of services, self-help groups utilize a helping technology not available in professional settings, where there is a clear separation between service providers and consumers. Not only does this approach give consumers greater control over the conditions of service but it enables people to meet their own needs by helping others, thereby enhancing their general sense of competency and their mastery of the particular problems with which they are trying to cope.[70]

Finally, in a highly industrialized society in which there is increased concentration of power in formal institutions, self-help groups can serve an important mediating or linkage function between small, relatively power-less primary groups such as the family and the large service bureaucracies, thereby alleviating people's sense of alienation and powerlessness.

For all these reasons, it seems essential for public policy to support the continued growth of mutual support groups designed to help people cope with problems of family living. This recommendation must be made with three caveats, however. First, because of current concerns regarding the cost of social services, there is a risk that self-help groups will be used as a substitute for needed professional services. Yet self-help groups are impor-tant precisely because they serve a function different from that of tradition-al family service agencies. Professional knowledge and skills are necessary to help people with many types of environmental, interpersonal, and intrapsychic problems. Much professional effort has been directed in recent years toward increasing our knowledge of family dynamics and improving our technologies for helping with specific types of family prob-lems. This progress will be wasted if cost considerations are permitted to dictate a widespread substitution of mutual helping for professional ser-vices in situations where expert knowledge is clearly needed.

Second, given the current widespread distrust of professional service organizations, there is a risk of over-romanticizing indigenous non-professional helpers. In the same way that the administrators of traditional service agencies may begin to serve their own vested interests rather than those of their clients, so the leaders of self-help groups may start to act in self-serving ways. Lack of professional training does not guarantee purity of motive any more than do years of formal education. Moreover, self-help groups are not subject to the same legal and ethical constraints as are the professional groups. Therefore, it is important that some minimal stan-dards be introduced for self-help groups receiving any type of public support to protect the members of such groups from abuses of power.

Third, it is essential to remember that most of the potential benefits of self-help groups derive from their diversity, their small, informal organiza-tional structures, their self-government, their diffuseness of relationships, and their non-instrumental goals. Unfortunately, public sanction and sup-port usually demand a tremendous elaboration of structures, formalization of policies, specification of objectives, and proliferation of record-keeping devices. Therefore, it is important that any effort to increase public support of self-help groups guard against developing regulations, funding mechan-isms, or administrative procedures that would subvert the very nature of the self-help groups it intends to benefit.

7   Families Are Important

It is not difficult to argue that concerns far removed from family well-being motivate many adults, to the detriment of family life. Many journalists, authors, clergymen, TV commentators, and documentaries have argued this point in recent years. After all, they allege, should one not so interpret divorce, desertion, long work hours and concentration on career, the growing presence in the work force of married women who have very young children, delayed childbirth after marriage, and the greater deliberateness in having children?

Moreover, the available statistics concerning people's life problems and deprivations prepare one for survey reports of high rates of dissatisfaction and malaise.[1] After all, as we saw in Chapter 1, marriage and birth rates have been declining while divorce rates have increased steadily, and the proportion of premarital births has increased. More children thus live in single-parent families. There is a high probability that children born now or in recent years will experience a "single-parent" family before age eighteen. Similarly, among women born since 1945, close to 40 percent may expect their first marriage to end in divorce. For those who remarry, an even higher percentage of their second marriages will end the same way. Rates for men are only a bit lower.

And for those to whom the optimum family environment is one in which one parent is home full time taking care of the children while the other goes out "to work," there is cause for alarm in the fact that, in March 1979, only 45 percent of all husband-wife families were families in which the wife was not in the labor force. The two-parent, two-wage-earner families are a majority among husband-wife families today.

Despite such findings, as we noted earlier, there is demographic evidence that the new life patterns that are developing may have quite positive connotations and that such indicators do not spell an end to family life.[2] In a world in which people experience many problems and tensions, personal happiness clearly is an "emerging ethic,"[3] and replies to "perceived quality of life" surveys are, in fact, consistently positive about life in general and families in particular.

Perceived Quality of Life

For some years now, in the United States and elsewhere, a tradition of research has grown up under the general heading of "perceived quality of life." In such studies an effort is made not to get respondents to talk particularly about needs or concerns but, rather, to assess their sum total living experiences. They are asked to rate specific life domains and to make holistic judgments as well. While a number of different investigations and research programs have played a part, much of the methodological and substantive contribution in the United States has come from the Institute for Social Research at the University of Michigan.[4] The increasing sophistication of the methods employed, the repetition of the surveys, and the constant refinement of reporting methods have created some confidence as to the reliability and validity of the results.

Since surveys of this type require a good deal of time to carry out, analyze, and report, the results are never completely "current." Nonetheless, there is remarkable consistency in findings from the late 1950s to the early 1970s. More recent individual surveys reinforce the conclusions.

First, there is in these studies stunning confirmation of the importance of the family to adult Americans. When asked to identify the two domains most important to them, 55 percent of the Americans polled named "a happy marriage" and 36 percent "a good family life." These are the top two selections, surpassing by far such alternatives as good government, good friends, one's house, an interesting job, the city, or even religion. ("Good health," the third domain chosen, ranks almost as high as "a good family life," and "religious faith," somewhat behind, ranks fourth.)[5] Not only are these domains rated high in importance, but the numbers of people dissatisfied with the current state of their lives in these domains is neither particularly low nor particularly high compared with other domains.[6]

The researchers at Yankelovich, Skelly and White, Inc., report findings of a similar trend in a number of national surveys over the past decade:

> Most Americans remain deeply committed to the idea and ideal of the family as an institution. . . .
> In 1978, 92 percent of all adult Americans interviewed in a nationwide Yankelovich survey said that the family is very important to them as a personal value;
> 83 percent indicated that they would welcome more emphasis on traditional family ties;
> 78 percent indicated that the family is the most meaningful part of life, compared to 9 percent who felt that way about work or leisure.
> . . . Regardless of how questions are asked about values, adult Americans say the family is considerably more important to them than other personal attachments such as work, leisure, and friendship.[7]

Focusing on the questions of concern to the 1980 White House Conference on Families, George Gallup also discovered the high salience of families in people's psychic economies: "No fewer than eight out of ten Americans eighteen years of age or older say their families are either the 'most' or 'one of the most' important elements of their lives."[8]

Second, most Americans are reasonably contented with their lives. For the period 1957–1972, the *Quality of American Life* reports assembled by Angus Campbell, Phillip Converse, and Willard Rogers show most respondents judging themselves as "very happy" and "pretty happy," with some tendency to fewer "very happy" responses. A "satisfaction" measure yields results quite similar to "happiness" measures, although younger respondents rate higher on self-reported happiness and older ones on life satisfactions.

Certainly, as we saw in Chapter 1, these families have "concerns" or "tensions." Of a total of 44 percent of all respondents (who report, overall, high rates of satisfaction and happiness), 18 percent were concerned about their health and 7 percent about the health of family members. Almost one-quarter were worried about some family matter, such as how the children were turning out. This compares with Ruth Clark and Greg Martire's report that 36 percent of parents with children under age thirteen and 44 percent of working mothers "say they worry about the job they are doing as parents."[9] Equal numbers were concerned about their jobs or education and some 20 percent were troubled about finances. One respondent in eight felt that the anxiety was "too much" and he or she could have a breakdown.

These data represent a challenge to any system of helping services, but they should be read, we repeat, against a backdrop of results in the *Quality of American Life* review that show marriage and family life as domains of high importance and of generally high satisfaction. It is not that there are no variations—the better-educated are somewhat less satisfied than the less-educated. Housewives and employed wives are quite alike in their reports of high satisfaction and in this regard are unlike the employed unmarried women, some of whom have children, although college-educated housewives are less satisfied and much less happy with their marriages. Whatever the psychological costs of marriage, the psychological costs of remaining single appear greater.[10]

These general tendencies are reflected in Frank Andrews and Stephen Withey's research, which, like the Campbell, Converse, and Rogers analyses, relates largely to the early 1970s. No matter whether on global assessments or with reference to specific domains, the most common evaluation is "mostly satisfied," although one person in ten responds as "mostly dissatisfied," "unhappy," or "terrible." For present purposes, it is of interest that despite much concern about government, foreign affairs, and the economy in the early 1970s:

> when it came to family decisions as to how the available income was to be spent, then a large majority felt satisfied, and many were pleased, with what they had and how available resources were being apportioned. . . . The financial strains, at least in 1972, had not as yet hit hard at family resources although there were portents of concern and some apprehension about the future.[11]

In a report of subjective self-evaluations, it is difficult to interpret absolutes. (What are the cut-offs in subjective self-assessments between "mostly dissatisfied" and "unhappy," that is, what are the objective referents?) However, there is a clear significance in the finding here too that in general Americans regard family more positively than they do government, foreign affairs, and the economy. We need not ignore alarms and problem areas in noting both the importance of family to people's perceived quality of life and the generally positive assessment of one's family and marital situation.

"Community" also elicits a generally positive assessment, as positive as the fact that there are easy intrafamilial agreements about resource disposal. Such ratings are far more positive than those about the economic situation, local government, national government, or the general state of the nation. While Americans are less pleased about practical local services (painting, repairs, appliances, food purchases) than they are with their community, they are as pleased with medical, hospital, police, fire, and garbage services, and with education.

Jobs and immediate neighborhood evoke a slightly more positive response than do community services, a response about the equal of that evoked by the community as a whole. Attitudes toward co-workers are equally positive, as are assessments about friends and associates. In general, all primary experience areas are more positively seen than are remote institutions. One is therefore not surprised to discover, as we note throughout this report, the many ways people seek to cope when things are not quite right in primary areas. The pattern clearly is strengthened by the stress within the culture on doing "your own thing," relating "well," maximizing satisfaction. Even though the categories "mixed response," "mostly dissatisfied," or "unhappy" would add up to fewer than 10 percent of all responses, one cannot ignore the absolute totals—the number of people who see themselves as in need of help or service or opportunity to act to improve things.

This point needs repetition with reference to the pattern of answers in other domains as well. For example, a series of scales about friends and

self, and about interpersonal relations, justify Andrews and Withey's conclusion that, despite all the change and stress, the family "in some form is
the most meaningful group for continued and intimate relations among
human individuals." Compared to assessments in all other domains, people express very positive feelings about their children, wives, husbands,
marriage, family life, things they do within the family, family responsibilities, and close relatives: "Here we have the strongest expressions of delight
and pleasure of any of the domains of life. People were so favorable that it is
easy to be misbelieving."[12]

Precisely because of the importance of the domain and the general
satisfaction, there is, again, need to attend to significant subgroups of
responses on some items that are "mixed," "mostly satisfied," or "unhappy." Of interest, too, is the fact that in contrast to family response,
there is less satisfaction in the responses about "self." While the majority
are at the positive end, they are more like assessments of neighborhood,
education, and the economy than like reactions to family and friends.
There are, in other words, significant numbers of areas of mixed and
negative assessments of one's self overall, one's achievements, aspects of
daily living, and one's ability to improve things. On the other hand,
experience in daily coping and religious experience are positively assessed.

We interpret all of this not as validating the various alarums about
massive alienation, anxiety, and crises, but as a report that, as we saw in
Chapter 1, there are significant numbers of Americans who are not fully
satisfied in a society that emphasizes self-fulfillment and satisfaction in
daily experience and relationships and that advertises the general well-
being of others through the media. These people who are not fully satisfied
include a smaller minority who label themselves as "unhappy" or "terrible"
in these more important areas. Nor are the numbers small. While only 4
percent use the ratings "mostly dissatisfied," "unhappy," or "terrible"
about their marriages, that 4 percent represents almost two million couples—and we know that there are "only" about one million divorces every
year. At the very least, the potential "pool," "target population," "market,"
for family and personal adjustment-related services, family life education,
and self-help activities includes these couples as well as a goodly proportion of the over five million female heads of families.

In contrast to some of the domains, responses about "self," even when
sustaining response averages at the positive end of the scales, are less often
completely "delighted" than responses on other items. And some 15 to 25
percent give responses that allow much room for improvement with regard
to ability to change things, ability to get a better job, health, sex life, sleep,
daily routines. In short, one does not require a problem or a crisis or a
pathology in the traditional sense to develop a motivation to do better—
assessments are relative between people and among domains of one's own

life—in a context of general overall happiness and satisfaction. All of which appears to contradict the diagnoses of those who preach that the society is characterized largely by alienation and gloom.

Efforts to specify these assessments by demographic subgroups yield less than one might predict. Indeed, the group-to-group variations remain quite small. However, for present purposes particularly, it is significant to note that unmarried adults are consistently lower on most perceived quality of life ratings and that unmarried parents clearly are in the most unsatisfactory situation. Blacks tend to report less satisfaction on many items than do whites.

Joseph H. Pleck, in a secondary analysis of data from a 1977 Quality of Employment Survey (another ongoing series at the University of Michigan), reports findings consistent with those above. His independent review of all other available research, with special reference to men's family roles, reinforces our own too. His conclusions from both his own analytic work with the data and from a literature review are of sufficient interest for an extended quotation:

> First, men's family role is far more psychologically significant to them than is their work role. It is clear that husbands spend less time in family tasks than in their jobs, and than employed wives spend in family tasks. But men nonetheless report their family role to be considerably more significant to them than their work role, and do so by a margin only somewhat less than women do. Likewise, men's family experience makes a much stronger contribution to their well-being than does their work experience, again only slightly less so than is the case for employed wives. These results concerning the significance of the family role to men are consistent with those of previous studies, although in light of the widespread currency of the stereotype of men as obsessed by work and oblivious to the family, these earlier results do not appear to be well known.
>
> To sum up the nature and consequences of men's family role, the family role is the most significant role in men's lives, although they spend less time in it than in their paid work, and positive experience in this role has greater consequences than does any other for men's overall well-being.
>
> It might be objected that the time men spend in housework and childcare more accurately reflects the family's psychological significance to them than do the questionnaire measures of involvement used here. Endorsing the importance of the family in general or one's own family in particular are so normative, it might be argued, that these responses reflect only platitudes, not real involvement. It is likely that the social desirability of pro-family statements affects these responses, but this

probable social desirability effect cannot be the only source of the present results. For one thing, the result appears on the item *family more, work less,* in which, unlike the other involvement items, involvement in the family is assessed in a format counterposing involvement in the family with earnings. This format provides those not really psychologically involved in the family a socially acceptable way of saying so. This counter-position should overcome the possible social desirability effects influencing the other items. (This item may be uncorrelated with the other items, and indeed be better than the others, for precisely this reason.) It is true that the proportion endorsing the family-involved response on this item is lower than on the other three. But even so, more men endorse the family-involved response on this item than the work-involved response, and the sex difference, though significant, is small.

For another thing, our assessment of the significance of the family role for men is not based simply on these direct self-reports. It is based in addition on the differential relationships of work and family variables to overall psychological well-being. These differential relationships should not be vulnerable to possible social desirability effects.

It should be noted, of course, that some men do fit the stereotype of being more involved in their jobs than in their families. . . . They are a small minority.[13]

A few specific domains in the several large quality of life surveys yield additional group results of some interest: there is no clear pattern of differences in responses to life satisfactions based on presence or absence of children or the age of the youngest child, but being married or not is significant for the response on several measures, especially being unmarried but having children. Social and economic status analyses yield some differences, but the patterns are complex. The less satisfactory situation for blacks is largely attributable to the larger number of poor in this group.

Two generalizations are worthy of specification: "All groups except those with broken marriages put marriage and their families high on their list of gratifications."[14] And "the picture of poorest quality of life appears among the group that is made up entirely of women with children who did not have a marital partner."[15]

The Social Indicators of Well-Being volume sums up a series of measures of global well-being that seem to have as much validity as the measures of specific life concerns that we have already reported. The most useful such measure reported ("Life 3") shows two-thirds of all Americans ranging between "pleased" to "mostly satisfied." One-sixth or one-seventh of respondents rank themselves even higher, and one-fourth or one-fifth consider themselves "less well off than mostly satisfied." Yet while summarizing this optimistic picture, we note the following specific: the small percentage rating their situation as "terrible" constitute a group of one-half million Americans.[16]

Again, while in the aggregate people consider their lives better than five years ago and are optimistic about the next five years, some one-third have noted no change over five years and almost one-third noted a decline in their situation. As much holds for the assessment of the future.

Overall assessments of one's well-being are similarly positive: 62 percent of respondents consider themselves better off than the typical American. There is a tendency to underestimate the sense of well-being felt by others. Still, 13 percent think of themselves as worse off than the typical American.

Thus, these and other measures find most Americans "pretty satisfied," "pretty happy," or better. Most affective self-assessments are positive. But the minority of negative ratings represent reports of significant numbers of people despite small percentages. Those in the lower socioeconomic status positions are less satisfied than those in high positions, the unmarried are less satisfied than the married, and unmarried people rearing children report the toughest situation of all, even though most of them expect to reach an average level of well-being within five years.

In concluding this section we need to repeat a useful distinction. Focusing on the "unhappy" or "less well off," we have reported a search for those who might be described as needing "help" in relation to problems, or as having an interest in self-improvement. Even the very satisfied, the most optimistic, and the most family-centered are clearly interested, as well, in the practical services and resources that facilitate family management and functioning, and economize on family routine time, without any assumption of dysfunction or problem at all.

The Importance of the Family

Some enthusiastic champions of family life education or personal social services may believe that their efforts will overcome everything. To them, the enrichment or strengthening or treatment of family life is the critical form of societal intervention. The research tells another story: family variables are critical in well-being, yet the elements susceptible to social service intervention are quite modest; but this does not make them insignificant. And the field is one in which full understanding of possibilities, results, limitations, does not yet exist.

First, as to the family's importance. A series of studies of income, status attainment, education, occupation, poverty, and equality tend to converge in their findings, even though none is definitive and all face methodological complexities. As much may be said of studies of socialization, personal characteristics, and cognitive capacity. Clearly, the family is a critical intervening variable, probably the critical variable in people's lives. Parents, income, occupation, and schooling are predictors of children's status through a causal nexus in which preparation for school, motivation, and cognitive capacity affect the type, nature, and quality of one's school experience and thus one's educational attainment, income, and occupation. Both income inheritance that "capitalizes" young people and the "investment" in them through the living standard and services provided while they are growing up serve to perpetuate in children the advantages and disadvantages, and thus the inequalities, in the families of their parents. Lee Rainwater and Martin Rein in their work on the economics of stratification describe the family as the center of an economic "claims system" that settles one's current standard of living, whatever its implication for the future.[17] Of course, a debate also rages about genetic endowment, but variability in life experience is largely explainable by these broad economic and social differences, while the evidence from genetics remains controversial and difficult to isolate. (Certainly people are not all genetically "equal," the issue being, however, whether racial, ethnic, or geographic groupings rather than environmental factors account for variability.)

These are old insights. Robert Nisbet cites Rousseau's advice that to improve education the family should be supplanted, thus protecting children from the prejudices of their fathers. The planners of the American anti-poverty war of the mid-1960s developed the Head Start program, an effort at compensatory education, offering cognitive stimulation for children growing up in poverty and deprived minority environments. Christopher Jencks identified the family as one of the prime conduits of social inequality, and even John Rawls considered and then flinched from the prospect of abolishing the family in the interests of equality.[18]

The research in several disciplines seeks to explain the process by which the family passes on its privilege or its disadvantage: an economist studies family inheritance and endowment;[19] an offshoot of another field of economics looks at the "quality" of time and resources that better-educated parents can invest in building up the "human capital" of their children; a psychologist studying the child's earliest years notes that privileged and educated parents are purveyors of a richer educational offering to a child before he gets to school;[20] sociological researchers note that some parents live with their children in environments that have better schools, recreational facilities, and public amenities than do others. Demographers studying mortality rates for persons in different living arrangements have argued that "healthier" people may tend to be selected more for some roles (marriage and having children) than are others, but, more likely, that some family statuses are more protective of health and physical well-being than are others; in other words, the living patterns of the married who have children may be more conducive to good health practices than the practices of many unmarrieds.

Family service and family life education programs, encounter groups, and community mental health centers do not affect well-being on this level. Income, occupation, resources, and social class are determined by societal forces beyond such programs and, in turn, affect much of the destiny of adults and their children. The importance of the family as an intervening variable has been noted, however, because its very significance and potency anchor the family within a cluster of social institutions and makes it available for intervention. And if the family is important to people, changes in the family also are, or will be, important.

Here, special insight comes from a study known as the "Panel Study of Income Dynamics," published in an ongoing series of analytic volumes under the title *Five Thousand American Families*. The study focus is on the determinants, sources, uses, and effects of income. This ambitious and valuable study began with one subsample of low-income families and another, a national cross section, in 1968. Successive waves of interviews have followed over eight years. The resulting studies have attended to many issues, and these data tapes have been useful to many independent investigators who have published elsewhere. For here, in a panel study, it is possible to study changes over time and to relate such changes to internal familial events and to societal developments. It also is possible to connect developments to many personal characteristics and elements of status. For present purposes, the main conclusions of *Five Thousand American Families* are dramatic and important:

> Family composition change is the most important of all the variables . . . in . . . changed well-being. Decisions about marriage, having children, and encouraging older children and other adults to stay in the household or leave it seem to be the main individual decisions that affect one's status.

> Changes in family income result largely from changes in the number of earners in a family, family size, entry into and leaving the labor force. Such factors are far more important than changes in wage levels and number of hours worked.

> And family composition is what is critical here. So, the major way to climb out of poverty is to get married, and the major way to fall in is to get divorced or leave the parental home.[21]

While economic factors causing changed family composition are the ones investigated by the Michigan analysts, they are able to explain only a portion of variations in changed family composition. The authors focus on such factors nonetheless in their search for policy relevance and access. They note that they have omitted "many obviously important psychological and sociological motives, such as love and societal pressures, which play a significant role in causing people to incur and maintain family obligations. In many cases, these factors are probably more important determinants of change than economic ones."[22]

The economic factors are studied as affecting family composition changes, which, in turn, have more impact on family economic well-being than any other identified variables. In general, the economic status of men is less affected by family compositional change than is that of women. Moreover, "changes brought about by marriage and remarriage that resulted in two-parent families were the most beneficial, while such changes as divorce, separation, splitting off and widowhood which resulted in a family with an unmarried household head were generally detrimental."[23]

When one studies aggregates, variables that affect large numbers at once and that are policy responsive, one concludes that broad economic trends and policies affect family composition changes, which, in turn, are the single major overall influences on economic well-being. But to understand individual behavior, it is appropriate—as noted in the Michigan reports— to look at sociological and psychological factors, variables that do not all point in the same way and that either may intervene between economic factors and family composition change or may be independent forces, also influencing such change, as seen by the two-panel dynamics schema reproduced in the figure.

The Michigan report states:

As we have seen . . . changes in family composition and the often related changes in labor force participation dominate the changes in a family's

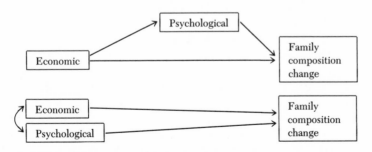

Possible Causal Patterns in Changes in Family Composition

Source: James N. Morgan, *Five Thousand American Families* (Ann Arbor, Mich.: University of Michigan, Survey Research Center of the Institute for Social Research, 1974), vol. 4, pp. 9–10.

well-being. There are two ways to look at this. One might argue that they are essentially random events or normal life cycle progressions which can be averaged out, controlled, or otherwise taken care of and are not very interesting in their own right. *Or one could argue that at least some of these changes, or their timing, might well be affected by people's purposes, desires, and reactions to their environment.* It might then be possible for public policy to have an effect on a family's economic well-being by altering either the environment or people's behavioral responses in such a way that family composition is changed.[24]

Full explication of these patterns and their relative importance—since both would appear valid—is important for social theory. For social programs, particularly family services of the many kinds we have described, both of the schema suggest that a case can be made for the services, as for the policy interventions. Income security programs, taxation, and economic policy generally will remain the major "wholesale" strategies for impact on family economic well-being, which, as we have seen, is the most critical consideration. But impact on psychological (and sociological) dimensions has major potential for affecting or mediating or changing the causal pattern. The nature of such possible interventions thus remains of interest. For, while major economic forces play their themes, people still have some choices about one or two parents working, about full- or part-time work, about placing children in child care programs, about having few or more children, about marrying and separating, about spending cautiously or living dangerously, about keeping a teenager in school or insisting on work, and about encouraging him or her to remain at home or to leave. In the words of the panel study analysts: "Perhaps this is the most important finding of all—*that the family and the responsibility that people have for one another* are still more important than any social policy or individual behavior in determining this changing distribution of well-being."[25]

Thus, family composition is a critical thing for people, and some of its elements can be affected by choice. Family services may influence such choice. The Michigan discussion is public policy–oriented in the macro sense: How does one improve economic well-being of the disadvantaged? But the question can be turned around: How can families discover their optimum goals? How can they implement them? The services discussed in this book have addressed questions of this order.

First, however, a word about the most ambitious of the recent attempts to look at "The Determinants of Economic Success in America." Christopher Jencks and a group of colleagues labored energetically, imaginatively, and long, asking *Who Gets Ahead?* and drawing upon five national surveys of twenty-five- to sixty-four-year-old men and six special-purpose samples. The Michigan Panel Study of Income Dynamics is only one of the surveys. While, at the end, the answer given remains partial and some of the interpretations are debated, it seems clear that background accounts "for something like 48 percent of the variance in occupational status and 15 to 35 percent of the variance in annual earnings. This is as strong an association as that between education and economic success. If our aim is to reduce the impact of being born to one set of parents rather than another, we still have a long way to go."[26] Other important influences on job status and income are test scores, which may or may not be proxies for "ability" and non-cognitive adolescent traits. Schooling, the "most readily observable predictor," may either be a rationing device, a source of knowledge, skill, and attitudes, or a major influence on aspirations, or some of each. The importance of schooling shows up even when other variables are controlled.

Obviously, family factors also affect schooling. Jencks sums up as follows: "Being white, having a father or mother with a lot of schooling, having a father with a high status occupation, having parents with high incomes, and coming from a small family all enhance a son's economic prospects."[27] The demographic background advantages associated with family work their effects significantly via cognitive skills developed before labor market entry; this does not say "whether men from privileged backgrounds do better on standardized tests for genetic or for nongenetic reasons."[28]

The overall conclusions are hardly definitive in their policy implications: Jencks draws a distinction between knowing that cognitive skills and educational attainment are the means through which background influences job status and income, and knowing that they are necessary elements in occupational success or should be. And he adds:

> We cannot even draw clear moral or political conclusions from the fact that family background affects life chances independent of test scores and education. Elitists have traditionally argued, for example, that family background affects economic success partly because those who are "properly" brought up have the "right" attitudes and values for top jobs. Our surveys do not measure these attitudes and values. But even if attitudes and values were to explain the "direct" effects of family background on economic success, what would we conclude? The answer would depend on whether the attitudes or values that explained the success of men from privileged backgrounds were only [what] we thought essential to maintaining the overall quality of life, or whether they were simply the hallmarks of some clubby snobbery. Without evidence on this, our data constitute neither an indictment nor an endorsement of the status quo.[29]

Richard DeLone argues that since families are mere "intermediate mechanisms" policy should aim at structural inequalities ("what families are") if such policy would change inequality.[30] While the policy logic is debatable and the debate goes on (given the uncertainties, why not attempt to address both causal and intervening elements on several levels?), the modern social research leaves us with Rousseau's insights, now quantified, specified, and weighted, but compounded by the uncertainties of complex multivariate analyses, measurement error, sampling error, and sampling restrictions. Clearly the family is and remains a central societal institution, a major factor in the life chances of children—and the correct object of policy, benefits, and services. But what kinds of policy, benefits, and services?

As we move from economic well-being to personality development, intellectual growth, and socialization, the acknowledgment of the family's strategic position is virtually universal, even though there are many schools of thought, countless interpretations of the process, and differing viewpoints as to the value and nature of societal interventions, if any. Burton White characterizes "the family as the first and most fundamental educational delivery system."[31] He concludes from his research that if the family does well during the first year, a child can probably survive a mediocre educational system. If a family does well, generally, professionals can provide effective training.

Both simple and complex societies have long acknowledged that adult care, love, and responsiveness are absolutely essential to the survival and normal development of infants. There are debates about genetic factors, often difficult to resolve because of the complexity of the research questions and the impossibility of carrying out controlled experiments, but there are no debates about an infant's physical helplessness and complete dependence on adult nurture. There are controversies about how much of a child's adult destiny is determined by age three or four or six, but there is no doubt that interaction with responsive, approving adults and attachment to them is the core process in cognitive and emotional development and child growth. There are shifting styles of child rearing and differing theories as to optimum parental styles, but no one disputes the importance of identifying a child-rearing mode consonant with its times if children are to thrive.

Indeed, when one states that the family is important, the non-economists and non-researchers think immediately of child rearing and socialization—the core family function, which remains while economic, protective, and educational activities are increasingly shared with or moved to other institutions. Some of the resistance to the development of socially sponsored child care arrangements, to be called upon by two-earner families with young children (or single-parent families in which the sole parent works), is a fear that the family may thus be giving up one of its most important remaining functions. The importance of the function and the dedication to it are exemplified by the extent of such fear despite the repeated evidence that parents are and remain the most important influences by far in the children's lives, whether or not they are exposed to other influences in child care and school programs.

The state of knowledge should not be exaggerated. There is a substantial gap between the certainties of the theoretical and didactic writing about child development, whether from one school of thought or another, and the actual research evidence. There are "certainties" in the literature (often contradictory certainties) about: what form of childbirth procedure is best; whether children should be breast fed or not; how infants are to be held and talked to; whether or not parents should respond to crying; toilet training and feeding styles; exposure or non-exposure of infants to substitute caretakers at different ages; the most desirable toys, playpens, clothing, temperature, cribs, types of food, and so on; the age at which peer group experience is possible and significant. Nonetheless, one often can trace shifts to fads, culture, marketplace sales pitches, and charismatic child care experts and not merely to certainties as to what induces child welfare. None of this is to argue that there is no knowledge. Within broad parameters, the range of the tolerable can be stated and the more desirable can often be pointed to. What is fascinating is the unquestioned agreement that the family chooses, implements, and shapes. Its importance is never questioned. If anything, the society would influence or empower the family, or attempt to make it more expert. And the argument clearly has validity.

The family environment and the family endowment remain important as children go from elementary to secondary to post-secondary education. As indicated earlier, parental education, income, occupation, race, and class predict a considerable part of what occurs in terms of social role and status as young people move through life. But correlations are not so high once environment, societal, and peer components and the influence of other institutions, particularly schools, also are taken into account. Nonetheless, because family background and circumstances continue to matter, and because many people feel that they should or could matter even more, the family remains a focus in efforts to affect children, youth, and adolescents. And even if the potential is constrained, it is significant enough not be be ignored.

It is not appropriate to pursue this discussion of the family as a focus as though only the child-rearing role and the economic effects have significance. For, in the modern world of small families, changed distribution of tasks among social institutions, and increased living time assigned to domains other than economic survival and child rearing, the family is also the haven for intimacy, emotional support, interpersonal fulfillment, expression of mutually developed values, and achievement of personal satisfactions. Here the variables are many, the research certainties even fewer, the controversies about role options and complementarities even more complex. What is certain, however, is that for adults the family is defined as critical to the perceived quality of life. The perception is apparently valid. And the search for qualitative "enrichment" seems constant.

Finally, the family is an appropriate focus with regard to its roles with the aged and the handicapped. Whatever the societal change, significant numbers of the aged (yet a minority) live with their adult children, who contribute to their support, care, and satisfaction late in life. Families, too, offer care and protection (often to a degree approximating the roles of paraprofessionals) for large numbers of the physically and mentally handicapped who would otherwise require protected residential arrangements or full time at-home companions.[32] The care of one's aged parents, of handicapped children, or of siblings is neither physically easy nor without a price in dollars, privacy, leisure, and the sacrifice of life alternatives. Sometimes people manage it willingly, well, and without aid. Sometimes they need and seek societal assistance—resources, guidance, emotional support.

The human capital theorists developing the discipline often now called "the new home economics" probably overstate the case (and obscure it with their specialized vocabulary) with the claim that "the family integrates the welfare of its members into an internally consistent family-utility function."[33] To affirm that the family may be viewed organically, operating with goals and preferences for the whole, is probably too much.[34] On the other hand, there would be broad interdisciplinary agreement with the view of Harold Watts, stated in a number of forums, that while the process may not be fully understood, the family is a key decision maker in the course of a developmental process for children (and other family members) involving an interaction of family, education, religion, health, and other institutions.

Without full understanding of the process it is not certain which interventions have effect and which do not, but there is widespread concern about the several components, and the efforts to intervene not only continue but expand.

From all that has been said about the family as a critical intervening variable, the Nelson Foote-Leonard Cottrell conclusions follow: "Whether one's interest . . . is in influencing single persons or whole societies, the point of greatest leverage for intervention is the family."[35] This, in all likelihood, is overstated. Yet the field of services to families is one such response. If we again caution that this service is in no sense a substitute for macro social policy, we also stress that it can be very useful. We turn now to an assessment of the field—whose components were introduced in the earlier chapters—and to some thoughts about the future.

Helping America's Families

How has the society responded? What is it likely to do? Americans agree overwhelmingly on the importance, indeed the centrality, of the family, but almost half of them began the 1980s feeling that family life had "gotten worse" over the previous fifteen years.[36] Improvements are being sought in two directions that certainly are not contradictory and that can be pursued simultaneously. On the one hand, there is the effort to deal directly with the underlying quality of the wider society: the economy, foreign affairs, politics, racial attitudes, equality for women, the physical environment, and the use of resources generally. On the other, there are the specific and immediate efforts to improve the quality of daily family life. In this book we have attempted an overview of the latter efforts.

The Overview

We have used the word "help" in a rather broad way. The help sought by individual families is influenced by the specific ways in which they define their own problems, needs, and wants. It is also shaped and constrained by the way in which the marketplace has perceived demand and possible response and has "invented" products and services. It is fashioned as well by assumptions made by the voluntary sector and government as to what is needed and what is appropriate. The point of departure always is a view of what the family should or can do by itself or in alliance with kin, friends, neighbors, or people in similar predicaments. There is hardly national consensus on this score.

What has emerged is diverse, disorganized, changing, and difficult to depict or assess. It must, however, be considered against the demographic and social trends affecting family life, as outlined earlier, and the problems, needs, wants, and capacity for self-help that shape the coping and management patterns and affect the demand for specific services.

On the level of daily experience, people do not necessarily connect what they are going through with broader trends and societal change. They identify needs and problems. And families and family members do have problems within their families: with their children or between husbands and wives or within the marriage and in their parenting roles and relationships. They have problems in their daily lives: at their jobs and in the ways in which their jobs, their family lives, and the communities in which they live interact. The problems may be interpersonal, situational, or both. Where problems and needs are perceived, they are often multiple and diverse. They may be acute—a sudden, overwhelming crisis when a member dies, becomes ill, leaves, loses a job—or chronic, as when families have to adapt to the presence of a child with a handicap or the long-term deterioration of a marriage relationship. Families have what we have been describing as normal life cycle and transitional problems, too, as adults adapt to becoming parents for the first time, or a mother accepts a full-time job, or a child first enters school, or parents adjust to the departure of children from home when they leave for college, jobs, and independent living.

The needs and problems have been analyzed and described more formally by scholars, who talk about societal changes and crises (unemployment, alienation), changes in family structure (divorce, remarriage, adoption), changes in family composition (the birth of a first child, the move of an elderly woman out of her own home into the household of a married daughter, a young man's move out of the parental home to establish his own household), or changes in family roles (the entry of a woman into the labor force when her child enters kindergarten, the joining of husband and wife in a family business after he had been the sole support with an outside job). Whether due to family structural, composition, or role changes, to societal events or trends, or to individual personality or personal history, problems may actually be experienced as intrapsychic or interpersonal role crises. Or they may not be seen as involving one's persona or role at all, but merely as problems requiring arranging for services, resources, facilities, information, or practical advice.

In brief, the experience for which help is sought may start with what are perceived as needs, or problems, or both. A problem, in turn, may be defined as a challenge or as an obstacle. It may be experienced as a source of mild discomfort, or severe stress, or overwhelming anguish. It may arise out of severe pathology or from ordinary, "routine" experience. It may be defined as a "family" problem, as a problem of the parent(s), or as a problem for, or created by, one particular member.

How the problem is defined—indeed whether or not it is defined as a problem, a need, a want, or something still different, as well as its salience and immediacy—will determine whether help is sought and the type of help sought and used. Variations in income, education, geography, occupation, or ethnicity lead to differences in how problems are defined and, ultimately, in the choice of help. Unfortunately these social categories also frequently affect access to needed services.

The ultimate consumers, the family group or family members, do not necessarily put together all of the things we have described or discussed

and think of it as one domain. The diversity of families, problems, perceptions, and services also leads to a diversity of definitions. In turning for
help, then, consumers may see themselves as attempting to meet a need
(daytime care for a three-year-old while her parents work, a home or a
school in a new community following a relocation, an "extra pair of hands"
for a single mother of two young children between getting up in the
morning and getting to work); to satisfy a desire or want ("adult
conversation," a vacation, some time for oneself); to make things better
(somehow to function better as wife, mother, father, husband, son, daughter, child); to deal with a serious problem (counselling and planning with a
long-unemployed husband, resolution of spouse differences as to whether
the wife should work, or intensive treatment for a schizophrenic child, an
impotent husband, a severely depressed wife, an adolescent on drugs).

The forms of help we have identified may be classified in four categories:
access and information, education, therapy or treatment or social care or
rehabilitation, practical services. They are found in all the sectors we have
explored—the marketplace, the public service system, the mutual aid
endeavors, and the not-for-profit sector. (See, for example, the sample
listing in the Appendix.) Moreover, despite variations, each of the four
kinds of help may be found in each sector. For example, there are extensive
information (access) services as well as some child care services found
within the public personal social services, which also arrange for substitute
care and residential treatment. Similarly, some community mental health
services offer intensive treatment of the mentally ill as well as marriage
counselling and family therapy and special groups for new parents or
parents of substance abusers, but also offer preventive educational programs. The voluntary agencies provide information, family treatment, and
some child care services and are now expanding advocacy and "family life
education." The church-related groups stress the educational component
as well as self-help and treatment on various levels. The marketplace
includes the whole gamut, with particular stress on "treatment" and the
supportive, facilitative, and expeditive services, a far wider range of practical services than what is available in either the public or the private
not-for-profit sector. Finally, self-help groups also cut across all these
areas, including new mothers' groups, women's consciousness-raising
groups; Alcoholics Anonymous, Recovery, and Parents Anonymous; cooperative child care, baby sitting, even house sitting (while neighbors or
friends are on vacation); as well as categorically focused and more general
advocacy and social action. Most arrange educational programs. Some refer
for service in rehabilitation and treatment programs.

Given the history of family services and their diversity of sponsorship,
funding, and definition of what is important, one would not expect each of
the systems to encompass everything and to be fully like the others—even

though all share some commitments to information, treatment, practical service, and education. The previous chapters do describe differences and possible advantages for each. They also make it difficult to ignore gaps and limitations in each and in the totality of what is offered. To illustrate:

Most of what is available in the public personal social services is inevitably targeted at the poor and disadvantaged, is focused on pathology and severe difficulty, is directed at categorical subgroups, often lacks a family orientation—and is in short supply.

A large part of the not-for-profit sector also is categorical and pathology-oriented, but some of it, particularly church-based or church-derived programs, has moved in quite different directions. But, while some agency somewhere offers almost all needed programs, the private sector ensures neither coverage nor accountability, nor provision for family-focused case integration. The self-help programs take off from both problem statuses and the normal life cycle concerns of everyday families, but by virtue of their very advantage, they may lack continuity, range, coverage, expertise, structure.

The marketplace has developed services of all the kinds described, but its dependence on profit limits its geographic coverage, its clientele, its choice of activities. Nor is there any way for it adequately to achieve coherence or service integration—something most consumers achieve for themselves, but which some troubled people need to count on as the responsibility of others. People with enough money can, of course, find market-related coordinated and comprehensive services, with experts responsible for "integrating" the service (travel agents, personal shoppers, interior designers, home-care contractors), but most consumers could not draw upon this capacity of the for-profit sector. It is useful to note that those who can buy such services do not view themselves as dependent or inadequate as a consequence.

We have found much that is admirable and exciting, and consumers clearly are using most available services, often to their full capacity. Yet there are problems characterizing the totality of the effort that go beyond coverage gaps and inadequate facilities. For one thing, even among those services specifically targeted on adults, most are directed at individuals or households, not at family units. At best, help may be described as "family-oriented"; that is, individuals are seen as the major consumer group, but they are assumed to be family members and thus may be assessed or considered or served in a family "context." This pattern is pronounced in the public sector services. An even stronger focus on family orientation can be found among the private family service agencies and the church-related groups. A focus on family units as a whole continues to be elusive, is often viewed as a specialty, and is seen as complicated and demanding. It remains the method of choice, despite cost and complexity, in certain direct-treatment situations, in social services relating to the break-up or protection of family in response to difficulties (foster care and adoption), and in family enrichment activities. Perhaps for most other services and forms of help, properly developed and implemented family alertness and orientation, rather than insistence on attention to and intervention within the entire family system, are the appropriate goals. This issue must be explored systematically and alternatives tested if the family service field is to develop and expand successfully. Practical services often are oriented to the individual, rather than to any family unit. Helping and treatment services will often fail without a family orientation, or perhaps a family approach, but society cannot ignore the needs of many who are not family unit members, out of choice or necessity.

Whether the future development is in the direction of more service and intervention directed at the family system as a unit, or merely toward a greater family awareness and concern ("orientation") while serving individuals, there is reason to urge some movement away from the current heavy emphasis in public and private personal social services on the organization of delivery systems around categorical "age" subgroups— children, youth, the aged—or around categorical "problem" subgroups— the abused, the neglected, the frail, the homebound, delinquents, runaways, and refugees. Certainly some of the services would be more effective were they addressed to family units or household residents, or so organized as to cope with the immediate human environment of the person to be helped. Even the categorical interest groups and organizational bureaucracies currently protecting their specialisms could come to see this as contributing to effectiveness and consistent with goals currently sought under such banners as "normalization," "deinstitutionalization," "mainstreaming," and community care.

Closely related to the categorical emphasis that may often block a family orientation—although it need not—is a related limitation of services now available. Much of what exists in the public and private not-for-profit sectors is directed toward pathology rather than toward normal life cycle or transitional problems. Even among those church-related services and movements focused on "enrichment" or "enhancement," the concern often seems to be with alleviating problems regardless of how they are defined by those experiencing them.

This point should not be misunderstood. Illness and disturbance demand treatment and rehabilitation and there are often shortages, poor services, and poorly organized delivery systems in need of reform. However, if the entire system of family helping is dominated by pathology and maladjustment, then "help treatment" becomes the most important form of help provided, even though it is certainly not the most frequently requested type of help. Furthermore, because of its dominance, a therapeutic perspective seems to spill over into the other types of help or service offered. Thus, family day care or center-based child care provided as a personal social service (clearly a "normal" need in normal families) still has some vestigial traces in many cities of a treatment or compensatory program. Help within the home (homemakers) is certainly defined this way, and indeed can only be provided to families with children on this basis by public and non-profit private agencies. Even many "educational" programs such as parent or family life education are often viewed as helping "interventions" for those to whom more clinically oriented treatment programs would not be accessible.

As a concomitant of the overemphasis on response to pathology, there arises the related problems of the paucity of help available for the new types of families and family life styles now becoming dominant or increasingly prevalent in our society, and for the range of widely experienced life cycle problems that continue to be ignored although they are increasingly important.

As we noted in Chapter 1, the two-parent, two-wage-earner family has now emerged as the single most important family type in the United States today, and most children are growing up in such families. Where children are concerned, another important family type is the single-parent family, usually female-headed, and usually involving a working parent; almost half the children born in the latter half of the 1970s are likely to experience living in such families before they are eighteen. For many there will be quick transitions into a two-parent family but the transitions still will be emotionally difficult. Yet despite the trend, and despite the fact that "reconstituted" families are becoming an increasingly important group in family service agencies, help is available for them largely as a therapeutic service, when they are in crisis or at least in severe pain. There is little if any help available for the large numbers of such families who are dealing with the complicated problems of a new kind of extended family (his, hers, ours), in addition to all the other demands involved in managing daily life. These are families in which daily routines are increasingly likely to include job as well as home and family responsibilities for both parents. Here is a "normal" need requiring help, mutual aid, and a sense of the universality of the experience, yet responses thus far are quite modest.

Elsewhere we have addressed the normal, generally experienced needs and requirements, by way of societal response in relation to families with two parents working outside the home or where the sole parent has an out-of-home job and the child or children are infants or toddlers. We have written of the need to develop family-child policy "packages" to include both family benefits (income supplements, such as family allowances, paid leaves from work with full job security for parents following the birth or adoption of a child, similar paid leaves to care for an ill young child at home) and family support services (all-day or part-day child care services for infants, toddlers, and pre-schoolers, and before- and after-school programs for pre- and primary-school-aged children).[37] In assessing what exists now within the public, private, and proprietary (for-profit) service sectors in the way of support services for normal families, we are struck by the lack of new, exciting, or even extensive examples of "family support" services. Indeed, the lack of creativity and the paucity of social innovation thus far are astonishing given the extensiveness of change in family life styles and the intensity with which families express a desire for help.[38]

The Next Phase

What do we then conclude? We launched this exploration, initially, because we had become increasingly conscious of a significant gap in social service provisions for families—in particular, families with children—and we wanted to know what could and should be done. We knew that by tradition the voluntary social agencies were more likely to be providing "family" services, but we also had the impression that a lot more was emerging in programs of religious groups, community groups, and self-help organizations, all of which were offering help to families. Given some of these new developments, we wondered what it all might mean. Did these developments explain or cause or justify the apparent failure on the part of the public sector to respond in a focused way to a large and an important need? Was public money now being spent in the not-for-profit sector for family-related services undermining, or further fragmenting, an already inadequate public system? Should one urge a more coherent family service system within the public social service system? Would, could, such a system play a major role in helping America's families seeking help?

Our conclusion is that what now exists in this field and what should emerge in the near future cannot be encompassed in one system nor should it. There is at this stage at least need for enrichment, expansion, clarification, experimentation—yes—and even for some coherence, but not for discouragement of the current pluralistic and diverse developments that respond to different types of families and different definitions of need. We here summarize the basis for this view and suggest some of the changes that are needed in the family services picture.

First, there has been, indeed, an enormous explosion in the number and variety of helping services for families, and these have emerged in some way in every sector, but most noticeably in the private market and in the variety of self-help and service activities undertaken in the voluntary, private not-for-profit sector. What we are seeing is a response to what families say they want and need, even if they say it unclearly and inconsistently. And the diversity of services that now exist seems an appropriate response in a loosely defined and unclear domain in which help and support mean different things to different people. We would conjecture that in time there will be a settling down and a clearer sense of what is important and why. Until then, however, it is impossible to determine exactly what of all this should be provided as well, or even perhaps primarily, within—or by funding from—the public personal social services system, to whom and why.

Second, as we indicated, there is still no generally accepted definition as to what a "family" service is. What these services seem to share is an effort to respond to changes in family composition, family structure, family roles, family life cycle problems, and societal developments impacting on the family per se. That is, these are services that are responding to such developments as more single-parent families, more working parents, more reconstituted families, more cohabitation and experimental marriages and family life styles, more families with responsibility for dependent members other than children (elderly parents, handicapped members), more small families, with fewer children, more mobile and isolated families. All of this is in addition to services responding to neglect, abuse, conflict, pathology, and family break-up.

As a consequence, not only are there more services of different kinds, but they have evolved to meet quite diverse needs. Therefore, they fit no readily identifiable criterion for "family" services, other than the criteria we posed at the onset: services that define their client-customer groups as "families" and/or services that families or individuals say they want to meet family-related needs or wants. We have suggested possible, more rigorous criteria and some differentiations between services addressing the family system per se and services so conducted as to be oriented to and constantly aware of the family while serving one or more members. We think both types are needed—for different purposes.

We mentioned earlier that these services offer individually, or in combination, information, education, treatment, or practical assistance. They take the form of help with the practical problems of daily living, in particular for families with less than the needed time, energy, and conventional aids; help with learning a new role or becoming more adequate in an existing one; help with changing a bad relationship or improving a good one. Depending on how the need or desire for help is defined, the specifics of the help sought will vary: to provide insight into how one's behavior may create problems for oneself and others, and how to change; to obtain information about a new role, situation, resource; to receive reassurance from discovering the universal nature of certain kinds of experiences and concerns; to facilitate access to resources and to expertise in specialized areas; to offer opportunity for self-improvement; to manage better one's home, one's day, one's family, one's life.

People of different classes, locations, backgrounds, ethnicity, education, experience, and problems or needs are comfortable—or uncomfortable—with different definitions of their problems and therefore with different types of help, and with the different institutions to which they might need to go for help. Certainly, the boundaries are still in flux. The phenomenon itself is one of change. It has its own dynamic, and we are not able, now, to "fix" the domain, nor would we want to. Indeed, it is this diversity that contributes to the sense of vitality we noted in what is occurring in many places.

Third, we would repeat, so as to emphasize, the growing need to develop far more practical services designed to alleviate some of the daily stress for families managing complicated lives, including jobs and home responsibilities, and to help families cope with normal life cycle and transitional problems. Here, we are convinced of the special need for creativity, social innovation, and experimentation regardless of where it occurs: public sector, private sector, marketplace. The challenge is to develop an improved social technology, to substitute for expensive, conventional, individual personal services in the marketplace or to provide such services in new ways at low cost. Even if the workday were shorter, lives are longer, and families are becoming increasingly more complex systems. New approaches to designing, organizing, and delivering services—and/or a new social technology of help—are what is needed if families with children are to manage in today's society.

Fourth, as experimentation proceeds in designing and developing family support services covering information, education, practical services, and treatment, we would expect and urge restructuring or realignment of the pattern that now prevails. As we have seen, the dominant components in the family service field now are the treatment services. We have noted that these are important; there may even be need for more. If the concept of a family support service is to provide help for average, normal families, however, such help cannot be provided where the primary focus is pathology and the primary goal treatment and rehabilitation—with all else secondary and peripheral. The core of a family support service must be the information, advice, education, and practical service component. Close linkages should exist between such a service and all sorts of therapeutic as well as social care services (nursing homes and adult homes, homemakers and home health aides, escort and shopping services for the frail, and so forth). Where such diverse services should be placed and how they should be delivered, in the context of a larger personal social service system, is a separate issue. Perhaps experience will suggest a division of labor among subcomponents of a larger system that will promote both access and efficiency while giving encouragement to the development of the separate information, education, treatment, and rehabilitation (including social care), as well as practical service, components. The challenge for now and the immediate future is the search for creativity, social invention, and a new social technology to help families as they change and adapt to new and changing conditions in a complex society. The issue of structure should not at this point stifle development.

Fifth, and last, we would point to a new issue (or a new phase of a very old issue) that seems to be emerging in the course of this and other fields of study, and that is the changing relationship between and among the three sectors discussed here: the public sector, the private for-profit sector, and the private not-for-profit sector. Not only are boundaries of the family services or "help for families" field unclear, but the traditional boundaries between the sectors are increasingly fuzzy. For some years now, public money has been supporting the not-for-profit sector in ways that have significantly shaped its activities and perhaps undone some of the unique characteristics of the not-for-profit. Moreover, private voluntary agencies have often used public funds to support their own initiatives, with little concern for how these reflected public priorities or affected the capacity of public agencies to meet their commitments. Now, something similar seems to be emerging in the marketplace as, through private insurance and public medical program reimbursement ("third party") or tax expenditures, public monies are entering the for-profit sector. There has been concern expressed by some about the ways that public services replace and even supplant private activities and responsibilities. We would add to this the question of how the market gets shaped, and indeed supported, by public funds provided directly or indirectly.

These brief remarks serve to introduce a topic that is moving to the top of the national agenda and that is illustrated in the family field, but hardly confined to it: the new mesh of the public, private for-profit, and private not-for-profit sectors in mixed economy societies as they realign themselves to the economic and social realities in the 1980s. One of the issues to be faced is especially relevant to the family field: to what extent is diversity so urgent as to argue for a competitive public-private "free market," devoid of any effort at rationalization, at conceptualizing the roles and relationships among sectors and program elements? We believe that the case for diversity and for a developmental approach has been made with reference to people's manifold needs, expectations, and definitions of what they want. Nor is technology so developed and knowledge so clear as to justify comprehensive and complete planning for a monolithic system. None of this, however, is a case for anarchy or laissez faire either. The diversity argument has other implications; the evidence that a developmental period is needed should not be ignored; but these things do not relieve those who expend public funds, funds that are a large component of the budget for many social services, from responsibility for some policy and program planning. Certainly citizens have a right to expect a minimum of service delivery capacity, some minimum of social policy protection, particularly for the most vulnerable and those in greatest need of service. On the other hand, to repeat, this is not a case for anything except some continued separation and independence of the several sectors. If any one of them is fully dependent on the others for support and financing, and if they are all completely meshed at the delivery level, diversity becomes a slogan that is never translated into reality.

Effects and Effectiveness

Some of our readers will want even more by way of evaluation. They will ask: "Do these services work? Do they help? What is the evidence?" The questions would appear to be premature if asked with reference to all family helping services at once, with expectation of a unified, sweeping answer. After all, we have pulled together a diversity of developments and suggested that they be viewed as potential components of a system to offer family supports and help. They are not institutionalized as one system now and it is not desirable that they be so institutionalized, even though pulling them together for analysis and planning purposes may be useful.

For this reason, we would respond that measurements of effectiveness should be addressed to system components, to specific sectors or subprograms, not to a field of family support services as such. There is also a good methodological reason for this view, familiar to researchers: very different criteria, instruments, and research designs are needed to deal with (to pick only a few illustrations) family therapy, marriage encounter weekends, family life education lectures, or child care programs.

Thought of in this way, there is a fairly long tradition of studying the effects of counselling and individual couple or family therapy, and some results are positive, others less so. What exists suggests room for improvement, and occasionally even how this might be done, but not for discontinuance. As much can be said for child care, rehabilitation, residential treatment, or group treatment methods.[39] At the same time we add that the research record is very uneven: there are program "fads," so that some are evaluated and others ignored. Samples are often poor, control groups lacking, criteria debatable, and instruments flawed. The field offers interesting and important challenges to research scholars. They will also want to tackle the neglected areas or the areas only now reaching a level of program specificity and stability meriting assessment of effects: much that occurs in family life education, practical services and self-help, and some of the newer therapeutic and counselling approaches.

To this another point should be added. As already suggested, it is also legitimate to apply the market model to the question of evaluation. Is there demand? Is there service take-up? Do consumers return? Behavioral and verbal indicia of consumer response are relevant in a field where needs and wants are in part subjective. Both in the marketplace, where people pay directly for services, and in all the other sectors that we have explored, there is evidence not only of need and demand, but also that many consumers find these services somewhat responsive. They may want more, perhaps better, programs, but they still are attracted by and endorse and pay for many of these programs. People refer their own family members, their relatives and friends. They join in as volunteers. They contribute.

We should not exaggerate. After all, other people with valid needs may be turned off and dissatisfied. There may be unreported damage done. There may be angry consumers. There may be unmet needs, unbalanced offerings, poor access and coverage, a lack of coherence, accountability, and integration. What exists, we conclude, is far from adequate and is flawed, but it is a beginning response to need. Better research and evaluation are needed, but they should be conducted with the expectation that their main effects could be to guide the improvement of program content and process. It is not likely that global research will "validate" something called "family support services" as a whole. It is more than likely that good research that tells how to do some things in other ways and better can have significant impact. Those who fund and sponsor research programs will find this a legitimate and attractive prospect.

A final observation may be in order as we close. While we have not explicitly made the point, we have described this growing field sufficiently for readers to know that the vast majority of current "consumers" of service are women. Even where the family as a whole is addressed, women often make the initial or only contacts and contracts, and carry the burden of application. This is consistent with the family ideologies and practices of modern societies.

This fact weakens the constituency for new services and the support for new initiatives. Women may be family service consumers, but they are, thus far, politically inactive and weak. Not that this is the only inhibiting factor. There is fear that government and government money will or could undermine family autonomy and privacy. There is a conviction that the marketplace can and will respond spontaneously and that no attention is needed. There is a belief that service will not only meet emerging needs but will change the family so as to create new needs.

These subjects need probing, debate, experimentation. The answers clearly are as relevant to men as to women—and we hope that we have demonstrated this. Families together, if they arrive at consensus, can become agents and forces for needed innovation and change. Our own exploration, in the tradition of all such journeys, may have raised more questions than it has answered; but some of the questions are new. It has also shown, we believe, that the questions are too important to be forgotten or ignored.

Notes

Preface

1. Kenneth Keniston and the Carnegie Council on Children, *All Our Children* (New York: Harcourt Brace Jovanovich, 1977), p. 79.

2. Advisory Committee on Child Development, National Research Council, *Toward a National Policy for Children and Families* (Washington, D.C.: National Academy of Sciences, 1976), p. 92.

3. Urie Bronfenbrenner, *The Ecology of Human Development* (Cambridge, Mass.: Harvard University Press, 1979). For example: "The availability of supportive settings is, in turn, a function of their existence and frequency in a given culture or subculture. The frequency can be enhanced by the adoption of public policies and practices that create additional settings and societal roles conducive to family life" (p. 7).

Chapter 1

1. Margaret Mead, "Can the American Family Survive?" *Redbook*, Feb. 1977, pp. 160, 438.

2. U.S. Bureau of the Census definition. See, for example, U.S. Bureau of the Census, "Money Income of Families and Persons in the United States, 1978," *Current Population Reports*, Series P-60, no. 123 (Washington, D.C.: U.S. Government Printing Office, 1980).

3. Rosabeth Moss Kanter, *Work and Family in the United States: A Critical Review and Agenda for Research and Policy* (New York: Russell Sage Foundation, 1977).

4. Family Service Association of America, official statement, mimeo., 1978.

5. Gerald Caplan, "The Family as Support System," as cited in "Report of the Task Panel on Community Support Systems," *Task Panel Reports Submitted to the President's Commission on Mental Health, 1978: Appendix* (Washington, D.C.: U.S. Government Printing Office, 1979), vol. 2, p. 168.

6. Robert A. Nisbet, "The Costs of Equality," in Michael Mooney and Florian Stuber, eds., *Small Comforts for Hard Times: Humanists on Public Policy* (New York: Columbia University Press, 1977), p. 48.

7. Mead, "Can the American Family Survive?" p. 160.

8. Mary Jo Bane, *Here to Stay* (New York: Basic Books, 1976).

9. Most of the data in this section are from the U.S. Bureau of the Census, *Current Population Reports*: Series P-20, No. 340, "Household and Family Characteristics: March 1978," (Washington, D.C.: U.S. Government Printing Office, 1979); and Series P-23, No. 107, "Families Maintained by Female Householders 1970–1979" (Washington, D.C.: U.S. Government Printing Office, 1980).

10. Subfamilies are those families living in a household headed by someone else.
11. Elizabeth Waldman et al., "Working Mothers in the 1970s: a Look at the Statistics," *Monthly Labor Review*, Oct. 1979, pp. 438–439. See also Beverly L. Johnson, "Marital and Family Characteristics of the Labor Force, March 1979," *Monthly Labor Review*, April 1980, pp. 48–52; U.S. Department of Labor, Bureau of Labor Statistics, *Perspectives on Working Women: A Databook, 1980.*
12. Derived from U.S. Bureau of the Census, "Fertility of American Women, June, 1978," *Current Population Reports*, Series P-20, no. 341 (Washington, D.C.: U.S. Government Printing Office, 1979), p. 2.
13. *Ibid.* and U.S. Bureau of the Census, "Patterns of Employment Before and After Childbirth, United States," *Vital and Health Statistics*, Series 23, no. 4 (Washington, D.C.: U.S. Government Printing Office, 1979).
14. U.S. Bureau of the Census, "Divorce, Child Custody and Child Support," *Current Population Reports: Special Studies*, Series P-23, no. 84 (Washington, D.C.: U.S. Government Printing Office, 1979); U.S. Bureau of the Census, "Perspectives on American Husbands and Wives," *Current Population Reports: Special Studies*, Series P-23, no. 77 (Washington, D.C.: U.S. Government Printing Office, 1978).
15. Paul C. Glick, "The Future of the American Family," in *Consequences of Changing U.S. Population: Baby Boom and Bust* (Hearings before the Select Committee on Population, U.S. House of Representatives, May 23, 1978; Washington, D.C.: U.S. Government Printing Office, 1978), pp. 287-306.
16. Still more are in families with separated parents who do not divorce.
17. For the review in the remainder of this chapter we are indebted to the research assistance of Dr. Sarah Rosenfield. Our overview concentrates on two major issues: the existence and perception of social and personal problems in the United States population and the distribution of these problems across major demographic groups; and data about where people go for help for their problems, and how help-seeking behavior varies by demographic characteristics. This review is selective in several ways. First we focus on "problems" that are most relevant to the family service domain. Second, we concentrate on recent empirical work, specifically in the 1970s. (When limited information is available on a particular issue, however, we refer to earlier research in the 1960s.) We seek to cover a broad range of data on problems and help-seeking behavior, including national sample polls as well as more traditional social science surveys.
18. Gerald Gurin, Joseph Veroff, and Sheila Feld, *Americans View Their Mental Health* (New York: Basic Books, 1960).
19. Joseph Veroff, Helen Melnick, and Richard Kulka, "Personal, Situational, and Interpersonal Attributions of Causes of Critical Life Problems," revision of a paper presented at the 85th annual meeting of the American Psychological Association, San Francisco, 1977; Richard Kulka, Joseph Veroff, and Eliazabeth Douvan, "Social Class and the Use of Professional Help for Personal Problems, 1957 and 1976," *Journal of Health and Social Behavior* 20 (March 1979): 2–17. The full report of this research is scheduled to appear after we go to press in two volumes whose titles are: Joseph Veroff, Elizabeth Douvan, and Richard Kulka, *The Inner American* and *Mental Health in America, 1957 to 1976* (New York: Basic Books, 1981).
20. Gallup Organization, *The Gallup Poll*, Aug. 11, 1977, and Sept. 29, 1977.
21. The exact frequencies of these responses are not reported.
22. Gallup Organization, "American Families, 1980: A Summary of Findings" (processed; Princeton, N.J.: The Organization, 1980), p. 31.

23. Veroff, Melnick, and Kulka, "Personal, Situational, and Interpersonal Attributions."

24. These responses are not cross-classified—that is, it is not known whether the same people reporting parent-child problems, for example, also report marital problems. This may be changed when the final report is published.

25. There are no other demographic characteristics included in these preliminary reports from the research. The categories of age groups are young (21–34 years), middle-aged (35–54), and old (55 +). Categories of education are grade school, high school, and college.

26. Herbert Yahraes, "Physical Violence in Families" (based on the research of Murray Straus and Richard Gelles), in Eunice Corfman, ed., *Families Today* (Washington, D.C.: National Institute of Mental Health, 1979), vol. 2, pp. 553–555.

27. Most of the studies cited here are based on large, representative samples of the United States population. For example, Morgan studied a national sample of 5,000 families, Glick and Norton (1971) used a sample of 28,000 households from the Survey of Economic Opportunity, and Norton and Glick (1976) used data from the National Center for Health Statistics and the Bureau of the Census. Bumpass and Sweet used 1970 National Fertility Study data on 5,442 women, and Miao used Bureau of the Census and Department of Labor data on large national samples. See James N. Morgan, *Five Thousand American Families: Patterns of Economic Progress*, vol. 1 (Ann Arbor, Mich.: University of Michigan, Survey Research Center of the Institute for Social Research, 1974); Paul C. Glick and Arthur J. Norton, "Frequency, Duration and Probability of Marriage and Divorce," *Journal of Marriage and the Family* 33 (May 1971): 307–317; Arthur J. Norton and Paul C. Glick, "Marital Instability: Past, Present, and Future," *Journal of Social Issues* 32, no. 1 (1976): 5–20, 441; Larry L. Bumpass and James A. Sweet, "Differentials in Marital Instability, 1970," *American Sociological Review* 37 (Dec. 1972): 754–766; and Greta Miao, "Marital Instability and Unemployment among Whites and Nonwhites: The Moynihan Report Revisited Again," *Journal of Marriage and the Family* 36 (Feb. 1974): 77–86.

To give an estimate of the current divorce rate, Norton and Glick show the average rate for the U.S. population in the 1972–1974 period to be 32 per 1,000 married women fourteen to forty-four years of age, totalling a mean of 907,000 divorces per year. This represents an increase over time from 1969–1971, when the average number of divorces was 702,000; in 1966–1968 the number was 535,000; in 1963–1965 the average was 452,000; and in 1960–1962, 407,000. More recent data show divorce rates per 100 in the population as follows: 1966, 2.5; 1971, 3.7; 1972, 4.1; 1973, 4.4; 1974, 4.6; 1975, 4.9; 1976 and 1977, 5.0; 1976, 5.1. The 1977 total was 1,090,000, and the 1978 total was 1,122,000.

28. Kanter reviews studies that link family disruption in general to low income, and Sawhill, Morgan, and Rainwater all find both divorce and separation rates to be higher in low income groups. See Kanter, *Work and Family*; Isabel V. Sawhill, "Marital Instability," unpublished manuscript, Urban Institute, as reviewed in George Levinger and Oliver C. Moles, "In Conclusion: Threads in the Fabric," *Journal of Social Issues* 32, no. 1 (1975): 193–207; Morgan, *Five Thousand American Families*; and Lee Rainwater, "Work, Well-Being, and Family Life," in James O'Toole, ed., *Work and the Quality of Life: Resource Papers on Work in America* (Cambridge, Mass.: MIT Press, 1974).

29. In their analysis of trends in marital instability from the 1920s to the 1970s,

Norton and Glick find that, although rates of divorce are still clearly high in the 1970s for lower-class groups, socioeconomic differences are declining (specific rates not given). See Norton and Glick, "Marital Instability."

30. Sawhill, "Marital Instability."

31. Miao, "Marital Instability and Unemployment."

32. Frank F. Furstenberg, Jr., "Work Experiences and Family Life," in O'Toole, ed., *Work and the Quality of Life*; R. Farley, *Black Families in the United States: Demographic Trends and Consequences* (Cooperative Research Project no. 10-P-56022/5-03; Ann Arbor, Mich.: University of Michigan, 1971); Robert Hampton, "Marital Disruption: Some Social and Economic Consequences," in Greg J. Duncan and James N. Morgan, eds., *Five Thousand American Families: Patterns of Economic Progress*, vol. 3 (Ann Arbor, Mich.: Institute for Social Research, 1975); and Norton and Glick, "Marital Instability."

33. Bumpass and Sweet, "Differentials in Marital Instability." See also Norton and Glick, "Marital Instability."

34. Morgan, *Five Thousand American Families*, vol. 1.

35. Bumpass and Sweet, "Differentials in Marital Instability."

36. Gallup Organization, *Gallup Poll*.

37. *Ibid.*

38. Yahraes, "Physical Violence in Families," pp. 553–554. Also Richard J. Gelles, *Family Violence* (Beverly Hills, Calif.: Sage Publications, 1979).

39. For an exceptionally helpful perspective placing unemployment in total family context see Mary Blehan, summarizing the work of Louis Ferman, in "Family Adjustment to Unemployment," in Eunice Corfman, ed., *Families Today* (Rockville, Md.: National Institute of Mental Health, 1979), vol. 1, pp. 413–440.

40. Michael J. Piore, "Upward Mobility, Job Monotony, and Labor Market Structure," in O'Toole, ed., *Work and the Quality of Life*; David Gordon, *Theories of Poverty and Unemployment* (Lexington, Mass.: D. C. Heath, 1972); Morgan, *Five Thousand American Families*.

41. Gallup Organization, "Family Financial Situation," *Gallup Opinion Index*, Report no. 117 (March 1975), p. 10, and "Family Financial Situation," *Gallup Opinion Index*, Report no. 124 (Oct. 1975), p. 21.

42. Gallup Organization, "Satisfaction Index," *Gallup Opinion Index*, Report no. 102 (Dec. 1973), pp. 19–26; and "Job Satisfaction," *Gallup Opinion Index*, Report no. 95 (April 1973), pp. 3–25.

43. U.S. Bureau of the Census, "Money Income in 1978 of Families and Persons in the United States," *Current Population Reports*, Series P-60, no. 123 (Washington, D.C.: U.S. Government Printing Office, 1980). See also George Masnick and Mary Jo Bane, *The Nation's Families, 1960–1990* (Cambridge, Mass.: Joint Center for Urban Studies of MIT and Harvard University, 1980).

44. Roper Public Opinion Research Center, "Areas of Happiness," *Current Opinion* 4, no. 3 (March 1976): 31, and George H. Gallup, *The Gallup Poll: Public Opinion, 1935–1971*, vol. 3: *1959–1971* (New York: Random House, 1972).

45. Gallup Organization, "Satisfaction Index."

46. Gallup Organization, "Job Satisfaction."

47. Stanislav V. Kasl, "Work and Mental Health," in O'Toole, ed., *Work and the Quality of Life*.

48. Piore, "Upward Mobility."

49. Thomas C. Harris and Edwin A. Locke, "Replication of White Collar–Blue Collar Differences in Sources of Satisfaction and Dissatisfaction," *Journal of Applied Psychology* 59, no. 3 (1974): 371–373.

50. Gallup Organization, "Job Satisfaction."

51. James House, "The Effects of Occupational Stress on Physical Health," in O'Toole, ed., *Work and the Quality of Life.*

52. John J. Schwab, George J. Warheit, and Eileen B. Fennell, "An Epidemiologic Assessment of Needs and Utilization of Services," *Evaluation* 2, no. 2 (1975): 64–76; John B. McKinlay, "Some Approaches and Problems in the Study of the Use of Services: An Overview," *Journal of Health and Social Behavior* 13 (June 1972): 115–152: John B. McKinlay, "Social Networks, Lay Consultation and Help-Seeking Behavior," *Social Forces* 51 (March 1972): 275–292; and William H. McBroom, "Illness, Illness Behavior and Socio-economic Status," *Journal of Health and Social Behavior* 11, no. 4 (Dec. 1970): 319–326.

53. Bruce Dohrenwend and Barbara Snell Dohrenwend, "Social and Cultural Influences on Psychopathology," *Annual Review of Psychology* 25 (1974): 417–452; "Sex Differences in Psychiatric Disorders," *American Journal of Sociology* 82 (1977): 1447–1454; "Reply to Gore and Tudor's Comments on 'Sex Differences in Psychiatric Disorders,' " *American Journal of Sociology* 82 (1977): 1336–1345; and "Report of the Task Panel on Nature and Scope of the Problems," *Task Panel Reports Submitted to the President's Commission on Mental Health, 1978* (Washington, D.C.: U.S. Government Printing Office, 1979), vol. 2, pp. 1–138.

54. See also Lenore Radloff, "Sex Differences in Depression: The Effects of Occupation and Marital Status," *Sex Roles* 1 (1975): 249–265; and Myrna Weissman and Gerald Klerman, "Sex Differences in the Epidemiology of Depression," *Archives of General Psychiatry* 34 (1977): 98–111.

55. Dohrenwend and Dohrenwend, "Reply to Gore and Tudor."

56. Veroff, Melnick, and Kulka, "Personal, Situational and Interpersonal Attributions."

57. Kulka, Veroff, and Douvan, "Social Class," p. 5.

58. David Mechanic, colloquium at Columbia University School of Public Health, Jan. 31, 1978.

59. Derek L. Phillips, "The 'True Prevalence' of Mental Illness in a New England State," *Community Mental Health Journal* 2, no. 1 (spring 1966): 35–40.

60. As reported in Emory Cowen, "Social and Community Interventions," *Annual Review of Psychology* 24 (1973): 423–472.

61. Dohrenwend and Dohrenwend, "Report of the Task Panel."

62. In reviews of studies and in their own research, Harris, Kulka et al., Anderson and Bartkus, and Cowen, for example, report that individuals in lower socioeconomic-status groups are less likely to go for professional help than individuals in higher social classes. See Sandra L. Harris, "The Relationship between Family Income and Number of Parent Perceived Problems," *International Journal of Social Psychiatry* 20 (spring-summer 1974): 109–112; Kulka, Veroff, and Douvan, "Social Class"; James G. Anderson and David E. Bartkus, "Choices of Medical Care: A Behavioral Model of Health and Illness Behavior," *Journal of Health and Social Behavior* 14 (Dec. 1973): 348–362; and Cowen, "Social and Community Interventions."

63. McKinlay, "Some Approaches and Problems."

64. Anderson and Bartkus, "Choices of Medical Care."

65. Edward Suchman, "Social Patterns of Illness and Medical Care," *Journal of Health and Human Behavior* 6 (spring 1965): 2–16; and Reed Geertsen, Melville R. Klauber, Mark Rindflesh, Robert L. Kane, and Robert Gray, "A Re-examination of Suchman's Views on Social Factors in Health Care Utilization," *Journal of Health and Social Bahavior* 16 (June 1975): 226–237.

66. McKinlay, "Social Networks"; Eliot Freidson, "Client Control and Medical Practice," *American Journal of Sociology* 65 (1960): 374–382; Freidson, *Patients' Views of Medical Practice* (New York: Russell Sage, 1961); Freidson, *Profession of Medicine* (New York: Dodd Mead, 1970).

67. Allan Horwitz, "Social Networks and Pathways to Psychiatric Treatment," *Social Forces* 56 (Sept. 1977): 86–105.

68. Kulka, Veroff, and Douvan, "Social Class."

69. Gurin, Veroff, and Feld, *Americans View Their Mental Health.*

70. Gallup Organization, "American Families, 1980," pp. 50–51.

71. For the period 1978–1979: things going "very well," 43 percent; things going "fairly well," 51 percent. The "very badly" response total declined from 1974–1975 to 1976–1977 to 1978–1979 from 17 percent to 10 percent to 6 percent. See "Opinion Roundup," *Public Opinion* 3, no. 1 (Dec.-Jan. 1980): 30.

Chapter 2

1. *New York*, May 1980.

2. Joanne Koch and Lew Koch, *The Marriage Savers* (New York: Coward, McCann and Geoghehan, 1976), p. 19.

3. Among the pioneers in the field was David Mace, who subsequently emerged as one of the leaders in the marriage enrichment movement described in Chapter 5.

4. For the early history, see David H. Olson, "Marriage and Family Therapy: Integrative Review and Critique," in William C. Nichols, Jr., ed., *Marriage and Family Therapy* (Minneapolis: National Council on Family Relations, 1974), especially pp. 15–16.

5. For a general introduction to the field of family therapy, see Vincent D. Foley, *An Introduction to Family Therapy* (New York: Grune and Stratton, 1974). A selected list of other important works in the field includes: Nathan Ackerman, *Treating the Troubled Family* (New York: Basic Books, 1966); Ivan Boszormenyi-Nagi and Geraldine Spark, *Invisible Loyalties* (New York: Harper and Row, 1973); Murray Bowen, *Family Therapy in Clinical Practice* (New York: Jason Aronson, 1978); Jay Haley, *Changing Families* (New York: Grune and Stratton, 1971); Haley, *Problem-Solving Therapy* (New York: Harper Colophon, 1978); Haley and Lynn Hoffman, *Techniques of Family Therapy* (New York: Basic Books, 1967); Sal Minuchin, *Families and Family Therapy* (Cambridge, Mass: Harvard University Press, 1974); Virginia Satir, *Conjoint Family Therapy* (Palo Alto, Calif.: Science and Behavior Books, 1967); Ross V. Speck and Carolyn L. Attneave, *Family Networks* (New York: Pantheon, 1973).

6. Foley, *Introduction to Family Therapy*, pp. 3–4.

7. It is noteworthy that in the current atmosphere four states have delicensed psychologists and at least one (Kansas) has delicensed family day care mothers.

8. See, for example, "Marriage Counselling," *Business Week*, May 1, 1978.

9. For descriptions of some of these programs, see Sheila H. Akabas, Paul A. Kurzman, and Nancy S. Kolben, eds., *Labor and Industrial Settings: Sites for Social Work Practice* (New York: Council on Social Work Education, 1979). See also *Meeting Human Service Needs in the Workplace: A Role for Social Work*, report of a Wingspread Conference (New York: Industrial Social Welfare Center, Columbia University School of Social Work, 1980). The program descriptions in the remainder of this section are from a report released by General Mills, Inc.

10. "In House Counsel Firms Offer Employees a New Benefit: Help in Personal

Problems," *Wall Street Journal*, Aug. 13, 1979. See also "Marriage Counselling," *Business Week*; "More Care Given Employees Psyches," *New York Times*, April 1, 1979.

For some discussion of what employers provide their employees and what some of the issues are, see Sheila B. Kamerman and Paul W. Kingston, "Employer Responses to the Family Responsibilities of Employees," a paper prepared for the National Academy of Science/National Research Council Panel on Work, Family, and Community, 1981.

11. These data are from the work of Alison Clarke-Stewart as summarized by David Harman and Orville Brim, Jr., in *Learning to Be Parents* (Beverly Hills, Calif.: Sage Publications, 1980), pp. 162–163.

12. Harold Goldberg, *The New Male* (New York: William Morrow and Co., 1979).

13. *Ibid.*, p. 214.

14. *Ibid.*, p. 194.

15. Dr. Joyce Brothers, *How to Get Whatever You Want Out of Life* (New York: Simon and Schuster, 1978).

16. Dr. Wayne W. Dyer, *Your Erroneous Zones* (New York: Avon, 1976), and *Pulling Your Own Strings* (New York: Avon, 1977).

17. Dyer, *Pulling Your Own Strings*, p. 12.

18. One example is Manuel J. Smith, Ph.D., *When I Say No I Feel Guilty* (New York: Dial Press, 1975).

19. Merle Shain, *When Lovers Are Friends* (New York: Lippincott, 1978.

20. Nathanial Lande, *Emotional Maintenance Manual* (New York: Rawson Wade, 1979), pp. 12–13.

21. "A Hot Line for Everyday Families," *New York Times*, Sept. 20, 1979.

22. One such service is *Psychology Today* "Cassettes," sold through the magazine.

23. For a report of how the food buying and meal patterns of American families have changed as a consequence of the growth in the numbers of women in the labor force, see "Food and the Working Wife," *New York Times*, May 23, 1979.

24. "Florida Geriatric Consultants," *New York Times*, Feb. 28, 1980.

25. A similar service is provided as a statutory personal social service in Britain, in the form of a "health visitor." Part nurse and part social worker, she provides this kind of help to every family with a newborn child. For some discussions of health visitors and how they work, see Alfred J. Kahn and Sheila B. Kamerman, *Not for the Poor Alone: European Social Services* (Philadelphia: Temple University Press, 1975; pbk. ed., New York: Harper Colophon Books, 1977).

26. *New York Times*, Oct. 6, 1977.

27. "Latest Wrinkles in Your Corner Supermarket," *U.S. News and World Report*, July 7, 1980.

28. This service has been written about in a number of magazine and newspaper articles. See, for example, Anne Taylor Fleming, "New Frontiers in Conception," *New York Times Magazine*, July 20, 1980.

29. "The Burgeoning Growth of Child Care Chains," *Business Week*, Jan. 21, 1980.

30. This estimate is derived as follows: T. W. Rodes and J. C. Moore, *National Child Care Consumer Study, 1975* (Arlington, Va.: Unco, Inc., 1976), calculated $6.3 billion in costs to consumers to which we have added the more recent estimate of $2.52 billion in public expenditures as reported in Congressional Budget Office,

Child Care and Preschool: Options for Federal Support (Washington, D.C.: U.S. Government Printing Office, 1978), p. x.

31. Katherine Senn Perry, *Child Care Centers Sponsored by Employers and Labor Unions in the United States* (Washington, D.C.: U.S. Department of Labor, Women's Bureau, 1980). Also Sheila B. Kamerman and Alfred J. Kahn, *Child Care, Family Benefits and Working Parents* (New York: Columbia University Press, 1981).

32. Kahn and Kamerman, *Not for the Poor Alone*.

Chapter 3

1. Harold Hagen and John E. Hansan, "How the States Put the Program Together," *Public Welfare* 36, no. 3 (summer 1978): 43–47.

2. *Ibid.*

3. "Report of the Task Panel on Community Mental Health Centers Assessment," *Task Panel Reports Submitted to the President's Commission on Mental Health, 1978: Appendix* (Washington, D.C.: U.S. Government Printing Office, 1979), vol. 2, p. 314. Also see Survey and Reports Branch, Division of Biometry and Epidemiology, National Institute of Mental Health, *Provisional Data on Federally Funded Community Mental Health Centers, 1976–77* (processed; May 1978), especially Tables 1, 9, and 12.

4. Neil Gilbert, "The Transformation of the Social Services," *Social Service Review* 51, no. 4 (Dec. 1977): 624–641. Also see Martha Derthick, *Uncontrollable Spending for Social Services Grants* (Washington, D.C.: Brookings Institution, 1975), and Alfred J. Kahn, "New Directions in Social Services," *Public Welfare* 34, no. 2 (spring 1976): 26–32.

5. Alfred J. Kahn, "Service Delivery at the Neighborhood Level: Experience, Theory, and Fads," *Social Service Review* 50, no. 1 (March 1976): 40.

6. *Ibid.*

7. Sheila B. Kamerman and Alfred J. Kahn, *Social Services in the United States* (Philadelphia: Temple University Press, 1976), pp. 194–195, 437–438, 471–478; Alfred J. Kahn, *Social Policy and Social Services* (2nd ed.; New York: Random House, 1979), pp. 171–173.

8. Kamerman and Kahn, *Social Services in the United States*, pp. 442–456.

9. Alfred J. Kahn and Sheila B. Kamerman, "The Course of the Personal Social Services," *Public Welfare* 36, no. 3 (summer 1978): 29–42.

10. Controller General of the United States, *Early Childhood and Family Development Programs Improve the Quality of Life for Low-Income Families*, Report to the Congress, HRD-79-40 (Washington, D.C.: General Accounting Office, 1979). See also Edward Zigler and Jeanette Valentine, eds., *Project Head Start: A Legacy of the War on Poverty* (New York: Free Press, 1979).

11. Controller General, *Early Childhood*.

12. Kahn and Kamerman, "The Course of Personal Social Services."

13. In 1980, RSA moved to a new Department of Education and was replaced by a Developmental Disabilities Administration. A fifth unit, the Administration for Public Services, was abolished and most of its staff was integrated into the categorical units. However, a new Office of Program Integration and Review, whose role and function are yet to emerge, could either considerably advance the cause of comprehensive service development or merely meet minimal federal Title XX technical and administrative responsibilities, leaving funds and initiatives to the

categorical "administrations" (Aged; Children-Youth-Families; Native Americans; Developmental Disabilities). Given block grant initiatives from the Reagan administration as we go to press, the latter prediction or more complete assignment of decisions to the states appears to be most realistic.

14. William Benton, *Social Services: Federal Legislation vs. State Implementation* (Washington, D.C.: Urban Institute, 1978). Also see Gloria Kilgore and Gabriel Salmon, *Technical Notes: Summaries and Characteristics of States' Title XX Social Service Plans for Fiscal Year 1979* (Washington, D.C.: U.S. Department of Health, Education, and Welfare, 1979), and *Social Services, U.S.A.*, issued periodically by the Office of Human Development Services, U.S. Department of Health and Human Services.

15. Office of Human Development Service, *Social Services, U. S. A.*, "Third Quarter Report," FY 1978 (Washington, D.C.: U.S. Department of Health and Human Services, 1980), p. 10.

16. Benton, *Social Services*.

17. The Cleveland Foundation and the American Public Welfare Association, *Strategy to Test Alternative Approaches for a Comprehensive Integrated System of Social Services* (Cleveland: The Foundation, 1978), and *Proposal for Personal Social Service Delivery Project* (Cleveland: The Foundation, 1978).

18. The American Public Welfare Association, "Social Welfare Goals for America's Next Decade," *Public Welfare* 35, no. 2 (spring 1977): 4–60. See reports on personal social services, child welfare, and aging.

19. Laurence E. Lynn, Jr., *The State and Human Services* (Cambridge, Mass.: MIT Press, 1980).

20. Steven P. Segal, "Community Mental Health," in Neil Gilbert and Harry Specht, eds., *The Handbook of the Social Services* (Englewood Cliffs, N.J.: Prentice-Hall, 1981), and Bernard L. Bloom, *Community Mental Health* (Monterey, Calif.: Brooks/Cole, 1977).

21. Reports of Task Panels on "Planning and Review," "Organization and Structure," "Community Mental Health Centers Assessment," *Task Panel Reports Submitted to the President's Commission on Mental Health*, pp. 239–339. For history, see pp. 316–318.

22. *Ibid.*

23. *Ibid.*, pp. 51, 101, 102. See also Carol Arntunia, John Kroll, and Stephanie Murphy, *Source Book of Programs, 1976: Community Mental Health Centers* (Palo Alto, Calif.: American Institute for Research, 1976); National Institute of Mental Health, "Provisional Data for Federally Funded Community Mental Health Centers, 1976–77" (mimeo.; Rockville, Md.: The Institute, 1977), p. 22, table 12.

Chapter 4

1. Salvatore Ambrosino, "Family Services and Family Service Agencies," in John Turner, ed., *Encyclopedia of Social Work* (17th issue; Washington, D.C.: National Association of Social Workers, 1977), vol. 1, pp. 429–434.

2. Patrick V. Riley, "Family Services," in Neil Gilbert and Harry Specht, eds., *The Handbook of the Social Services* (Englewood Cliffs, N.J.: Prentice-Hall, 1981).

3. For a discussion of these programs as the core of a family service agency, see Salvatore Ambrosino, "Integrating Counselling, Family Life Education, and Family Advocacy," *Social Casework* 60, no. 10 (Dec. 1979): 579–585.

4. Dorothy Fahs Beck and Mary Ann Jones, *Progress on Family Problems* (New York: Family Service Association of America, 1973).

5. Riley, "Family Services," p. 7.

6. For a review of the research on family service agencies, see Scott Briar and Jon R. Conte, "Families," in Henry S. Maas, ed., *Social Service Research: Reviews of Studies* (Washington, D.C.: National Association of Social Workers, 1978), pp. 9–38.

7. See, for example, Sara E. Bonkowski and Brenda Wanner-Westly, "The Divorce Group: A New Treatment Modality," *Social Casework* 60, no. 9 (Nov. 1979): 552–557.

8. See, for example, Janice Prochaska and Jane R. Coyle, "Choosing Parenthood: A Needed Family Life Education Group," *Social Casework* 60, no. 5 (May 1979): 289–295, and Roberta Wooten, "Family Services: Family Life Education," in Turner, ed., *Encyclopedia*, vol. 1, pp. 423–429.

9. In addition to the references provided in Chapter 2, note 5, see Max Siporin, "Marriage and Family Therapy in Social Work," *Social Casework* 61, no. 1 (Jan. 1980): 11–21.

10. Briar and Conte, "Families," esp. pp. 22–26.

11. Fahs Beck and Jones, *Progress on Family Problems*. See also Briar and Conte, "Families."

12. Family Service Association of America, *Annual Report* (New York: FSAA, 1978).

13. Ellen Manser, *Family Advocacy: A Manual for Action* (New York: Family Service Association of America, 1973); Patrick V. Riley, "Family Advocacy: Case to Cause and Back to Case," *Child Welfare* 50 (July 1971): 374–383; Robert Sunley, "Family Advocacy: From Case to Cause," *Social Casework* 51, no. 6 (June 1970): 347–357. On the integration of counselling, family life education, and advocacy, see Ambrosino, "Integrating."

14. Fahs Beck and Jones, *Progress on Family Problems*.

15. Family Service Association of America, *Overview of Findings of the FSAA Task Force on Family Life Education, Development and Enrichment* (New York: FSAA, 1976).

16. *Ibid.*, pp. 1–24.

17. *Ibid.*, p. 2.

18. Family Service Association of America, *Workshop Models for Family Life Education*: Donal P. Riley, Kathryn Apgar, and John Eaton, *Parent Child Communication* (New York: FSAA, 1977); Diana Richmond Garland, *Couples Communication and Negotiation Skills* (New York: FSAA, 1978); Betsy Nicholson Callahan and Vivian Freeman, *Career Planning for Women* (New York: FSAA, 1978); Betsy Nicholson Callahan, *Separation and Divorce* (New York: FSAA, 1979).

19. Ambrosino, "Integrating."

20. Dale Hoffman, "Learning How to Be a Parent," *New York*, May 15, 1978, pp. 62–66; quotation, p. 61.

21. David Harman and Orville G. Brim, Jr., *Learning to Be Parents* (Beverly Hills, Calif.: Sage Publications, 1980). This book updates Orville G. Brim, Jr., *Education for Parenting* (New York: Russell Sage Foundation, 1959).

Also see Wooten, "Family Services: Family Life Education"; Steven L. Schlossman, "Before Home Start: Note Toward a History of Parent Education in America, 1897–1929," *Harvard Educational Review* 46, no. 3 (Aug. 1976): 436–467; Eleanor Braun Luckey, "Family Life Education Revisited," *Family Coordinator* 27, no. 1 (Jan. 1978): 69–73; James W. Croake and Kenneth E. Glover, "A History and Evaluation of Parent Education," *Family Coordinator* 26, no. 2 (April 1977): 151–158.

22. Aline B. Auerbach, "Parent Groups in Education," mimeo. paper presented before the American Orthopsychiatric Association, New York, 1954, cited by Harman and Brim, *Learning to Be Parents*, p. 176.

23. Harman and Brim, *Learning to Be Parents*, ch. 9.

24. Harman and Brim develop "the principle of situation specificity" as their main principle for this evolving field. *Ibid.*, p. 43.

Chapter 5

1. Veroff, unpublished 1976 study, cited in "Report of the Task Panel on Community Support Systems," *Task Panel Reports Submitted to the President's Commission on Mental Health, 1978: Appendix* (Washington, D.C.: U.S. Government Printing Office, 1979), vol. 2, p. 192; Seward Hiltner, *Pastoral Counseling* (New York and Nashville: Abingdon, 1949), p. 18.

2. We use the term "church" here to mean all religious institutions regardless of denomination.

3. National Conference of Catholic Bishops and United States Catholic Conference, *A Vision and Strategy* (Washington, D.C.: U.S. Catholic Conference, 1978), pp. 7–11.

4. Don Demarest et al., *Marriage Encounter: A Guide to Sharing* (St. Paul, Minn.: Carillon, 1977), p. 3.

5. Leon Smith, *Family Ministry: An Educational Resource for the Local Church* (Nashville: Discipleship Resources, 1975), foreword, intro., ch. 1, and (quotation) p. 7.

6. *Ibid.*, pp. 9–10.

7. *Ibid.*, p. 10.

8. For another illustration see the periodic mailing of materials and the various communications workshops and laboratories organized by Frank and Loraine Pitman as co-directors of family education of the Division of Homeland Ministries, Christian Church (Disciples of Christ), based in Indianapolis.

9. The Most Reverend John R. Quinn, President, National Conference of Catholic Bishops, foreword to *Vision and Strategy*, quoting the Papal Committee for the Family, *The Family in the Pastoral Activity of the Church*.

10. John L. Thomas, *The American Catholic Family: A Sociological Perspective* (pamphlet; Washington, D.C.: U. S. Catholic Conference, 1974), p. 14.

11. Fr. Gabriel Calvo, "Reflections," *Marriage Encounter* 8, no. 6 (June 1979): 10, 4. While Fr. Calvo launched the large Catholic movement, earlier work in the U.S. had been begun by David and Vera Mace, Len and Antoinette Smith, Herbert Otto, and Sherod Miller, who are mentioned elsewhere in this chapter.

12. G. William Sheek, "Theological Perspectives on the Relationship between Public Policy and Family Life," processed Dec. 1979, p. 5.

13. Commission on Marriage and Family Life, *Models of Ministry* (Washington, D.C.: U.S. Catholic Conference, 1979).

14. On ACME see David Mace and Vera Mace, *We Can Have Better Marriages if We Really Want Them* (Nashville: Abington, 1974). David Mace, a leading family sociologist and both teacher and administrator in the marriage counselling and enrichment fields, is co-author with his wife of a series of relevant volumes. ACME is a "couple" membership organization that undertakes educational, promotional, referral, and self-help activities through local chapters.

The quotation is from a personal communication dated July 30, 1980, from Dr.

Joe E. Leonard, Jr., Department of Educational Planning Services, Family Ministries, American Baptist Churches, USA, Valley Forge, Pennsylvania.

15. Department of Education, U.S. Catholic Conference, *Marriage and Family Enrichment: A Resource Guide* (Washington, D.C.: U.S. Catholic Conference, 1979).

16. Evelyn M. Duvall, *Family Development* (4th ed.; New York: Lippincott, 1971).

17. The national coordinating agencies are the Council of Jewish Federations and Welfare Funds and the Association of Jewish Family and Children's Agencies.

18. Hiltner, *Pastoral Counseling*, p. 18.

19. *Ibid.*, pp. 19–20.

20. *Ibid.*, ch. 1. See pp. 30–32.

21. In a self-report survey in 1979, the American Association of Pastoral Counselors, a certifying group whose members probably constitute the most highly trained component of the profession, found the following distribution among settings: 43 percent in pastoral counselling centers; 22 percent in congregations; 13 percent in chaplaincy; 6 percent in mental health facilities; 6 percent in university and seminary settings. About half were responsible to an ecclesiastical organization for their counselling (American Association of Pastoral Counselors *Newsletter*, Feb. 1980, p. 1.

22. Full-time programs are manageable with three full days a week.

23. The Association for Clinical and Pastoral Education is an ecumenical, interfaith association composed of clinical pastoral educators, theological school representatives, representatives of clinical agencies and health and welfare institutions, and others. It defines standards and accredits centers for clinical pastoral education and certifies supervisors. The work derives from pastoral activity and chaplaincies in hospitals, prisons, and mental health clinics and was originally inspired by Dr. Richard Cabot and Anton Boiser. There are now some 800 certified supervisors and 350–400 agencies certified as training centers. Some 5,000 theological seminary and post-seminary students participate in training each year, 60 percent of them part time. The basic task is to train parish clergy to integrate counselling into their normal functions. Those who take part in a "second rung" of advanced training become qualified for the American Association of Pastoral Counseling and the American Association of Marriage and Family Counselors. About one third of the participants in training are Catholic and two-thirds Protestant.

24. Carroll A. Wise, *Pastoral Counseling: Its Theory and Practice* (New York: Harper and Brothers, 1951), pp. 67–68.

25. Fr. Tom Hill, "Family Encounter" in *Marriage Encounter* 9, no. 1 (Jan. 1980): 6–11.

26. Demarest et al., *Marriage Encounter*, p. ix.

27. *Marriage Enrichment Resource Manual* (St. Paul, Minn.: National Marriage Encounter, 1978).

28. "Marriage Counseling," *Business Week*, May 1, 1978, p. 110. A full report is to be published as Larry Hof and William R. Miller, *Marriage Enrichment: Philosophy, Process, and Programs*.

29. Russell L. Wilson and June N. Wilson, "The Family Enrichment Weekend," in Herbert A. Otto, ed., *Marriage and Family Enrichment* (Nashville, Tenn.: Abingdon, 1976), pp. 39–40.

30. For a full overview, see Otto, ed., *Marriage and Family Enrichment*, and Demarest et al., *Marriage Encounter*.

31. Demarest et al., *Marriage Encounter*, p. 40. W = Writing; E = Exchange; D = Dialogue; S = Select Question for Next Dialogue.

32. Otto, ed., *Marriage and Family Enrichment*, p. 11.

33. *Ibid.*

34. Gerald Summerford, "The Grayness Syndrome," *Marriage Encounter* 8, no. 5 (May 1979): 22.

35. Fr. Gabriel Calvo, "Reflections," p. 12.

36. Otto, ed., *Marriage and Family Enrichment*, pp. 14–15.

37. Mace in *ibid.*, p. 176.

38. Personal communication, Dr. Daniel B. Wackman, Interpersonal Communications Programs, Inc., April 2, 1980. The more recent assessment is Karen Smith Wampler and Douglas H. Sprenkle, "The Minnesota Couple Communication Program: A Follow-Up Study," *Journal of Marriage and the Family* 42, no. 3 (Aug. 1980): 577–584.

39. Bernard G. Guerney, Jr., *Relationship Enhancement: Skill Training Programs for Therapy, Problem Prevention, and Enrichment* (San Francisco: Jossey-Bass, 1977). See also Charlotte Dickerson Moore, "Fortifying Family Ties," in Eunice Corfman, ed., *Families Today* (National Institute of Mental Health Science Monographs no. 1; Washington, D.C.: U.S. Government Printing Office, 1979), vol. 2, pp. 929–969.

40. Elam W. Nunnally, Sherod Miller, and Daniel B. Wackman, "The Minnesota Couples Communications Program," *Small Group Behavior* 6, no. 1 (Feb. 1975): 57.

41. See Otto, ed., *Marriage and Family Enrichment*.

42. "Family Cluster Training Events" (brochure; Rochester, N.Y., spring-summer 1980). Also personal communication, Dr. Margaret M. Sawin, April 10, 1980.

43. *Ibid.* Also see Margaret Sawin, *Family Enrichment with Family Clusters* (Valley Forge, Pa.: Judson, 1979), and the discussion in Otto, ed., *Marriage and Family Enrichment*, pp. 20–21.

44. Otto, ed., *Marriage and Family Enrichment*. Also see his article, "Marriage and Family Enrichment Programs in North America," *Family Coordinator* 24, no. 2 (April 1975): 137–142.

45. Otto, ed., *Marriage and Family Enrichment*.

46. A sophisticated research review and a proposal for a sequential model integrating attitudinal and behavioral change objectives is offered by Larry Hof, Norman Epstein, and William R. Miller, "Integrating Attitudinal and Behavioral Change in Marriage Enrichment," *Family Relations* 29, no. 2 (April 1980): 241–248.

47. *Ibid.*

Chapter 6

1. Maurice Jackson, "Their Brothers' Keepers" (mimeo.; Berkeley, Calif.: Pacific School of Religion, 1963), cited in Alfred H. Katz, "Self-Help Organizations and Volunteer Participation in Social Welfare," *Social Work* 15 (Jan. 1970): 52.

2. Alfred H. Katz and Eugene I. Bender, *The Strength in Us* (New York: New Viewpoints, 1976), p. 36.

3. "Groups Help Those Who Help Themselves," *Hastings Center Report* 7 (Oct. 1977): 3.

4. Most of our historical material has been drawn from the writings of Alfred Katz. For additional information, see Alfred H. Katz, "Self-Help Groups," in John Turner, ed., *Encyclopedia of Social Work*, vol. 2 (Washington, D.C.: National Association of Social Workers, 1977), pp. 1254–1260; and Alfred H. Katz and Eugene Bender, "Self-Help Groups in Western Society: History and Prospects," *Journal of Applied Behavioral Science* 12 (July-Sept. 1976): 265–282.

5. Petr Kropotkin, *Mutual Aid: A Factor of Evolution* (New York: New York University Press, 1972), cited in Katz and Bender, *The Strength in Us*, ch. 2.

6. Matthew P. Dumont, "Self-Help Treatment Programs," *American Journal of Psychiatry* 131 (June 1974): 631.

7. Katz, "Self-Help Groups," p. 1256.

8. Dumont, "Self-Help Treatment Programs," pp. 631–632, 634.

9. See, for example, Sol Tax, "Self-Help Groups: Thoughts on Public Policy," *Journal of Applied Behavior Science* 12 (July-Sept. 1976): 448–454; Victor W. Sidel and Ruth Sidel, "Beyond Coping," *Social Policy* 7 (Sept.-Oct. 1976): 67–69; Katz and Bender, *The Strength in Us*; and Anthony J. Vattano, "Power to the People: Self-Help Groups," *Social Work* 17 (July 1972): 7–15.

10. Tax, "Self-Help Groups," p. 449.

11. Morton A. Lieberman and Leonard D. Borman, "Self-Help and Social Research," *Journal of Applied Behavioral Science* 12 (July-Sept. 1976): 457.

12. Gustave A. Decocq, "European and North American Self-Help Movements: Some Contrasts," in Katz and Bender, *The Strength in Us*, ch. 19.

13. Richard Steinman and Donald M. Traunstein, "Redefining Deviance: The Self-Help Challenge to the Human Services," *Journal of Applied Behavioral Science* 12 (July-Sept. 1976): 351.

14. Dumont, "Self-Help Treatment Programs, pp. 632, 633.

15. C. G. [Colin Greer], "A Cautionary Note," *Social Policy* 7 (Sept.-Oct. 1976): 3.

16. Vattano, "Power to the People," p. 8. See also, minutes of meeting, Committee of Community Social Researchers, Community Council of Greater New York, Oct. 11, 1977, pp. 3–4.

17. Frank Baker, "The Interface between Professionals and Natural Support Systems," *Clinical Social Work Journal* 5 (summer 1977): 147.

18. William B. Cameron, *Modern Social Movements: A Sociological Outline* (New York: Random House, 1966), p. 10, cited in Katz and Bender, *The Strength in Us*, pp. 29–30.

19. Marie Killilea, "Mutual Help Organizations: Interpretations in the Literature," in Gerald Caplan and Marie Killilea, eds., *Support Systems and Mutual Help: Multi-disciplinary Explorations* (New York: Grune and Stratton, 1976), pp. 37–93, 39. See Killilea's entire article for a full discussion of these various interpretations.

20. Michael Rossman, "Self-Help Marketplace," *Social Policy* 7 (Sept.-Oct. 1976): 86–91.

21. Vattano, "Power to the People."

22. Alan Gartner and Frank Reissman, *Self-Help in the Human Services* (San Francisco: Jossey-Bass, 1977), ch. 1.

23. Gerald Caplan, *Support Systems and Community Mental Health* (New York: Behavioral Publications, 1974), p. 2, cited in Killilea, "Mutual Help Organizations," p. 41.

24. Caplan, *Support Systems and Community Mental Health*, pp. 5–6, cited in

Gerald Caplan, "The Family as a Support System," in Caplan and Killilea, eds., *Support Systems and Mutual Help*, p. 20.

25. Ross V. Speck and Carolyn L. Attneave, *Family Networks* (New York: Vintage Books, 1974); Alice H. Collins and Diane L. Pancoast, *Natural Helping Networks* (Washington, D.C.: National Association of Social Workers, 1976); and Phyllis Rolfe Silverman, "The Widow as a Caregiver in a Program of Preventive Intervention with Other Widows," in Caplan and Killilea, eds., *Support Systems and Mutual Help*, ch. 10.

26. Katz and Bender, *The Strength in Us*, p. 9.

27. See, for example, Thomas J. Powell, "The Use of Self-Help Groups as Supportive Reference Communities," *American Journal of Orthopsychiatry* 45 (Oct. 1975): 756–764; Leon H. Levy, "Self Help Groups: Types and Psychological Processes," *Journal of Applied Behavioral Science* 12 (July–Sept. 1976): 310–322; and Steinman and Traunstein, "Redefining Deviance."

28. Edward Sagarin, *Odd Man In: Societies of Deviants in America* (Chicago: Quadrangle, 1969), p. 21, cited in Katz, "Self-Help Groups," p. 1258.

29. Katz and Bender, *The Strength in Us*, p. 39.

30. *Ibid.*, pp. 37–38, 41.

31. Steinman and Traunstein, "Redefining Deviance," pp. 352–355.

32. Levy, "Self Help Groups," pp. 312–313.

33. Powell, "The Use of Self-Help Groups," pp. 758–759.

34. Katz and Bender, *The Strength in Us*, p. 113.

35. Steinman and Traunstein, "Redefining Deviance," pp. 354–355.

36. Katz and Bender, *The Strength in Us*, pp. 112–122.

37. *Ibid.*, pp. 122–124.

38. Dumont, "Self-Help Treatment Programs," p. 633.

39. David Spiegal, "Going Public and Self-Help," in Caplan and Killilea, eds., *Support Systems and Mutual Help*, pp. 135–154.

40. Eugene C. Durman, "The Role of Self-Help in Service Provision," *Journal of Applied Behavioral Science* 12 (July–Sept. 1976): 433–437.

41. Frank Riessman, "How Does Self-Help Work?" *Social Policy* 7 (Sept.-Oct. 1976): 41–45.

42. Levy, "Self Help Groups," pp. 315–320.

43. Killilea, "Mutual Help Organizations," pp. 39 and 67–75. It should be noted that Killilea's review was written before the publication of the special issues on self-help by *Social Policy* (vol. 7 [Sept.–Oct. 1976]) and the *Journal of Applied Behavioral Science* (vol. 12 [Sept.-Oct. 1976]), from which much of the earlier material in this section is drawn. Hence, she does not refer to the work of some of these authors. With the exception of Levy's analyses of psychological processes, however, she touches on all the major themes in the literature on self-help.

44. See, for example, Vattano, "Power to the People"; Powell, "The Use of Self-Help Groups"; Katz, "Self-Help Groups"; and Baker, "Interface between Professionals and Natural Support Systems."

45. Baker, "Interface between Professionals and Natural Support Systems," pp. 144–145.

46. Ralph W. Tyler, "Social Policy and Self-Help Groups," *Journal of Applied Behavioral Science* 12 (July–Sept. 1976): 444–448.

47. Katz, "Self-Help Groups," pp. 1259–1260.

48. Sidel and Sidel, "Beyond Coping," pp. 67–69.

49. Phyllis R. Silverman and Hope G. Murrow, "Mutual Help during Critical Role Transitions," *Journal of Applied Behavioral Science* 12 (July-Sept. 1976): 411.

50. *Ibid.*, pp. 411–412.

51. *Ibid.*, pp. 412–417.

52. Ethel P. Gould, "Special Report: The Single-Parent Family Benefits in Parents Without Partners, Inc.," *Journal of Marriage and the Family* 30 (Nov. 1968): 666.

53. Katz and Bender, *The Strength in Us*, pp. 69–70.

54. Robert S. Weiss, "The Contribution of an Organization of Single Parents to the Well-Being of Its Members," in Caplan and Killilea, eds., *Support Systems and Mutual Help*, p. 178.

55. Katz and Bender, *The Strength in Us*, p. 70.

56. Caplan, "The Family as a Support System," pp. 22–31, 32–36.

57. Carol Swenson, "Social Networks, Mutual Aid and the Life Model of Practice," in Carel B. Germain, ed., *Social Work Practice: People and Environments* (New York: Columbia University Press, 1979), pp. 213–238.

58. Speck and Attneave, *Family Networks*, p. 7, for the quotation above. See these authors for a fuller description of this approach.

59. Bruce M. Pringle, "Family Clusters as a Means of Reducing Isolation among Urbanites," *The Family Coordinator* 23, no. 2 (April 1974): 175–180.

60. See Collins and Pancoast, *Natural Helping Networks*, for a fuller description of this program and the natural helping network strategy.

61. Mildred Fine Kaplan et al., "A Self-Help Telephone Service for Women," *Social Work* 21 (Nov. 1975): 519–520.

62. See Phyllis R. Silverman, "The Widow as a Caregiver," and Ruby B. Abrahams, "Mutual Helping: Styles of Caregiving in a Mutual Aid Program—the Widowed Service Line," in Caplan and Killilea, eds., *Support Systems and Mutual Help*, for further information on these programs. Published since our review is Phyllis R. Silverman, *Mutual Help Groups: Organization and Development* (Beverly Hills, Calif.: Sage Publications, 1980).

63. "Report of the Task Panel on Community Support Systems, Submitted to the President's Commission on Mental Health, February 15, 1978," in *Task Panel Reports Submitted to the President's Commission on Mental Health, 1978: Appendix* (Washington, D.C.: U.S. Government Printing Office, 1979), vol. 2, p. 210.

64. Killilea, "Mutual Help Organizations," pp. 78–82.

65. Katz and Bender, "Self-Help Groups in Western Society," pp. 281–282.

66. Durman, "The Role of Self-Help," pp. 437–443.

67. Minutes, Committee of Community Social Researchers, p. 4.

68. See *Report to the President from the President's Commission on Mental Health, 1978* (Washington, D.C.: U.S. Government Printing Office, 1978).

69. See Eugene Litwak, "Theory of Natural Support Systems and Self-Help Groups," paper presented at the annual meeting of the American Psychiatric Association, Atlanta, Ga., May, 1978 (mimeo.), for further elaboration of this concept.

70. This is the "helper therapy" concept first identified by Frank Reissman. See Reissman, "How Does Self-Help Work?" for further discussion.

Chapter 7

1. For example, see Murray S. Weitzman, "Finally the Family," in Conrad Taeuber, spec. ed., *America in the Seventies: Some Social Indicators (The Annals,* vol. 435; Philadelphia: American Academy of Policital and Social Sciences, Jan. 1978), pp. 61–82.

2. See Mary Jo Bane, *Here to Stay* (New York: Basic Books, 1976); George Masnick and Mary Jo Bane, *The Nation's Families, 1960–1990* (Cambridge, Mass.: Joint Center for Urban Studies of MIT and Harvard University, 1980).

3. Marvin Sussman, "Family, Kinship and Bureaucracy," in Angus Campbell and Phillip E. Converse, ed., *The Human Meaning of Social Change* (New York: Russell Sage Foundation, 1972), pp. 146–153.

4. Major sources are Campbell and Converse, ed., *Human Meaning*, 1978; Taeuber, spec. ed., *America in the Seventies*; Angus Campbell, Phillip E. Converse, and Williard L. Rogers, *The Quality of American Life* (New York: Russell Sage Foundation, 1976); and Frank M. Andrews and Stephen B. Withey, *Social Indicators of Well-Being: Americans' Perceptions of Life Quality* (New York: Plenum, 1976).

5. Campbell, Converse, and Rogers, *Quality of American Life*, Tables 3 and 4, and Taeuber, spec. ed., *America in the Seventies*, p. 19.

6. *Social Indicators, 1976* (Washington, D.C.: Bureau of the Census, U.S. Department of Commerce, 1977), chart J, p. xliii.

7. Ruth Clark and Greg Martire, "Americans, Still in a Family Way," *Public Opinion* 2, no. 5 (Oct.-Nov. 1979): 16.

8. Gallup Organization, "American Families, 1980: A Summary of Findings" (processed; Princeton, N.J.: The Organization, 1980), p. 1.

9. Clark and Martire, "Americans," p. 19.

10. *Ibid.*, p. 438.

11. Andrews and Withey, *Social Indicators of Well-Being*, pp. 250–281, 255.

12. *Ibid.*, p. 265.

13. Joseph H. Pleck and L. Lang, "Men's Family Role: Its Nature and Consequences" (Wellesley, Mass.: Wellesley College Center for Research on Women, 1978?). See also Eunice Corfman, reporting on the research of Joseph Pleck in "Married Men: Work and Family," in Eunice Corfman, ed., *Families Today* (National Institute of Mental Health Science Monographs no. 1; Washington, D.C.: U.S. Government Printing Office, 1979), vol. 1, pp. 387–412.

14. Andrews and Withey, *Social Indicators of Well-Being*, p. 304.

15. *Ibid.*, p. 305. See also Elizabeth Douvan, Joseph Veroff, and Richard Kulka, "Family Roles in a Twenty-Year Perspective," *Economic Outlook, USA* 6, no. 3 (summer 1979): 60–63.

16. *Ibid.*, p. 312.

17. Lee Rainwater, Martin Rein, and Joseph Schwartz, "Income Claims Systems in Three Countries: A Stratification Perspective," *Joint Center Family Policy Notes*, no. 16 (Cambridge, Mass.: Joint Center for Urban Studies of MIT and Harvard University, 1980).

18. See Robert Nisbet, "The Costs of Equality," in Michael Mooney and Florian Stuber, ed., *Small Comforts for Hard Times: Humanists on Public Policy* (New York: Columbia University Press, 1977), p. 47. For detail, the two Christopher Jencks volumes are Christopher Jencks et al., *Inequality* (New York: Basic Books, 1972), and *Who Gets Ahead?* (New York: Basic Books, 1979). See also John Rawls, *A Theory of Justice* (Cambridge, Mass.: Harvard University Press, 1971), pp. 300 ff., 511–512.

On Head Start, see Edward Zigler and Jeanette Valentine, eds., *Project Head Start: The Legacy of the War on Poverty* (New York: Free Press, 1979).

19. John A. Brittain, *The Inheritance of Economic Status* (Washington, D.C.: Brookings Institution, 1977), and John A. Brittain, *Inheritance and the Inequality of Material Wealth* (Washington, D.C.: Brookings Institution, 1978).

20. "Variations in what children learn in school depend largely on variations in what they bring to school" (Christopher Jencks as quoted by Brigitte Berger in "A New Interpretation of the I.Q. Controversy," *Public Interest* 50 [winter 1978]: 37).

21. James N. Morgan, *Five Thousand American Families: Patterns of Economic Progress* (Ann Arbor, Mich.: Survey University of Michigan, Research Center of the Institute for Social Research, 1974), vol. 1, pp. 337, 42–43, 75.

22. *Ibid.*, vol. 4, p. 8.

23. *Ibid.*, p. 16.

24. *Ibid.*, vol. 1, p. 99. Emphasis added.

25. *Ibid.*, p. 338. Emphasis added.

26. Christopher Jencks et al., *Who Gets Ahead?* pp. 230–231. See also Table, p. 62.

27. *Ibid.*, p. 62.

28. *Ibid.*, p. 75.

29. *Ibid.*, pp. 83–84.

30. Richard H. DeLone, *Small Futures* (New York: Harcourt Brace Jovanovich, 1979).

31. Burton White, *The First Three Years of Life* (Englewood Cliffs, N.J.: Prentice-Hall, 1975), p. 4.

32. For some discussion of this issue, see Robert M. Moroney, *Families, Social Services and Social Policy: The Issue of Shared Responsibility* (Washington, D.C.: U.S. Government Printing Office, 1980).

33. Theodore W. Schultz, ed., *Economics of the Family* (Chicago: University of Chicago Press, 1974). See Schultz, "Fertility and Economic Values," p. 11.

34. Zvi Griliches, "Comment," in Schultz, ed., *Economics of the Family*, pp. 546–548.

35. Nelson N. Foote and Leonard S. Cottrell, Jr., *Identity and Interpersonal Competence: A New Direction in Family Research* (Chicago: University of Chicago Press, 1955), p. 14.

36. Gallup Organization, "American Families, 1980."

37. Sheila B. Kamerman and Alfred J. Kahn, *Child Care, Family Benefits, and Working Parents* (New York: Columbia University Press, 1981).

38. For some discussion of this for a selected group of families, see Sheila B. Kamerman, *Parenting in an Unresponsive Society: Managing Work and Family Life* (New York: Free Press, 1980).

39. Alfred Kadushin, "Children in Adoptive Homes" and "Children in Foster Families and Institutions," and Scott Briar and Jon R. Conte, "Families," in Henry S. Maas, ed., *Social Service Research: Reviews of Studies* (Washington, D.C.: National Association of Social Workers, 1978), contain extensive references to a series of relevant research literature reviews.

Index

261

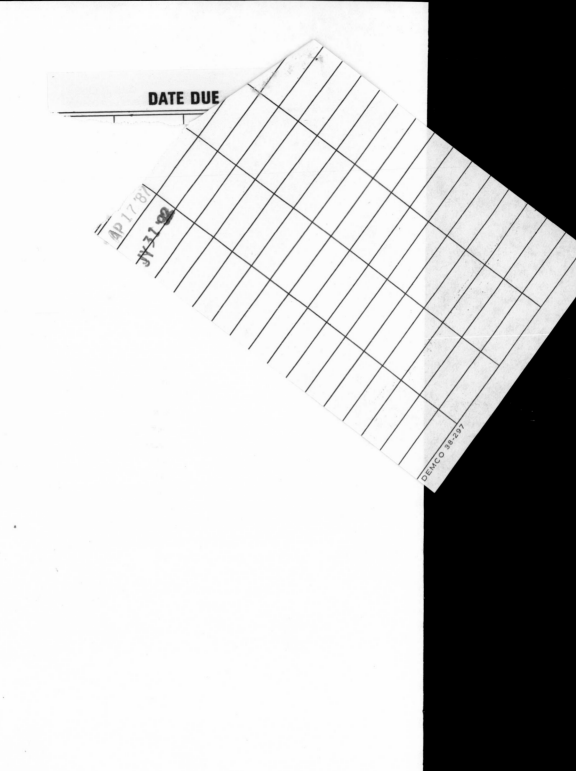